Unions, Immigration, and Internationalization

EUROPE IN TRANSITION: THE NYU EUROPEAN STUDIES SERIES

Unions, Immigration, and Internationalization: New Challenges and Changing Coalitions in the United States and France

Leah A. Haus

UNIONS, IMMIGRATION, AND INTERNATIONALIZATION
© Leah A. Haus, 2002

First published 2002 by
PALGRAVE MACMILLAN
175 Fifth Avenue, New York, N.Y. 10010 and
Houndmills, Basingstoke, Hampshire RG21 6XS
Companies and representatives throughout the world.

PALGRAVE MACMILLAN is the global academic imprint of the Palgrave Macmillan division of St. Martin's Press, LLC and of Palgrave Macmillan Ltd. Macmillan® is a registered trademark in the United States, United Kingdom and other countries. Palgrave is a registered trademark in the European Union and other countries.

ISBN 0–312–29494–8

Library of Congress Cataloging-in-Publication Data

Haus, Leah A., 1960–
    Unions, immigration, and internationalization : new challenges and changing coalitions in the United States and France / Leah A. Haus
        p. cm.
    Includes bibliographical references and index.
    ISBN 0–312–29494–8
      1. Labor unions—United States—History—20th century. 2. Alien labor—United States. 3. Emigration and immigration—Government policy—United States. 4. Labor unions—France—History—20th century. 5. Alien labor—France. 6. Emigration and immigration—Government policy—France. I. Title.

HD6508 .H344 2002
331.6′2′0973—dc21   2002024879

A catalogue record for this book is available from the British Library.

Design by Newgen Imaging Systems (P) Ltd., Chennai, India.

First edition: July, 2002
10 9 8 7 6 5 4 3 2 1

Printed in the United States of America.

Contents

Acknowledgments

This book builds on conference papers and articles that I wrote during the 1990s. Earlier versions of parts of the argument and data in this book were published in "Openings in the Wall: Transnational Migrants, Labor Unions, and U.S. Immigration Policy," *International Organization* Spring 1995; and "Labor Unions and Immigration Policy in France," *International Migration Review* Fall 1999.

Many people gave comments on earlier conference papers and articles that helped with revisions and, among other things, convinced me to consider norm liberalization since the early twentieth century. For constructive criticisms or helpful discussions at different times in the last decade I particularly thank Kitty Calavita, Muzaffar Chishti, Robert Keohane, Mark Kesselman, Ted Perlmutter, Mark Schumacher, Catherine Wihtol de Wenden, and Aristide Zolberg. Anonymous reviewers have also played an important role at various stages. For crucial comments, I am particularly indebted to the anonymous reviewers for the journal *International Organization*, and to the journal's former editor, John Odell. I also thank one anonymous reviewer of a draft of the entire book for giving helpful comments, particularly with regard to the concluding chapter.

I am deeply grateful to the many current and former union officials who agreed to be interviewed for this study and who gave their time generously, and to the people who gave essential help in union libraries and archives. I thank Martin Schain for introductions in France. I thank those who worked on the book at Palgrave, particularly Annje Kern, Ella Pearce, and Toby Wahl. Research grants were provided by Vassar College, the American Political Science Association, and New York University.

Abbreviation List

AEL	Asiatic Exclusion League
AFL	American Federation of Labor
ACWA	Amalgamated Clothing Workers of America
ACTWU	Amalgamated Clothing and Textile Workers of America
CFDT	Confédération Française Démocratique du Travail
CGT	Confédération Générale du Travail
CGTU	Confédération Générale du Travail Unitaire
CIO	Congress of Industrial Organizations
ECHR	European Convention for the Protection of Human Rights
EU	European Union
HERE	Hotel Employees and Restaurant Employees International Union
INS	Immigration and Naturalization Service
IRCA	Immigration Reform and Control Act
ILGWU	International Ladies Garment Workers Union
ILO	International Labor Organization
SCIRP	Select Commission on Immigration and Refugee Policy
SEA	Single European Act
SEIU	Service Employees International Union
SFBTC	San Francisco Building Trades Council
SGI	Société Générale d'Immigration
TUC	Trades Union Congress
UBC	United Brotherhood of Carpenters and Joiners of America
UFCWU	United Food and Commercial Workers Union
UFW	United Farm Workers
UMW	United Mine Workers of America
UNITE	Union of Needletrades, Industrial and Textile Employees

Foreword

Martin A. Schain, Series Editor

This is the third volume in the *Europe in Transition Series*, and an important new departure. It is the first monograph in the series that focuses on immigration. We are interested in new work in this area that treats immigration in comparative perspective, and we are particularly pleased to bring you this innovative study by Leah Haus that contributes to our understanding of the impact of immigration on unions in France and the United States.

Unions, Immigration, and Internationalization is a major analysis of the way that unions in France and the United States have dealt with immigration during two different historical periods. It challenges the conventional wisdom that argues that unions tend to favor immigration restriction because immigrants undermine their control over the labor market. It also probes the complexity of the relationship between unions and immigrant workers, as well as the ways that unions in two countries have dealt with the challenges of globalization.

The comparison between France and the United States focuses on two countries for which immigrant labor has been important since the nineteenth century. Economic growth and expansion have been directly linked to relatively open immigration policies, and both countries have struggled to incorporate immigrant communities over a long period of time. In both France and the United States, unions have been important agents of incorporation for diverse immigrant communities.

This rich and probing analysis helps us look at the relationship between unions and immigration with fresh eyes. Through Haus's work we gain deeper understanding both of the past and the future impact of the dynamics of globalization.

CHAPTER 1

Introduction

The Question

Immigration policy was an important and controversial item on the political agenda of countries such as the United States and France in the late twentieth century, and remains so as we enter the new millennium. The debates brought out different views on the ability of governments to control migration in an era of economic internationalization. Different views also surfaced on the rights of governments to control migration when this hit on the human rights of the migrants. At a more specific level, the policy conflicts centered on such issues as amnesty programs for illegal, undocumented immigrants; inspections for, and expulsions of illegal, undocumented immigrants; criteria for entrance of legal permanent immigrants; and expanding quotas for temporary work permits.

Controversies over immigration policy are not new. Debates took place in the earlier years of the twentieth century in France and the United States, when both countries experienced high rates of immigration from Eastern and Southern Europe. Then, as now, a range of societal groups fought to obtain their preferred outcome on immigration policy.

But, despite the repeated controversies in both time periods, there is something new going on today. The social coalitions and cleavages that form in immigration policy debates are not the same now as they were then. Most notably, labor unions have changed coalitions. In the past it was often thought that unions would pressure for restrictionist immigration policy measures so as to reduce the flow of labor into the country and to thereby improve wages and work conditions. In the early twentieth century, unions did sit in the restrictionist coalition. But in the late twentieth century, labor unions in France and the United States often departed from the restrictionist coalition and sat with liberal groups in immigration policy debates. This study seeks to explain why. How do we account for this change in the immigration policy preferences of unions between the early and late twentieth century? Why did the conventional wisdom become outdated?

The Argument

This study considers unions in France and the United States: two post-industrial democracies with weak labor movements; and two countries that experienced substantial immigration flows in the early twentieth century as well as in the post-World War II period. The concluding chapter branches out to consider other countries, particularly the United Kingdom.

The argument of this book is that one needs to consider the challenges and consequences of various forms of internationalization to understand why unions changed coalitions. Many union leaders considered that economic internationalization undermined the full effectiveness of certain restrictionist immigration policy measures that aim to control migration, making it pointless to agitate for such measures; and an internationalization of human rights concerns encouraged union leaders to oppose certain restrictionist immigration policy measures that hit on the rights of migrants. Meanwhile, many union leaders saw support for certain non-restrictionist measures (or opposition to certain restrictionist measures) as a way to facilitate organization, which is an alternative strategy to restrictionism for improving wages and work conditions.[1]

Scholars in the late twentieth century have debated the themes of the ability and right of governments to control migration in an era of economic internationalization and in an era of the internationalization of human rights concerns. Just as academics have debated these themes, it is reasonable to expect that protagonists over policy, such as unions, have also thought about these themes and that their views on these subjects might affect their tactics. It is also reasonable to expect that protagonists over policy, such as unions, have changed their views on these themes since the early twentieth century, and that these changes contribute to an explanation for why unions defected from the restrictionist coalition more often in the late twentieth century than in the early twentieth century.

The subject of migration has always posed dilemmas for organized labor. At the beginning of the twentieth century, migration, along with other major issues such as national self-determination, colonialism, and war, posed concrete issues that tore the Left in different directions. These issues caused "internal turmoil" for the Second International, an organization designed to promote international ideas, contacts, and coordination of socialist labor movements in the period 1889–1914. It was the successor to the First International, where Karl Marx had concluded the Inaugural Address with the appeal: "Workmen of all countries, Unite!"[2] In the early twentieth century for the most part labor unions in countries of immigration joined the restrictionist coalition.

A more lengthy and detailed explication of the argument for why unions changed coalitions follows.

The Problem with the Conventional Wisdom[3]

In the past it was often thought that unions favored restrictionism. This expectation rested on a loosely framed theoretical model, which posited that one should expect unions, on the basis of economic interest, to seek to restrict access to the labor market by outsiders. This expectation that unions favor restrictionism so as to reduce the labor supply and improve wages and work conditions implicitly assumes that unions consider states to have the ability and/or right to control migration flows. One may be less likely to pressure for restrictionist legislation if one did not expect the legislation to have effective and/or desirable outcomes. This assumption for the most part helped to explain union preferences in the early twentieth century. For example, a report from the American Federation of Labor (AFL) in 1921 noted that it had "urged the complete restriction of immigration for at least two years,"[4] and in 1924 the AFL stated that its preferred outcome was the "total suspension of immigration for a period of five years or longer."[5]

The above assumption has held less explanatory power in the late twentieth century. Our understanding of unions' immigration policy preferences is enhanced by instead assuming that unions consider that the state's ability and/or right to control migration flows, while considerable, is incomplete. For example, the Immigration Committee of the Los Angeles Federation of Labor, AFL-CIO, noted in 1993 that: "We are living in an era where the movement of labor, like capital, is increasingly common and difficult to regulate. The world has become a smaller place and organized labor is adjusting."[6] Likewise the Head of the Immigration Section of the major French union confederation, the

Confédération Générale du Travail (CGT) in France, wrote in 1994 that: "We know likewise that the question of the 'regulation' or of the 'management' of international migration flows is to say the least difficult or even impossible."[7]

The Role of the State in Controlling Migration

Ability

Some observers consider that the state's ability to completely control migration has declined due to *economic internationalization* and the emerging transnationalization of the labor market. Technological revolutions such as declining transport costs, which sharply raise the supply of tourists and students who can overstay visas, necessitating internal patrol for effective immigration control, and improved communication technology, which intensifies the transnational social networks sustaining migration flows, are said to have reduced the state's ability to fully control migration flows.[8]

To the extent that unions share this general view, this reduces the expected benefits of restrictionism for unions. If unions question the state's ability to fully control migration, then certain measures intended to further restrict migration would be considered unlikely to attain their stated goal.

Rights

Some observers consider that there has been an internationalization of human rights concerns, or norm liberalization, in the post-World War II period, which has reduced the choices available to the state and increased the constraints against adopting certain control measures (such as expulsions and repatriations) that undermine the rights of migrants in their role as human beings.[9]

To the extent that unions share this view, and have internationalized their concerns for human rights to include the rights of migrants, this increases the expected costs of restrictionism for unions. If unions question the state's right to fully control migration, then those measures intended to further restrict migration that clash with liberal norms would be considered undesirable.

In summary, the first reason why unions more often departed from the restrictionist coalition in the late twentieth century than in the early twentieth century is because they changed their views on the role of the state in controlling migration. They questioned the ability of the state to completely control migration and/or the right of the state to completely control migration. This does not imply that unions believe that the state has no control over its borders. They do not believe this. Nor does it imply that unions have become staunch supporters of the liberal and individualistic philosophy behind international human rights conventions (or practitioners of international class solidarity). They are not, and there is some coded illiberalism and nationalism in unions on immigration policy issues. Moreover, moving beyond the subject of migration, unions' stress on the need to uphold human rights in the context of trade agreements may be a convenient cover for protectionism. But this cover for protectionism is reversed on immigration issues, where upholding human rights generally increases rather than decreases inflows. Despite these caveats, when one takes the early twentieth century as a baseline for comparison, it is apparent that unions have partially modified their views on these themes over time in regard to migration (as have many academics).

If unions assume that the state's ability and/or right to control migration flows, while considerable, is incomplete, one would not expect unions to pressure for an unattainable or undesirable outcome of further restrictionism. Instead one may expect unions to focus on an alternative outcome, such as organizing immigrant workers.

Organizing/Inclusion and Exclusion

Restrictionism and organizing immigrants are two alternative and at times conflicting strategies for raising wages and work conditions. The rationale for restrictionism is that it limits the labor supply and thus provides a means to improve wages and work conditions. Organizing immigrants likewise provides a means to improve wages and work conditions for both immigrant and native workers. Absent organization, immigrant workers are more likely to undercut unionized native workers.

Unions have different identities and have adopted a variety of approaches to organizing in general. For example, U.S. construction craft unions in the early twentieth century were exclusionary; French unions have inclusive ideals but they do not actively organize anyone; some inclusive U.S. unions do actively organize. These diverse approaches to organizing can be expected to influence the extent to which unions regard immigrant incorporation into unions as an effective alternative strategy to restrictionism.

If unions are inclusive and active organizers, one may expect that, seeking to improve wages and work conditions, they will more seriously consider the strategy of organizing immigrants as an alternative to the strategy of restrictionism. In contrast, exclusive unions (U.S. construction craft unions for many years) face an incentive to exclude immigrants from union membership, which is a prerequisite for access to the more desirable union jobs, and are thus more likely to remain attached to restrictionism as a route to raising wages.

The Link between Organizing and State Control

There have always been tensions between the strategies of organizing and restrictionism. Unions that had a restrictionist posture in the early twentieth century were likely to alienate immigrants and thus hinder effective organization. Unions that tried to organize immigrants in the early twentieth century, such as the United Mine Workers, faced this dilemma. On the one hand such unions had an incentive to pressure for restrictionism: to control the labor supply; and on the other hand they had an incentive to refrain from restrictionism: to avoid alienating immigrants from unions.

Unions more often came down on the side of organizing rather than restrictionism in the late twentieth century because on the one hand, as explicated above, the anticipated benefits of restrictionism declined due to changing views on the role of the state in controlling migration (certain restrictionist measures are deemed ineffective or undesirable). And on the other hand the tensions between restrictionism and organizing increased. Restrictionism came to be seen as increasingly incompatible with, or an impediment to, effective organization because of economic internationalization. In other words, the practical reasons for unions to oppose certain restrictionist measures, or to favor certain open or non-restrictionist measures, so as to facilitate organization increased for those who consider that the state's ability to control migration has declined. Some specific examples of why include:

1. If one questions the government's ability to fully control migration flows, one would expect that if legal immigration is banned, then people will come anyway but in an unauthorized manner. Thus restrictionist measures that aim to block entrance and increase exit of *legal* immigrants (such as the nonrenewal of permits in France; or a reduction in the size of legal immigration quotas in the U.S.) would be deemed to have the effect of increasing the quantity of *illegal* immigrants who, lacking legal protection, are less likely to join unions than legal immigrants.

2. Restrictionist measures that seek to increase exit of illegal immigrants (such as sanctions against employers of illegal immigrants, inspections of worksites where they are employed, and expulsions for those who lack legal status) would alienate immigrants from unions and thereby undermine effective organization and, if one questions the ability to fully control migration, more illegal immigrants will simply emerge as replacements. Moreover, these restrictionist measures, such as calling in the Immigration and Naturalization Service (INS) to inspect a worksite, can be used by the employers of the illegal immigrants to break an organizing drive.

3. Non-restrictionist immigration measures, such as amnesty for illegal immigrants, enables these workers to gain legal status and increases their legal protection and shadow of the future, raising their ability and incentives to participate in union activities. Moreover, helping applicants with the bureaucratic procedures in the amnesty program is a service that unions can provide to encourage the applicants to join the union.

Summary

To summarize the argument of this study: unions see less rationale for pressuring for certain restrictionist measures in the late twentieth century than they did in the early twentieth century for two interconnected reasons.

1. Union views on the changing role of the state in an era of (a) economic internationalization, and (b) internationalization of human rights concerns. Unions see some restrictionist measures as (a) ineffective in controlling migration, and/or (b) undesirable because they undermine the rights of migrants in their role as human beings.

2. Union views that support for restrictionist measures would hinder effective organization for practical reasons that were intensified in an era of economic internationalization, or support for some non-restrictionist measures would facilitate organization, which is an alternative strategy to restrictionism for improving wages and work conditions for those unions that have an inclusive approach.

It is important to clarify that unions do not oppose all restrictionist measures, or favor open borders. Most union leaders consider that the state retains considerable, but incomplete, ability and right to control migration. The argument presented leads one to expect that unions would support those non-restrictionist measures (or oppose those restrictionist measures) that most clearly impact on organizing. These would not be patrol measures at the territorial borders. Rather they would be internal patrol measures that indirectly or directly impact on the workplace and organizing, such as amnesty and employer sanctions. The argument presented also leads one to expect that unions would support those non-restrictionist measures (or oppose those restrictionist measures) that most clearly uphold liberal democratic principles, which entail granting access to legalization and citizenship to those people who are members of the society by virtue of living in the community for a period of time, and to those people with family ties to a member of the society.[10]

The General and the Unique

A number of studies have explored whether the policy preferences of societal groups, and policy outcomes, have diverged or converged in the face of common external challenges such as economic internationalization.[11] A few of these studies focus on labor unions and have pointed to divergence in union responses to, first, the economic crisis of the 1970s and, second, deepening economic internationalization later in the twentieth century. These studies highlight the path-dependent nature of unions, which adapt to new circumstances in ways that fit with their pre-existing ideas, values, and habits.[12] Union identities, or "distinctive ways of mapping the world, values and goals," have been shown to serve as a prism through which unions interpret and accommodate new challenges.[13]

This book undertakes a comparative study so as to explore whether, and if so, why unions diverge in their response to the challenge of immigration in an era of deepening internationalization. Unions in both the United States and France share some important features such as low union density and little input into government policymaking. But they have very different identities. French unions are ideological and class-oriented. Ideational concerns weigh heavily in their policy preferences. As noted by George Ross in a study of union responses to economic crises, "'ideological' factors had had, and have, considerable weight in forming the orientations of French unions."[14] By contrast, U.S. unions are pragmatic and incrementalist, and concerns over immediate interests weigh heavily in their policy preferences.

The study shows that at one level French and U.S. unions, despite their different identities, adopted quite similar responses to global level changes. In both cases the unions changed coalitions. Both French and U.S. unions in the late twentieth century refrained from the restrictionist temptation to which their counterparts in the early twentieth century gave in. Deepening internationalization helps to explain why they changed coalitions in both cases.

But at another level the unique identities of different unions remained influential. Unions in both countries filtered the global changes through their own specific lenses, and the particular identities of labor movements remained significant in determining policy preferences. Different aspects of internationalization, while impacting in both cases, carried different weight among unions in the two countries. In other words, there was some variation in each case in the causes behind the common outcome of changing coalitions.

A brief indication of some of these specific features follows here as an introduction to the case studies and so as to supplement the more general argument presented above.

The pragmatic U.S. unions showed greater concern for the ways in which certain immigration laws served as practical impediments to organizing than did their French counterparts, who are known for their general inactivity when it comes to organizing. In the United States the changes in union immigration policy preferences were driven by a rejuvination of the organizing agenda, which sought to reverse the declining union density that may itself have partly resulted from the increasing capital mobility associated with economic internationalization.[15] As an increasing number of unions began to take organizing seriously, they came into direct contact with immigration policy issues because many of their potential members were legal or illegal, undocumented immigrants. Restrictionist measures were having a debilitating effect on organizing drives. Unions simultaneously reconsidered their views on the ability of the state to completely control migration in an era of economic internationalization and drew skeptical conclusions that presented the other reason for departing from the restrictionist coalition. Due to their views on the changing role of the state, they saw little to lose in departing from the restrictionist coalition.

This combination of reasons for resisting restrictionism (skepticism about the state's ability to completely control migration; and the debilitating impact of certain restrictionist measures on organization) is seen, for example, in statements by the Service Employees International

Union (SEIU). In the early 1990s the SEIU changed positions and began to fight for the repeal of employer sanctions legislation that is intended to restrict illegal immigration by penalizing employers who knowingly hire undocumented immigrants. On the one hand, employer sanctions legislation was impeding organization. As noted by the SEIU president:

> Employer sanctions legislation has done nothing to improve the lot of low-wage workers in the building service industry. Rather, their principal effect is to prevent a union from organizing workers employed by nonunion contractors. This dramatically increases the value of undocumented workers to contractors and building owners.[16]

And on the other hand, for the SEIU, the government lacked the ability to completely control migration in an era of economic internationalization, and the legislation was ineffective in obtaining its stated goal of deterring illegal immigration. As noted in a resolution approved by the SEIU in 1992: "... push factors will continue to encourage people to seek a better life in the United States—no matter how punitive U.S. immigration policy becomes. It is clear that under any scenario, undocumented workers will continue to be a major part of the low-wage service work force in many areas."[17]

French union officials (like their U.S. counterparts) began to question the state's ability to fully control migration flows as they devoted increasing attention to the general subject of economic "globalization" in the 1990s. But the highly ideational French unions showed greater concern for normative issues relating to the state's right to control migration than did their pragmatic U.S. counterparts, who comparatively rarely mentioned normative issues. For example, French unions strongly opposed the restrictionist Debré Laws that were proposed by the Minister of the Interior, Jean-Louis Debré, in 1997. One union confederation, the Confédération Française Démocratique du Travail (CFDT), explained its opposition as follows: "The National Assembly, in its first reading, ignored humanitarianism and realism by adopting and toughening the Debré bill on immigration."[18]

French unions hold inclusive ideals but the identity of most French unions has traditionally not involved much active organizing of anyone. Thus it is not surprising that organizing concerns were a less significant factor behind their change in coalitions than was the case for U.S. unions.

Alternative Possible Explanations

Undesirable Jobs

It could alternatively be argued that unions refrained from restrictionism because immigrants take undesirable low-wage jobs that native workers don't want. Thus there is little pressure for restrictionism. Similarly, it could be argued that unions covering declining industrial sectors (such as apparel) have an incentive to support openness to ensure the supply of labor necessary to prevent the exit of capital to low-wage countries. Absent immigration, it is unlikely that these jobs would continue to exist in the United States and France.[19] Foreigners are thus not displacing native workers.

This line of reasoning does help to explain union immigration policies. It will be seen in the case studies that for the most part it was those unions that cover sectors where the undesirable low-wage jobs are located (for example, janitors) that defected from the restrictionist coalition in the late twentieth century. In contrast, unions remained restrictionist with regard to "higher-level" jobs, such as information technology and engineering in the United States, where the AFL-CIO sought to restrict the number of temporary non-immigrant visas through which many of the foreign workers in these "higher-level" jobs enter the country.

However, this explanation has several weaknesses. First, it does a better job of accounting for union immigration policies in the declining manufacturing sector, where capital can exit abroad, than in the service sector. Service sector jobs (for example, janitors, domestic home workers, hotel/restaurant workers) are on-site. Capital lacks an easy escape route abroad in these growth on-site sectors. Yet unions covering the service sector, most notably the SEIU in the United States, have led the fight against further restrictionism.

Second, and of more importance, this alternative argument fails to explain *change* in unions' immigration policy preferences over time, and change is the focus of this study. This alternative argument would lead one to expect to see a constancy over time in the immigration policy preferences of unions that cover sectors with undesirable low-wage jobs. For example, it fails to explain why the United Mine Workers union failed to resist restrictionism in the early twentieth century; it fails to explain why a number of U.S. unions changed their policies toward illegal immigration in the late twentieth century; and it fails to explain why the French CGT changed aspects of its immigration policy in the late twentieth century in the direction of liberalization, despite high unemployment levels in France. The jobs did not suddenly become undesirable in the late twentieth century. What did change was an increasing attention to economic internationalization by unions (like everyone else), an internationalization of human rights concerns on the agenda of global politics beginning after World War II, and then intensifying in the post-Cold War era; and, for the United States, a rejuvination in the organizing agenda of the labor movement.

Broader Political Dynamics

It will be seen in the case studies that union immigration policy preferences in the late twentieth century relate to broader political dynamics.

In France these broader political dynamics have played out with particular regard to the National Front, a political party that has been a significant actor on the French political scene in the late twentieth century. Unions have strongly opposed the National Front, and have thus at times opposed restrictionist immigration policy measures so as to avoid playing into the hands of the National Front, among other reasons.

In the United States these broader political dynamics have played out with particular regard to maintaining cohesion with liberal groups that emerged after World War II. Unions have thus at times opposed certain restrictionist immigration policy measures so as to accommodate the preferences of partners such as Latino groups, whose support may be needed by labor on other non-immigration related issues.

In sum, for broader reasons, unions might support liberal immigration policy preferences that do not necessarily accurately represent their own preferences.

This alternative argument, while contributing to a more complete interpretation of unions' immigration policy preferences, alone is inadequate. First, it begs the question of why union statements on the reasons for their immigration policy preferences in both countries give substantial attention to other factors that directly relate to the argument presented in this book. Statements do also at times mention issues related to these broader political dynamics, but it is certainly not the only focus of attention. There is no particular reason why unions would distort the explanations in their statements to such an extent.

Second, this alternative possible argument borders on circularity with the question posed in this study. It fails to really address the question posed. Rather it re-emphasizes the puzzle posed. It begs the question of why broader political dynamics have played out differently on immigration issues today from the early twentieth century. For example, with regard to France, the argument that unions have resisted restrictionist immigration policy proposals so as to block the National Front, while contributing to our understanding, alone is unsatisfactory. It poses the puzzle of why unions have responded to the National Front in the way that they have. They could alternatively have reacted to the National Front in a manner similar to political parties, which have often sought to coopt potential National Front voters by supporting restrictionist measures.[20] It leaves unaddressed why unions have not likewise played the restrictionist card with the hope of diluting support for the National Front and of encouraging some French workers to join or remain in unions, particularly in the case of the CGT, which covers sectors where there are a fair amount of National Front sympathizers. Something else must also be going on to explain *why unions have instead defected from the restrictionist coalition*, unlike political parties in the late twentieth century and unlike some unions in the early twentieth century. Radical right-wing groups were present on the French political scene in the inter-war years.[21] Many unions nonetheless sat in the restrictionist coalition then on immigration issues even though they opposed such groups on a number of other issues. Why have unions reacted differently now from then? How do we understand the direction of dynamics? Why has the National Front elicited a response from unions of opposition rather than cooptation? This brings one back to a focus on norm liberalization and the internationalization of human rights concerns so as to get at this puzzle.

There has been some liberalization in the universe of discourse in both France and the United States since the early twentieth century in general, and on immigrant-related issues in particular. This change in discourse, in conjunction with the emergence of organized liberal groups and immigrant associations that oppose restrictionism and that barely existed in the early twentieth century, alters the likely consequences for union leaders should they actively pursue illiberal policies. An illiberal position on immigration today places one in what is considered in contemporary discourse to be the "right-wing" political camp in a more pronounced way than was the case in the early twentieth century; and an illiberal position today risks alienating the liberal groups that barely existed in the early twentieth century and whose support may be needed on other non-immigration related issues.

At the same time, there has been some internationalization of human rights concerns among union officials since the early twentieth century. In sum, normative discourse and views on this subject differ today from then, and have contributed to mitigating the restrictionist temptation.

Plan of the Book

The next chapter discusses the broader scholarly literature that relates to the main themes of this study: economic internationalization, internationalization of human rights norms, and organizing immigrants.

The causes of union immigration policy preferences in the early twentieth century and in the late twentieth century in the United States and in France are explored in the case studies presented in chapters three through six.

The material on U.S. unions in both time periods supplements a focus on the confederation level with in-depth discussions of individual unions at a disaggregated level so as to more thoroughly test the arguments presented. For example, the analysis of the sources of U.S. unions' immigration policy preferences in the early twentieth century covered in chapter three includes, among other cases, a study of the principal inclusive, organizing union then—the United Mine Workers (UMW). This provides a basis for comparison with inclusive, organizing unions in the late twentieth century, such as the SEIU, covered in chapter four. This comparison of unions with an active organizing approach in both time periods helps to assess the impact of concerns about economic internationalization and internationalization of human rights concerns in the recent time period.

Immigration issues in France are primarily addressed at the level of confederations. Unlike the United States, individual unions comparatively rarely addressed immigration policy issues in the post-war era. Thus the material on French unions in chapters five and six focuses on the main confederations in both time periods and gives less attention to individual union federations. Nonetheless, case studies are presented for both time periods on unions in the construction sector, which is a sector where many immigrants worked.

The concluding chapter asks to what extent the findings of this book are unique to the specific cases of the United States and France, or may be generalizable to other liberal democratic post-industrial countries. The chapter proposes factors that may generate a variation in union immigration policy preferences (such as the level of union density or strength), for testing in future research work on other countries; and it includes a case study that analyzes British unions' immigration policy preferences in the late twentieth century.

Sources

This book draws on intensive case studies that are focused at the leadership level and the official policy of unions in the United States and France in the early and late twentieth century. The research considers union statements. Statements of unions, like those of everyone, may include rhetoric, and the study thus also gives attention to the extent to which unions backed their statements with actions, time, and other resources.

The sources used are both written and oral, and all translations were done by this author. Written sources include union documents, union newspapers, union periodicals, union press releases, U.S. congressional hearings, and the transcripts of the Select Commission on Immigration and Refugee Policy. Some of the written sources were gained from national archives and union archives. The archives consulted include the following. For France: the National Archives, the Departmental Archives of the Rhône-Alpes, the CGT's archives, and the CFDT's archives. For the United States: the National Archives, the Tamiment Labor Archives, the United Mine Workers Archives, and the George Meany Memorial Archives. Written sources were also gained from the reading rooms or libraries of various unions in both countries.

Oral sources are drawn from numerous interviews that were conducted by the author in France on various occasions between 1995 and 1999 (Lyon, Montreuil, and Paris); the United States on various occasions between 1992 and 2000 (Los Angeles, New York City, and Washington, D.C.); and England in June 2001 (London). The interviews were conducted on the condition of anonymity. The interviewees were primarily current (or retired) union officials, although some interviewees represented a variety of other organizations involved in immigration policy controversies. Conversations with about five union officials were repeated several times or more during the years 1992–2000. In addition, the author was permitted to attend some union meetings in France.

In most cases the material gained from interviews was cross-checked normally with written sources, or at times with other interviewees. When thorough cross-checking was not possible the material has either been omitted or introduced with the words "apparently" or "it seems."

CHAPTER 2

Explaining Union Immigration Policy Preferences: Economic Internationalization, Internationalization of Human Rights, and Organizing Immigrants

There is much literature in the field of political economy that seeks to explain the policy preferences of societal groups to international economic flows.[1] Like this book, some of the literature has sought to understand why policy preferences change at different historical periods. For example, Helen Milner asked why France and the United States resisted the protectionist temptation in trade policy during the 1970s, unlike in the inter-war years.[2] But this existing body of literature has focused on the policy preferences of societal groups to trade and capital flows, and has tended to overlook reactions to migration flows. More broadly, the study of the causes and consequences of migration, as well as reactions to migration, has been largely divorced from the mainstream study of international political economy.

Analyzing responses to migration may be messier than analyzing responses to capital flows or trade. The subject is more complex because "a person is not a shirt."[3] But this does not mitigate a need for understanding responses to migration.

Scholarship that does exist on the immigration policy preferences of societal groups, and coalition formation, at a more general level has been represented in the work of Aristide Zolberg.[4] Zolberg presented a model which posited that, on the basis of economic interest, one should expect organized labor to seek to restrict access to the labor market by outsiders. His model considered migrants in their role as both economic and socio-political actors, and he pointed to a likely split in the usual coalitions that form in other issue areas. He suggested that on the Right, immigration policy split business and cultural conservatives. Business had an interest in openness to increase the labor supply and, at times, the supply of strikebreakers; whereas cultural conservatives, seeking to retain cultural homogeneity, had an interest in restricting entrance of immigrants from new source countries. On the Left, immigration was said to split the liberal-labor coalition. Liberal and ethnic groups had an interest in openness to protect the human rights of migrants and to permit family reunion for transnational relatives; whereas labor groups were thought to favor restrictionism to limit the labor supply and avoid greater job competition. Thus one would expect the emergence of so-called odd-couple coalitions between business and liberal/ethnic groups; and between labor and cultural conservatives.

These odd-couple coalitions pointed to by Zolberg did emerge in debates on immigration policy in the early twentieth century. The mainstream of labor movements sat in the restrictionist coalition at that time. But there has been a change in coalitions in the late twentieth century. Labor organizations have often defected from the restrictionist coalition. Instead there has been a fragile liberal-labor coalition (which has at times sat on the same side of the fence as business, albeit with very different motives). This change in coalitions calls for an analysis of why this has occurred.

The Role of the State: The Internationalization of the Economy and of Human Rights

There has been a proliferation of debates in migration studies about the role of the state in the late twentieth century. The debate fits within the broader discussions about "globalization" in the academic and policy arenas. Groups concerned with public policy have addressed this debate, and the subject has elicited a variety of responses. Unions, like a range of other societal actors, have thought about the subject, and, as will be seen in later chapters, their views on these broader themes have impacted on their immigration policy preferences. This is a good part of the reason why the conventional wisdom (that unions sit in the restrictionist coalition) has become outdated—it implicitly assumes that unions consider that the state has the ability and/or right to fully control migration.

The academic debates in migration studies have centered on the state's ability to effectively control migration in an era of economic internationalization, and the state's right to control migration in an era of the internationalization of human rights concerns.

Economic Internationalization

An enormous amount of work in the field of international political economy has discussed the subject of economic internationalization in the late twentieth century.[5] At times this literature has stressed the uneven nature of economic internationalization in different areas today, and the importance of considering the regional prism.[6] Deepening economic regionalization has also been the subject of a great deal of discussion in academia and in the world beyond, particularly in the context of the European Union but also in other areas such as NAFTA.

Within the field of migration studies, scholars have put forward their different notions on the capacity of the state to manage migration in the contemporary era of economic internationalization. Some emphasize continuity between past and present, and suggest that the capacity of the state to control migration today is similar to (or greater than) the early twentieth century. It is this view that underlies the conventional wisdom that unions sit in the restrictionist coalition. One would not pressure for further restrictionist measures if one did not think that such measures would be effective.

Other scholars instead stress change, and indicate that broader transformations in the global political economy have complicated the state's capacity to fully manage migration flows in the late twentieth century.

Continuity

Scholarship that brought attention to the state's role in determining migration flows was work by Aristide Zolberg. Zolberg critiqued overly economistic theories of migration (both liberal economic theory and historical-structural theory) for failing to explain why migration flows are not greater than they are. By focusing on the role of the state and its restrictionist rules of entrance and exit, Zolberg provided the missing link to explain why migration flows are not greater than they are.[7] There are alternative explanations to Zolberg's focus on the state to explain absence of movement, such as attachment to the home community, and lack of networks and resources.[8] Nonetheless, as Zolberg stresses, governments' restrictionist rules of entrance and exit undoubtedly block much migration that would otherwise occur.

Zolberg shows that governments have at times initiated migration through liberalization of rules of entrance. They have also suppressed migration flows through restrictionist rules of entrance since the late nineteenth century, when the supply of potential migrants began to exceed demand; and in the earlier mercantilist era, through policing exit when populations were viewed as valuable economic and military assets.[9] Zolberg expects receiving states to raise restrictionist barriers to entrance in hard times or periods of global economic crisis, when both the pressures for protectionism in developed countries and the pressures for emigration from developing countries, which are hit harder by global recession, increase. He argues that:

> Under these conditions, restrictive measures were designed to achieve two distinct but complementary objectives: (1) to protect domestic society against deleterious processes generated by international market forces; and (2) to enhance national security in the face of rising international tensions. Protection was of concern to both workers threatened by unemployment and elites faced with the mounting burden of maintaining and managing populations that were no longer self-subsistent in a period of economic crisis.[10]

Zolberg clarifies that migration redistributes wealth from native workers in developed countries to immigrants arriving from developing countries through access to employment and collective goods, threatening domestic management, and that there is "every reason to expect that the affluent group will consolidate its protective wall."[11]

Building on Zolberg's focus on the state, some scholars have argued that the state's capacity to control migration has increased in the late twentieth century. For example, this conclusion is reached by Gary Freeman, who qualifies his argument to focus on the differential experiences in immigration policy performance. He argues that the capacity of governments to control migration varies according to the specific task (for example, legal immigration, illegal immigration, and temporary worker programs) and according to the specific country (for example, the United States is less effective than Australia due to the differences in their physical locations). He concludes that:

> There is no doubt that the democracies have more and better means to control their borders, monitor foreigners within their territory, and manage international flows than they did twenty, fifty, or one hundred years ago. The long-term trend is undeniably toward greater, not less government effort and capacity to control international migration.[12]

Finally, scholars who argue that little has changed with regard to the role of the state in the global economy in the twentieth century point out that economic interdependence and the cross-border flows of capital, goods, and people were also high in the early twentieth century.[13] The transnational social networks that sustain chain migration, and are sometimes said to complicate the effectiveness of government policy in the late twentieth century, also existed in the early twentieth century. In other words, features that are sometimes viewed as challenging to the state in the late twentieth century are not so new.

The quantity of migration flows into both France and the United States was high in the early twentieth century. Transnational social linkages existed then, like now, and they were a significant factor sustaining migration flows through chain migration. The means of communication were letters and reports from returning migrants; and remittances were either mailed or brought back by returning migrants. Some examples follow.

With regard to France, in the late nineteenth century thousands of workers commuted across the French–Belgium border on a daily basis to work in the French textile factories or metal works.[14] In the early twentieth century Italian workers in the industrial region of Longwy (in the Northeast of France) often came from the same Italian villages as chain migration set in. Italian workers quite often worked in Longwy from April to October and returned to Italy for the winter. Others stayed in France for several years, and returned to Italy after they had saved enough money to buy a plot of land or small store.[15]

With regard to the United States, historical studies of migration include many examples of how friends or family members provided information about wages and work conditions to people back home, encouraged or even paid for them to undertake the trans-Atlantic voyage, and helped find employment and places of residence for the newcomers.[16] Polish villagers knew about pay scales and job opportunities in the United States from letters sent back by migrants. These letters were regarded as communal property in the villages, and this correspondence was seen as a social obligation.[17] A U.S. Immigration Commission study in 1908–1909 noted that approximately 60 percent of new immigrants from Southern and Eastern Europe stated that their passage had been arranged by immigrants already in the United States.[18] Many migrants came to the United States as "Birds of Passage" intending to save money and then return home. While some of the "Birds of Passage" ended up staying, quite a few retained transnational links and returned home to settle.[19]

Despite these significant transnational social networks, the state clearly had great control over migration flows and the ability to cut the chain migration resulting from transnational social networks at that time. This can be seen by the changes in migration flows following the enactment of restrictionist immigration policy measures. The 1921 Emergency Quota Law in the United States was designed to reduce immigration from the new source countries of Eastern and Southern Europe. The quantity of Polish immigrants dropped from 95,089 in 1921 to 28,635 in 1922. The quantity of Italian immigrants dropped from 222,260 in 1921 to 40,319 in 1922. The 1924 National Origins Act in the United States, among other things, excluded Japanese from migration to the United States. The quantity of Japanese immigrants dropped from 8,801 in 1924 to 723 in 1925.[20] When the French government imposed restrictionist measures (such as the denial of permits and repatriations) in the recession of 1927, the net balance of migration flows changed dramatically from 113,426 more entrances than exits in 1926 to a *reverse flow* of 25,657 more exits than entrances in 1927.[21]

Change
Other scholars point to changes in the government's capacity to manage migration in the late twentieth century due to broader transformations in the global political economy. For example, Saskia Sassen argues that economic internationalization, or the formation of transnational economic spaces, and the emergence of an international human rights regime have changed the "substantive nature of state control over immigration."[22] She critiques the notion that there is a crisis and points to the lack of realism in the popular dramatic images of an invasion. Instead, Sassen argues that there is a management problem and, concurring with Wayne Cornelius et al,[23] points to a growing gap between national immigration policy goals and outcomes. Sassen places international migration in the context of broader changes in the global political economy and points to the linkages between migration and other political economic issues—linkages that undermine the effectiveness of the old rules of the game or traditional immigration policy that "continues to be characterized by its formal isolation from other major processes, as if it were possible to handle migration as a bounded, closed event."[24] She argues that the restructuring of the global economy through capital mobility reinforces labor migration,[25] and that the broader dynamics in the global political economy and the emergence of an international human rights regime:

> Reduces the autonomy of the state in controlling immigration: large-scale international migrations are highly conditioned and structured, embedded

in complex economic, social, and ethnic networks. States may insist on treating immigration as the aggregate outcome of individual actions, but they cannot escape the consequences of those larger dynamics. A national state may have the power to write the text of an immigration policy, but it is likely to be dealing with complex, transnational processes that it can only partly address or regulate through immigration policy as conventionally understood.[26]

Similar views are held by Douglas Massey et al who, upon exploring the explanatory value of a variety of different theories of migration in different regions of the world, conclude that there are multiple causes for migration (such as the incorporation of peripheral areas into the global economy and the demand stemming from the structural segmentation of the labor market in developed countries). They argue that these causes are not easy to control, and thus immigration "cannot simply be turned on and off like a tap."[27] This is a very different picture from that of early twentieth-century France when, as shown by table 5.2 in chapter five, and as described by Gary Cross, "the state opened and closed the frontier to labor immigration as if it were a faucet."[28] Writing about the late twentieth century, Massey et al conclude that:

> As long as the world's powerful, capital-rich economies are incorporated within global trade, information, and production networks, they will tend to receive international migrants. In both theoretical and practical terms it has proved difficult to lower barriers to the movement of capital, information, and goods while at the same time raising barriers to the movement of workers. Immigration is simply the labour component of globalizing factor markets.[29]

Finally, while transnational social linkages were strong in the early twentieth century as noted above, studies on the contemporary period suggest these linkages have intensified in recent years as a result of reduced transportation costs and improved communication technology, which have made the world a smaller space, increasing the difficulties of effectively managing migration. Transnational communication today is instantaneous. Letters take less time to reach their destinations and have been supplemented with telephones, cameras, radios, televisions, fax, and email, making it easy for people in, for example, Santo Domingo to learn quickly about job opportunities in New York City. Television and foreign direct investment are said to have intensified ideological links and spread Western consumption expectations, raising aspirations above a level that can be met in developing countries and thus increasing the pressures to migrate.[30]

Numerous works point to the intensification of transnational social linkages and transnational communities in the late twentieth century. For example, one of every six Salvadorians lives in the United States, U.S. style fast-food restaurants, such as Wendy's, pervade San Salvador; and teenagers lobby their parents to leave for the United States.[31] In the Dominican Republic migration has become self-reinforcing, as migrants reinforce the advertising messages of foreign firms by returning with electrical appliances and other mass consumer goods that create expectations that are unattainable for others unless they join the migratory flows.[32]

In summary, scholars have articulated different views on continuity and change in the role of the state in managing migration in the late twentieth century. This debate has permeated both academia and the public policy arena. As will be seen in later chapters, the views of union leaders began to incline toward change in the late twentieth century and to indicate that in their view the government's ability to control migration, while still substantial, is nonetheless incomplete. Thus they saw less reason to seek further restrictionist measures, which would be unlikely to attain their stated goal. This consideration (along with skepticism about the right of the state to fully control migration), constitutes part of the argument to explain why unions defected from the restrictionist coalition more often in the late twentieth century than they did in the early twentieth century.

Internationalization of Human Rights Concerns

Human rights concerns are a relatively new issue in international politics. They have emerged alongside a liberalization of normative discourse and practice in democracies such as the United States after the civil rights movement, and France, which extended the vote to women after World War II.

The subject of human rights reached the global agenda in the aftermath of World War II and intensified at an unprecedented rate in the late twentieth century. There are differing views on the practical impact (or lack thereof) of this change, and on the implications of this change for state sovereignty. For some, human rights issues have contributed to a blurring of the line between international and domestic law, and exclusive domestic jurisdiction has become increasingly conditional on adherence to international principles such as human rights norms.[33] Others point out that, while human rights politics today do at times challenge some aspects of conventional notions of sovereignty, this is nothing new in so far as relations between rulers and the ruled in one state have continuously been an issue of concern to outside actors, and national autonomy was always subjected to challenges in previous eras in other ways, such as through a concern for religious or minority rights.[34] Despite these differences, most observers agree that, while human wrongs continue to take place as before, the increased attention given to human rights concerns is a new development on the global agenda.

Human rights first became an issue on the agenda of international politics with the abolition of slavery and the slave trade in the nineteenth century, when Britain violated the norm of non-intervention (particularly against Brazil) so as to end slavery.[35] The rights of workers were then given some marginal attention in the global arena after World War I, when the allied governments, seeking to avoid the outbreak of social conflict and to prevent a spread of the revolutionary movement in Russia, established the International Labor Organization (ILO) in 1919, a tripartite institution with representation by government, business, and labor. The ILO has since drawn up various conventions to protect workers' rights on such issues as freedom of association, organizing and bargaining rights, and workplace health and safety standards. The ILO has also drawn up a number of conventions that seek to protect the rights of migrant workers, such as the 1925 Equality of Treatment (Accident Compensation) Convention, ratified by 120 countries by 2001; the 1962 Equality of Treatment (Social Security) Convention, ratified by 38 countries by 2001; and the 1975 Migrant Workers' Convention, ratified by 18 countries by 2001. The ILO has also engaged in a range of studies, reports, and seminars concerned with migrant workers' rights.

It was only after the Holocaust and World War II that human rights issues gained a more widespread place in international discussions. One way in which this was manifested was through the setting of international human rights standards in various agreements such as the Universal Declaration of Human Rights (adopted unanimously by the UN General Assembly in 1948); the Genocide Convention (1948); the Convention Relating to the Status of Refugees (1951); and, following decolonization and the associated increase in the number of African and Asian states in the United Nations, the International Convention on the Elimination of All Forms of Racial Discrimination (1965); the Convention on the Elimination of Discrimination Against Women (1979); the Convention Against Torture (1984); the Declaration on the Right to Development (1986); and the Convention on the Rights of the Child (1989).[36]

Human rights politics gained increasing salience on the global agenda in the late twentieth century when, on the one hand, the end of the

Cold War opened a space for change by ending ideological bipolarity and reducing incentives for the United States and the Soviet Union to continue supporting repressive governments that systematically violated human rights; and, on the other hand, there was a proliferation of human rights non-governmental organizations that pushed for change, such as Amnesty International, Human Rights Watch, the International Commission of Jurists, Doctors Without Borders, and many others. The UN held a special Conference on Human Rights in 1993, and the General Assembly approved the establishment of a High Commissioner for Human Rights the same year.

These changes in the global arena in the 1990s were sufficient to lead Henry Kissinger (a former U.S. Secretary of State and National Security Adviser, and a well-known adherent of the Realist state-centric tradition of international politics), to write at the turn of the millennium that "In less than a decade, an unprecedented movement has emerged to submit international politics to judicial procedures. It has spread with extraordinary speed. ..."[37]

This development was particularly clear in regard to war crimes tribunals. While the idea for setting up an international tribunal to judge war crimes and crimes against humanity was first proposed after World War I, at that time nothing came of it. The Nuremberg War Crimes Trials of Nazi leaders in 1945–46 set certain limits on the norm of state sovereignty, and set the precedent for the war crimes tribunals of the post-Cold War era.[38] Discussions about establishing a permanent international criminal court were held in the early 1950s, but they were then stalled, and atrocities such as the "Killing Fields" in Cambodia passed without trial. It was only at the end of the Cold War, in 1989, that the UN General Assembly requested that work begin again on drawing up a permanent International Criminal Court, and this time the discussions were successful in large part due to the lobbying efforts of the numerous relatively new non-governmental human rights organizations.[39] International Criminal Tribunals were established for Rwanda and the Former Yugoslavia in the 1990s, and a permanent International Criminal Court (ICC) to uphold international laws banning genocide, war crimes, and crimes against humanity was established in 1998. Ratifications proceeded much more quickly than had been predicted, and by June 2001 the Statute had already been ratified by thirty-six governments, more than half of the sixty needed for the ICC to come into force.[40] Another example of the increasing salience and internationalization of human rights issues in the late twentieth century was the British decision to detain Augusto Pinochet, former President of Chile, when he visited Britain in 1998. The British decision, which placed the principle of universal jurisdiction above that of sovereign immunity, was taken in response to an extradition request from a Spanish judge who sought to try the former Chilean President for crimes committed against Spanish people in Chilean territory.

The internationalization of human rights, like the internationalization of the economy, has been uneven in different regions of the world. The change in the human rights sphere has been most intense in Europe, where the governments of newly established democracies at the end of World War II pushed to set up the European Convention for the Protection of Human Rights (ECHR) so as to block domestic threats from the totalitarian Right and Left, and to thereby lock in and consolidate democracy and prevent international aggression.[41] The ECHR, which came into force in 1953, has much more meaningful monitoring and enforcement procedures than do other international human rights conventions, and governments have consistently complied with ECHR judgments on a broad range of issues, such as treatment of prisoners, military codes, wiretapping, and censorship of the press.[42] The ECHR (which is a completely separate institution from the European Union) has become more encompassing over time. First, its membership base expanded to over forty countries by the turn of the millennium, with a major enlargement occurring in the 1990s when the new democracies of Eastern Europe joined. Second, the number of petitions submitted to the ECHR has grown dramatically over time. The number of private petitions to the ECHR rose from 138 in 1955 to 4,750 submitted in 1997. The numbers continued to grow in the 1990s: French nationals submitted 392 petitions in 1995 and 448 petitions in 1997; German nationals submitted 180 petitions in 1995 and 298 petitions in 1997; the number of petitions from Italy increased from 567 in 1995 to 825 in 1997; and the number from the United Kingdom rose from 372 in 1995 to 400 in 1997.[43] The ECHR has consistently declined to consider most of the petitions submitted to it, but the number of cases considered over time, like the number of petitions submitted, has gone up; and when the ECHR has considered a petition, the petitioner has often won the case against the government. The ECHR decided 17 cases from 1959 to 1976, 50 cases from 1978 to 1984, 141 cases from 1985 to 1990, and 213 cases from 1991 to 1993. A significant number of these cases involved aliens.[44]

The regional agreements designed to uphold human rights in the Americas, while more elaborate than human rights conventions in Africa, Asia, or the Middle East, have been weak by comparison with the

European Convention. The Inter-American Commission of Human Rights has produced reports that have helped to publicize human rights violations, but its decisions have rarely been implemented.

The United States itself has had a markedly poor record in ratifying international human rights conventions by comparison with other liberal democracies, presenting a puzzle as to why this has been the case. For example, the United States took forty years to ratify the Genocide Convention, and when the United States did finally ratify the Convention, it attached conditions to its approval that heavily diluted the substance of its commitment. The United States voted against the International Criminal Court when its founding treaty was created in 1998. Although the United States has since signed this treaty, it has not ratified it, whereas many U.S. allies have ratified the ICC treaty. The United States has not ratified any ILO conventions on migrant workers, whereas a number of other liberal democratic post-industrial countries have, for example France, Germany, Italy, Sweden, Denmark, and the United Kingdom. Nonetheless, U.S. federal courts have increasingly cited the Universal Declaration of Human Rights, and a substantial proportion of the cases where the Human Rights Declaration has been cited have involved immigration issues. The Universal Declaration was cited in seventy-six federal cases between 1948 and 1994. Seventy of those cases occurred after 1970, and fifty-nine of them took place after 1980. 49 percent of the total seventy-six cases involved immigration issues.[45]

The internationalization of human rights issues has implications for migration politics, the subject to which this section now turns. As articulated by Joseph Carens, liberal democratic principles entail granting access to citizenship to those people who are members of the society by virtue of living in the community for a period of time, and to those people with family ties to a member of the society.[46] Thus, one would expect a liberalization of norms since the early twentieth century to particularly impact on immigration policy toward those people who live and work in the country, but who lack legal status and legal equality (such as undocumented or illegal immigrants); or toward those people who have not yet entered the country but who have moral claims resulting from family ties to members of the society (that is, family reunion migration). A liberalization of norms would be less likely to impact on immigration policy preferences toward those people who have not yet entered the country and who lack close social links with members of the society.

Various scholars who consider that the relationship between states and migrants is changing in the late twentieth century have developed arguments that focus on norm liberalization or the internationalization of human rights concerns as the explanation for this change. These approaches generally share the view that the relationship between states and migrants has changed in the late twentieth century due to an increasing prominence of norms that uphold human rights and that question the right of the state to control migration. Some of these studies focus on immigrant policy rather than immigration policy, but they overlap with this study in terms of thematic concerns and thus warrant brief reference here. The most convincing evidence presented to support these arguments is drawn from the role of the judiciary in upholding the rights of migrants as human beings.

The changing approach, and crucial role of the judiciary was pointed out by Peter Schuck in his influential article in 1984.[47] Schuck, focusing on the U.S. case, argued that transformations in immigration law reflected what he referred to as a weakening in the notion of national sovereignty. Court decisions have increasingly departed from the classical legal order, bringing immigration law belatedly into line with the mainstream of public law in the United States. The new legal doctrine was exemplified in *Plyer v. Doe* in 1982, when the Supreme Court's ruling compelled a state to provide free public education to the children of undocumented aliens. Schuck attributes these legal transformations to structural changes in objective circumstances; to a new social reality where new social contracts between undocumented aliens and American society are being negotiated each day; and to changes in ideology and the emergence of a new legal consciousness reflecting communitarian norms.

Schuck's emphasis on a changing ideology was expanded on by James Hollifield, who argued that the emergence of new legal cultures and human rights-based politics at the domestic level of analysis constrained the state and decreased the state's capacity to control migration in liberal democracies such as France, the United States, and Germany. For example, in France, the Council of State cancelled attempts by the government to inhibit family reunification in the late 1970s so as to uphold the rights of migrants.[48]

The role of changing norms was taken to a global level of analysis by Yasemin Soysal, drawing on the sociological institutionalist literature and complementing Sassen's focus on changes and dynamics in the economy at the global level of analysis. Soysal's focus is on the subject of immigrant incorporation (not immigration policy), and she argues that there has been an erosion in the distinction between formal citizens and resident aliens in terms of their rights and duties. Immigrants have increasingly been incorporated into the society and polity of the countries in which they reside, even without formal citizenship status. Soysal attributes this to a change in global discourse and global culture, as "human rights are now a pervasive feature of global public culture,"[49] and "global discourses and models increasingly penetrate national frameworks."[50] For Soysal, the change in global culture has generated a more universalistic or "postnational" model of membership, in which "what were previously defined as national rights become entitlements legitimized on the basis of personhood."[51] A similar approach has been adopted by David Jacobson, who emphasizes the role of international human rights conventions, which, working their way through domestic judicial systems, "are becoming the vehicle that is transforming the nation-state system."[52]

The most convincing evidence given by Soysal and Jacobson to support their arguments focuses on the role of the judiciary. But generally their studies lack detailed in-depth case studies or process tracing needed to explore to what extent there is a causal connection between changes in the so-called global culture and local trends and local attributes or behavior.[53] They fail to consider alternative possible causal explanations for the rise in rights given to resident aliens. For example, governments may see this as the route to avoid riots and promote domestic social peace.[54] Subsequent work by Amy Gurowitz that sought to test arguments that point to the role of international norms shows that they played a role in changing Japanese policies toward Koreans and recent migrant workers in Japan by providing pro-immigrant actors with a tool to use in domestic policy conflicts.[55]

Despite important differences in the level of analysis, through a focus on the judiciary these studies all suggest that human rights norms have played an increasingly important role in the formulation of immigration or immigrant policy in liberal democracies in the late twentieth century.

This book expands on this theme by focusing on unions and their changing norms on immigration policy. While unions still display some illiberalism at times, they have nonetheless shown greater normative concern for the rights of migrants in their role as human beings than did their counterparts in the early twentieth century, and they have opposed those restrictionist measures that most clearly clash with liberal principles. This is evident in both countries when viewed in historical perspective. However, French unions, with a more ideological identity than their pragmatic U.S. counterparts (and facing a deeper human rights regime at the external regional European level than is the case for U.S. unions), articulated greater concern for human rights issues and much more often pointed to regional and international conventions to legitimize and strengthen their position in domestic conflicts than did U.S. unions.

This skepticism about the right of the state to completely control migration (along with skepticism about the ability of the state to fully control migration), constitutes part of the argument to explain why unions changed coalitions.

If unions consider that the state's ability and/or right to control migration flows, while considerable, is incomplete, one would not expect unions to pressure for those restrictionist measures that they deem to be ineffective and/or undesirable. Instead, one may expect unions to focus on an alternative strategy for raising wages and work conditions, such as organizing immigrants.

Organizing Immigrants

Before discussing the existing literature on organizing immigrants, and its relation to the argument presented here, it is appropriate to briefly digress and provide summary background material on the different identities of unions, particularly with regard to organizing. These diverse identities and approaches to organizing have mattered, and have impacted on the ways in which unions have viewed and filtered the broader changes discussed above.

Diverse Union Identities and Organizing

Different unions and labor movements have diverse identities, or lenses, habits, and values through which they interpret and react to the external environment. One aspect of identity that is of particular concern to this study is the union's approach toward membership or organizing. There is substantial diversity in unions' approaches to organizing among the cases analyzed in this study, ranging from the exclusionary U.S. construction craft unions, to the inclusive but inactive French unions, to some inclusive and active U.S. unions (United Mine Workers in the early twentieth century and the Service Employees International Union in the late twentieth century).

The mainstream of the labor movement in the United States in the early twentieth century was dominated by the American Federation of Labor (AFL). The AFL had an anti-radical, or conservative, ideology, and considered that "capitalism preserved certain conditions which were valuable for the survival of liberty despite its evident flaws and injustices ... [and] consel[led] that industrial capitalism should be reformed rather than repudiated."[56] A significant portion of the AFL membership was in the building trades, and the construction craft unions were well known for their exclusionary ideology that upheld the importance of father-son solidarity. Craft unions, representing skilled workers with some power in the labor market, had an institutional structure that was designed to control job placement through the hiring hall, providing the unions with an incentive to exclude immigrants from membership so as to preclude them from the more desirable union jobs.

Although there were some inclusive, organizing U.S. unions in the early twentieth century (most notably, the United Mine Workers), the main spurt to an inclusive organizing approach in the United States came with the formation of the Congress of Industrial Organizations (CIO) in 1936 which, unlike the AFL, held the belief that unskilled workers should be organized.

Inclusive U.S. unions have had a pragmatic, incremental (rather than a revolutionary) approach to change. Revolutionary movements in the United States, such as the Industrial Workers of the World, were small and short-lived. Inclusive U.S. unions have been more active organizers than their French counterparts. Among other things, U.S. unions, unlike their French counterparts, have salaried organizers. The amount of financial resources, time, and energy devoted to organizing by U.S. unions has varied among unions and over time. The Service Employees International Union (SEIU) was the most dynamic union in this regard in the late twentieth century, and the AFL-CIO began to devote substantially more energy and resources to organizing when the former President of the SEIU, John Sweeney, became President of the AFL-CIO in 1995.

The differences in approaches to organizing in the United States began to break down in the later twentieth century as the construction craft unions began to give attention to organizing after a sharp decline in union density, the lines between craft and industrial unions became blurred, and unions increasingly sought members in any economic sector rather than focusing on a single sector.

Most French unions (including construction unions) had inclusive ideals in both the early and the late twentieth century. The principle of industrial unionism gained more widespread acceptance in France than in the United States in the early twentieth century. It was generally accepted by all the French union confederations by the inter-war years. But French unions have not generally engaged in active organization of workers, be they native or immigrant. French unions have "tiny organizational apparatuses."[57] The historically under-institutionalized nature of the French industrial relations system, the notable shortage of union funds, which stunts the ability to provide selective private material benefits to potential members and to provide strike funds, the absence of salaried organizers, and the reliance on volunteer militants has resulted in a situation where "the real cement of French unions has traditionally been the *ideological commitment* of its militants, a sense of devotion to the 'working class' ..."[58] (emphasis in the original).

France has had a plurality of union confederations in the twentieth century that have shared the feature of a strong ideological commitment, although they have had different views over how to promote social change in practice. The most prominent of these confederations in the early twentieth century were the moderate Confédération Générale du Travail (CGT), with an ideology that was reformist and to a certain extent class collaborationist; and the revolutionary Confédération Générale du Travail Unitaire (CGTU), which split from the CGT in 1921, became "bolshevised" and dominated by the Communist Party, and approached issues through the prism of Marxist concepts, class conflict, and international class solidarity. The CGT and the CGTU reunified in 1936. In the post-World War II era the main confederations were the CGT, which became dominated by members of the former CGTU and had close links with the Communist Party; and the Confédération Française Démocratique du Travail (CFDT), which emerged in 1964 from a Catholic union movement after a period of deconfessionalization when it abandoned "older Christian doctrines of class harmony and adopt[ed] more aggressive class conflictual perspectives."[59] The CFDT, following a radical and militant period, shifted to a more moderate, reformist "recentering".

Despite their differences, for the most part French unions have been "class oriented, as opposed to particularistic."[60] In contrast to the pragmatic, incremental approach of the inclusive U.S. unions that focus on more immediate interests, inclusive French unions have shown a strong ideational component and a revolutionary, transformative ideology that never took on the same prominence in the United States.

In summary, the case studies included in this book include unions with diverse identities in general, and to organizing more specifically. This provides an opportunity to explore to what extent and in what way diversity matters in the face of global changes. As will be seen in later chapters, unions filtered the global changes in ways that reflected their specific identities.

To return now to the subject of existing scholarship on organizing immigrants. This literature has focused on immigrant incorporation into (or exclusion from) unions.[61] Although this literature on organizing immigrants does not directly address unions' immigration policy preferences, it does nonetheless give some insights that point to the need to consider the relationship between organizing and immigration policy preferences. It suggests that there may be tensions between restrictionist immigration policy measures and effective organizing.

Existing Literature on Organizing Immigrants in France

With regard to France, literature on the early twentieth century points to a variety of government actions, such as expulsions from the country and harassments at union meetings, that intimidated immigrant workers from joining unions.[62] These examples given on expulsions implicitly brings to attention the need to consider connections between immigration policy measures and the (in) effectiveness of organizing immigrants (although this connection is not explicated in this literature). It shows that restrictionist immigration policy measures, such as expulsions, can impede organization. It thus provides a rationale for why unions that seek to effectively organize immigrants might resist certain restrictionist immigration policy measures.

Literature on organizing immigrants in the late twentieth century in France implicitly brings to our attention another linkage between effective organization and union immigration policy preferences. This literature points to ways in which unions adapted certain policies to take into consideration the specific needs and concerns of immigrant workers so as to encourage them to join unions. Religion is often focused on as the specific concern that needed to be accommodated so as to facilitate organization. As shown by René Mouriaux and Catherine Wihtol de Wenden, when the workers at the Renault automobile factory at Billancourt autonomously submitted a petition to the management asking that a mosque be built in the factory, the CGT, although initially divided on the issue, then supported the petition.[63] As one CGT official stated:

> This demand for a prayer room, we blocked it from the list of demands for several years. We said "we are not a church, we are secular." When the petition was put forward, our position changed as we found ourselves facing a situation that included a mass of people. If we had blocked the demand, we risked pushing the believers to oppose us ... nonetheless the issue caused a fair amount of upheaval at the CGT.[64]

Management also accommodated the request so as to maintain peace and productivity at the factory.[65]

One part of the argument of this book builds on that line of reasoning, but focuses on immigration policy preferences (rather than religion) as the specific concern that unions have come to accommodate. It asks if unions adapted their immigration policy preferences (for example, by favoring amnesty or regularization programs) so as to accommodate the specific needs and concerns of immigrants and thus facilitate organization in the late twentieth century. Later chapters show that unions viewed their support for non-restrictionist measures such as amnesty programs as a way of meeting the specific needs of immigrants so as to facilitate organization.

Existing Literature on Organizing Immigrants in the United States

Quite a lot of literature on organizing immigrants in the United States explicitly or implicitly critiques the view that immigrants are difficult to organize. This literature argues that immigrants (legal and undocumented) can be organized under certain conditions; and the arguments are substantiated by in-depth case studies.

A classic work along these lines is Victor Greene's case study of the Slav immigrant workers in the Pennsylvania anthracite coal mines at the turn of the century. Greene critiqued what was at that time the conventional wisdom that immigrants impeded organization due to language barriers, or by acting as strike breakers or by being forced by poverty to work for low wages. Instead he argued that immigrants were organizable. He pointed to alternative causes for the failures in organization in the 1870s and 1880s, such as the power of operators, defective and conservative union leadership, and rivalry between different labor organizations.[66]

A later study by Hector Delgado similarly critiqued the conventional wisdom on the "unorganizable," but he focused on undocumented immigrants later in the twentieth century. Delgado's book involves a case study of a successful organizing drive among undocumented immigrants working in a waterbed factory in Los Angeles in the mid-1980s so as to shed light on factors that facilitate organization. Likewise, a recent volume, edited by Ruth Milkman, explores the conditions that facilitate, or impede, immigrant unionization through studies of cases from the late twentieth century in California.[67]

This historical and contemporary scholarship on organizing immigrants in the United States, while giving valuable insights for this study, does not directly broach the linkage between organizing and union immigration policy preferences. The argument of this study is in part that unions refrained from advocating certain restrictionist immigration policy measures so as to facilitate organizing, which is an alternative strategy for raising wages. While tensions between restrictionism and organizing have always existed, these tensions have been heightened for those who consider that the role of the state in managing migration has declined in the late twentieth century. For example, as mentioned in the previous chapter, increasing restrictions against legal immigrants would be expected to increase the quantity of illegal immigrants, who may be more difficult to organize than legal immigrants.

In short, the existing literature on organizing immigrants does not directly get at the question posed in this study: why unions more often defected from restrictionism in the late twentieth century than they did in the early twentieth century. The next section turns to literature that discusses unions' immigration policy preferences.

Unions' Immigration Policy Preferences

There is a marked absence of work on unions' immigration policy preferences in the United States and France in the late twentieth century. However, there is some for earlier time periods. But this literature often discusses unions' immigration policy preferences as a sub-issue rather than as the central focus, or dependent variable of the studies. Of more importance, this literature does not set out to consider the late twentieth century and thus misses the puzzle posed here, and likewise overlooks how changing union views on the ability and/or right of the state to control migration in the late twentieth century may impact on unions' immigration policy preferences.

Existing Literature on Unions' Immigration Policy Preferences in the United States

Gwendolyn Mink analyzes the reasons for the AFL's nativist immigration policy preferences in the early twentieth century. She argues that immigration from new source countries in the late nineteenth and early twentieth century, in conjunction with mechanization, increased the leverage of employers and threatened the privileged position of craft unions. The possibility of responding to the new unskilled and semi-skilled immigrants by organizing them would "have challenged the monopoly of craft-based unionism over working-class organization."[68] Thus the craft unions instead lobbied for immigration restriction and engaged in "legislative struggles to secure a closed-shop society."[69]

However, Mink's central concern is different. She seeks to understand the connection between the trade union response to immigration and the political development of American trade unionism (the American version of labor politics); or, more broadly, American political history.

Likewise Kitty Calavita discusses unions' immigration policy preferences in the early twentieth century, in mid-century toward the Bracero Program, and in the 1970s toward California's "employer sanctions" legislation.[70] But the central focus of her work instead seeks to interpret U.S. immigration policymaking and the dynamics behind it. For Calavita, immigration law is symbolic law, reflecting the contradictions inherent to immigration in democratic capitalist societies. Understanding the role of the state is central to Calavita's work, which is grounded in a dialectical-structural model of the state while also taking human agency seriously. But, as explaining unions' immigration policy preferences is not her central goal, she does not address a central concern of this book: how the views of unions' on the state's role may impact on their immigration policy preferences.

Existing Literature on Unions' Immigration Policy Preferences in France

The connection between the role of the state and unions' immigration policy preferences has been mentioned by both Gary Cross and Léon Gani in their studies on France in earlier time periods.

Cross, in his study on the politics of immigration in France in the inter-war years, published in 1983, suggests that at that time strong state control over migration mitigated the need for unions to resort to violence or to shout loudly for restrictionism. He argues that the "state in fact controlled immigration in order to minimize potential French labor unrest. ... Central ... was government control over the entry of aliens into France and thus their access to her job market. The state opened and closed the frontier to labor immigration as if it were a faucet."[71] At times of rising unemployment (such as 1927 and 1932), the government adopted various restrictionist measures such as the denial of permits and repatriations. More foreign workers left France than entered France. Thus, while the demands of business had substantial influence over government policy, the "state was not, however, simply the 'executive committee of the bourgeoisie.'"[72]

Cross' suggestion that strong state control resulted in less loud restrictionism by unions than might otherwise have occurred provides a convincing account of the inter-war period. But the position of unions in the late twentieth century provides a puzzle for his argument. Migration was reduced when the government halted labor migration in

1974. But, unlike times when restrictionist measures were imposed in the early twentieth century, in the late twentieth century, despite the imposition of measures designed to reach "zero immigration," entrances remained significant and certainly were not less than exits. The pattern in the late twentieth century showed that the government could no longer open and close the frontier to labor immigration "as if it were a faucet" as it had done in the early twentieth century. After 1974 the government sought to further restrict migration during a period of high unemployment. But entrances to France remained significantly higher than exits. The logic of Cross' argument would lead us to expect that this appearance of declining state ability to turn the tap on and off (by comparison with the inter-war years) in conjunction with high unemployment would lead unions to protest loudly for restrictionism. But, *in reverse* of this expectation, unions have opposed further restrictionist proposals or laws. This presents the puzzle as to why.

Data in Léon Gani's review of unions' immigration policy preferences in France, published in 1972, suggest part of the answer. Gani's data indicate that unions may abandon a restrictionist posture due to a notion that such a posture is not grounded in reality. But the rationale for why unions saw restrictionism as unrealistic in earlier time periods differs from the rationale presented in this book for the late twentieth century. Gani noted that after a decade of calling for a halt to immigration in its resolutions on immigrant workers, a faction emerged at the CGT Congress in 1963 that questioned the validity of continuing to demand a halt to immigration. Subsequent resolutions on immigrant workers did not include this demand.[73] Gani explains that this new approach resulted from a sense that immigration would inevitably continue given the government and employers' search for profits.[74] In other words, the union's identity, or way of mapping the world, mattered. The CGT held an instrumentalist view of the state, seeing business and the state as one and the same, and this impacted on its stance to immigration policy.

This reason for a sense of inevitability differs from the argument of this study, which is that even if the government seeks to restrict immigration it will not be able to completely succeed. As will be seen in chapter six, contrary to instrumentalist notions of the state, the government did then impose restrictionist measures in the 1970s, thereby undermining the rationale for unions to maintain the reasoning behind the sense of inevitability explained by Gani for an earlier time period. Not surprisingly, the CGT then, in the late 1970s (several years after Gani's book was published), returned to an explicitly restrictionist posture.[75] This begs the question of to what extent and why unions have since refrained from advocating restrictionist immigration policy measures in the 1980s and the 1990s—years of high unemployment generating conditions that for theoretical and for historical-empirical reasons might be expected to elicit a restrictionist response by unions. A thorough answer to this question requires considering a variety of factors, but a good deal of understanding is gained by considering unions' views on the changing role of the state resulting from economic internationalization and the internationalization of human rights concerns.

Conclusion

Previous scholarship did not pose the question raised in this study, and thus it is not surprising that the literature to date does not provide a satisfactory answer. Nonetheless, literature exists on a range of themes that need to be considered to address the puzzle posed in this book. This study builds on, and connects, this broader scholarship relating to, first, internationalization and, second, organizing immigrants so as to develop an argument that explains why unions changed coalitions in immigration policy debates.

CHAPTER 3

In Pursuit of Complete Control: Labor Unions and U.S. Immigration Policy in the Early Twentieth Century

Immigration policy generated major controversies in the United States in the early twentieth century. This chapter focuses on the immigration policy preferences of unions at that time so as to give a baseline for comparison with unions' immigration policy preferences in the late twentieth century, which constitute the subject of the subsequent chapter.

Unions pressured for protectionism in the early twentieth century. Representatives of the Left went as far as to seek support for their immigration policy stance at the level of the Second International. The American delegates submitted restrictionist immigration policy resolutions to the Second International's meeting in Amsterdam (1904), and then again at the International's meeting in Stuttgart (1907) (a meeting that was opened by a demonstration of 50,000 workers). The U.S. delegates were unsuccessful in gaining support at these meetings, which were held in Europe, from where many of the aspiring migrants came. Other delegates rejected the American position and the American motions were defeated.[1]

The historical cases selected for study here have been chosen so as to explore the impact of different approaches to organizing on unions' immigration policy preferences in the early twentieth century. This chapter thus supplements a review of the AFL's position with a case study of the exclusionary construction craft unions that sought to limit union membership; and, of more interest, a case study of the inclusionary United Mine Workers (UMW), which was the largest union that engaged in active organizing at that time. The study of the UMW was chosen so as to assess whether organizing pressures alone (a concern to avoid alienating potential immigrant members) pushed the union to depart from restrictionism in the early twentieth century, at a time when unions more likely considered that government immigration policy control measures would be effective and desirable. The data show that the UMW at that time did not oppose restrictionist proposals, presenting a puzzle as to why organizing unions in the late twentieth century did do so.

Immigration into the United States: Background

Migration Flows

Improved transportation systems in the mid-late nineteenth century facilitated a new wave of trans-Atlantic migration. The development of the railroad system in Europe integrated people living in rural areas into the trans-Atlantic network by giving them easier access to ports of departure for the United States; and the transition from sailing ships to steamships in the 1860s and 1870s improved safety and sharply reduced the time that it took to cross the Atlantic.

Immigration into the United States increased rapidly at the beginning of the twentieth century. The total inflow was over 1 million in 1905 and for several years after that. The sharp increase at that time came from the new source countries of Southern, Eastern, and Central Europe. For example, the number of immigrants from Italy rose from 12,354 in 1880 to 215,537 in 1910; and the number of immigrants from Russia and the Baltic states increased from 5,014 in 1880 to 186,792 in 1910. At the same time there was a significant reduction in the number of immigrants from the old source areas of Britain, Ireland, Scandinavia, and Germany.[2]

Migration was actively encouraged by steamship agents who recruited passengers for shipping companies, often promising to connect the immigrant to a job once in the United States. The activities of steamship agents were reinforced by family and friends already in the United States and by return migrants, who often gave aspiring migrants crucial information about jobs, in addition to giving financial resources for the trans-Atlantic voyage.[3]

Most immigrants to the United States in the early twentieth century were unskilled, and they often came from rural regions. The overwhelming majority, upon entry to the United States, stated that they

Table 3.1 Immigration flows into the United States: 1900–1939

Year	Immigrants from all countries	Year	Immigrants from all countries
1900	448,572	1920	430,001
1901	487,918	1921	805,228
1902	648,743	1922	309,556
1903	857,046	1923	522,919
1904	812,870	1924	706,896
1905	1,026,499	1925	294,314
1906	1,100,735	1926	304,488
1907	1,285,349	1927	335,175
1908	782,870	1928	307,255
1909	751,786	1929	279,678
1910	1,041,570	1930	241,700
1911	878,587	1931	97,139
1912	838,172	1932	35,576
1913	1,197,892	1933	23,068
1914	1,218,480	1934	29,470
1915	326,700	1935	34,956
1916	298,826	1936	36,329
1917	295,403	1937	50,244
1918	110,618	1938	67,895
1919	141,132	1939	82,998

Source: U.S. Immigration and Naturalization Service, *Statistical Yearbook of the Immigration and Naturalization Service, 1992* (Washington, D.C.: U.S. Government Printing Office, 1993), p. 25.

had no occupation or were farm laborers and foremen; laborers; or craftsmen, foremen, and operatives.[4] Once in the United States, most of the new immigrants went to work in the growing urban regions and the industrial sector of the U.S. economy, where technological developments increased the demand for unskilled workers, who came to replace skilled craftsmen. Immigrant workers were concentrated in such sectors as mining, garments, steel, and the automobile industry.[5]

Immigration Policy

The United States enacted immigration laws that applied differential treatment to different regions of the world in the early twentieth century.

The most restrictionist measures were applied to people from Asia. The Chinese Exclusion Act, which barred immigration from China, was enacted in 1882. It was initially instituted as a temporary measure, and was then made permanent in 1904. The same exclusionary treatment was extended to people from all other countries in Asia in 1924, when

Table 3.2 Unemployment rates as a percentage of the civilian labor force: 1900–1937

Year	Unemployed percentage of civilian labor force	Year	Unemployed percentage of civilian labor force
1900	5.0	1919	1.4
1901	4.0	1920	5.2
1902	3.7	1921	11.7
1903	3.9	1922	6.7
1904	5.4	1923	2.4
1905	4.3	1924	5.0
1906	1.7	1925	3.2
1907	2.8	1926	1.8
1908	8.0	1927	3.3
1909	5.1	1928	4.2
1910	5.9	1929	3.2
1911	6.7	1930	8.7
1912	4.6	1931	15.9
1913	4.3	1932	23.6
1914	7.9	1933	24.9
1915	8.5	1934	21.7
1916	5.1	1935	20.1
1917	4.6	1936	16.9
1918	1.4	1937	14.3

Source: U.S. Bureau of the Census, *Historical Statistics of the United States, Colonial Times to 1970* (Washington, D.C.: Bureau of the Census, 1975), part 1, p. 135.

those aliens who were ineligible for U.S. citizenship (that is, all Asians) became barred from immigration into the United States.[6]

The other main concern of the restrictionists was immigration from the new source countries of Southern and Eastern Europe. Discussions on measures to curtail this new immigration focused on two issues: a literacy test and the enactment of a national origins quota system.

Restrictionists put a lot of time into obtaining a law that would require immigrants to pass a literacy test. The measure was approved by Congress in 1896, 1913, 1915, and 1917, but it was barred by a presidential veto each time. However, in 1917 the restrictionists had sufficient votes in Congress to override the presidential veto, and the literacy test was enacted into law. The measure banned adult immigrants who were unable to read a passage in some language. Advocates of the law stated that it would reduce immigration by 25 percent. The main victims would be from the new source countries of Southern and Eastern Europe, where the illiteracy rates were higher than in the old source countries.[7]

The other measure that was designed to restrict immigration from the new source countries was a national origins quota system, which was initially enacted as a temporary measure in the Emergency Quota Law of 1921 (a year of high unemployment, as can be seen from table 3.2) and was then revised and made permanent in the National Origins Act of 1924.

Under the Emergency Quota Law of 1921 each country was assigned an admissions quota that was to be 3 percent of the number of foreign born of its nationality present in the United States at the time of the 1910 census. This would enable immigration from old source countries to continue at the pre-war level, while sharply reducing immigration from the new source countries.

The quota system was revised in the National Origins Act of 1924. The size of the quota was reduced to 2 percent of the number of foreign born in the United States in the baseline year, and the baseline year was moved back to 1890. This had the effect of sharply reducing the size of the quotas for the new source countries. For example, the Italian quota was reduced from 42,000 to 4,000; and the Polish quota was reduced from 31,000 to 6,000.[8]

Western Hemisphere countries were exempted from the national origins quota system, ensuring business of a source of labor from Mexico and Canada. Restrictionists sought to reduce Mexican immigration by incorporating the Western Hemisphere into the national origins quota system in the late 1920s, but they failed to attain their goal.

Restrictionists likewise failed in their attempts to enact new laws to suspend, or further curtail, immigration during the Great Depression. However, although laws were not changed, restrictionism was sharply increased in the 1930s by administrative measures. First, to restrict entrance, the administration began to seriously implement the previously enacted public charge clause, which barred immigration for those aspiring immigrants who consular officials stated were likely to become a public charge.[9] Second, to increase exit, many Mexican workers were repatriated.[10]

Unions' Immigration Policy Preferences

The American Federation of Labor

The AFL pressures for restrictionism

The conventional wisdom that unions favor restrictionist immigration policy measures so as to reduce the labor supply, pushing them into

an "odd-couple" coalition with cultural conservatives, helps to understand the AFL's position in the early twentieth century. The Federation
at times sought measures that aimed to *completely* restrict migration.
Measures that aimed to completely restrict migration were sought either
against migrants from specific countries, or against migration in general
at specific time periods.

The most extreme position taken by the AFL was with regard to
immigrants from Asia. The AFL consistently advocated expanding the
coverage of the Chinese Exclusion Act to all immigrants from Asia, and
it regularly approved reports and convention resolutions that favored a
complete halt to this immigration. For example, a committee report
adopted at the 1909 AFL Convention noted that "Japanese, Koreans, and
Hindoos are constantly arriving in ports ..." and recommended "that the
Chinese Exclusion Act be so extended that it will apply to all Asiatic
races."[11] A similar report was again adopted at the 1912 Convention, and
a resolution calling for the extension of the Chinese Exclusion Act to
apply to all "Asiatics" was approved in 1913. This policy was reiterated in
the early 1920s, when the main focus of concern was the so-called
Japanese invasion.

The reasons given by the AFL to explain its fight to completely
halt Asian immigration at times referred to economic issues, and explicitly focused on racial issues. For example, one resolution, which was
approved in 1904 and was then considered and approved regularly at the
AFL's annual conventions for several more years after that, stated that:

> Whereas, the American public sentiment against the immigration of
> Chinese labor, as expressed and crystalized in the enactment of the Chinese
> Exclusion Act, finds still stronger justification in demanding prompt and
> adequate measures of protection against the immigration of Japanese and
> Korean labor, on the grounds, first, that the wage and living standard of
> such labor are dangerous to, and must, if granted recognition in the
> United States, prove destructive of the American standards in these essen-
> tial respects; secondly, that the racial incompatibility, as between the
> peoples of the Orient and the United States, presents a problem of race
> preservation which it is our imperative duty to solve in our own favor, and
> which can only be thus solved by a policy of Exclusion; and ...
>   therefore be it
>   Resolved, that the terms of the Chinese Exclusion Act should be
> enlarged and extended so as to permanently exclude from the United
> States and its insular territory all classes of Japanese and Koreans ...[12]

These issues were repeated in other reports and resolutions. For example, AFL President Samuel Gompers, when urging support for the

renewal of the Chinese Exclusion Act in 1902, argued that:

> The introduction or continuance of an element so entirely at variance
> with our economic, political, social and moral conceptions, and so utterly
> incapable of adaptation to the Caucasian ideals of civilization, is not only
> dangerous to us as a class, but is destructive of the very institutions we are
> so earnestly striving to uphold ... every incoming coolie means the
> displacement of an American, and the lowering of the American standard
> of living ...[13]

The AFL also advocated restricting immigration from the new source
countries of Eastern and Southern Europe. The AFL's approach was in
line with the recommendations of the Dillingham Commission, an immigration commission appointed in 1907. The Dillingham Commission's
forty-two volume report, presented in 1910, recommended that the
United States adopt measures designed to restrict further admission of
unskilled labor, among other issues, and it particularly favored the adoption of a literacy test so as to increase restrictionism.[14] The report received
a strong endorsement from the AFL, and AFL President Gompers urged
locals to read the summary statement of the report and to disseminate its
conclusions in local newspapers.[15]

The Dillingham Commission's Report (with which the AFL agreed)
pointed to both racial and economic motivations for restrictionism.
It often portrayed the immigrants from the new source countries of
Southern and Eastern Europe as inferior to old stock immigrants and
argued that they were "far less intelligent" than the old source immigrants.[16] Half of the lengthy report was devoted to the economic effects
of immigration, concluding, without giving supportive evidence, that
the "new" immigration had been detrimental for existing labor standards, and had weakened labor organizations.[17]

The AFL favored the enactment of a literacy test to restrict immigration from the new source countries of Eastern and Southern Europe. It
was thought that this test would be more likely to block migration from
these countries, while allowing for continued migration from the old
source countries.[18] As noted in Gompers' report to the AFL Convention
in 1902:

> This regulation will exclude hardly any of the natives of Great Britain,
> Ireland, Germany, France, or Scandinavia. It will exclude only a small
> proportion of our immigrants from North Italy. It will shut out a consid-
> erable number of South Italians and of Slavs and others equally or more
> undesirable and injurious.

A provision of this kind will be beneficial to the more desirable classes of immigrants, as well as to ourselves. It is good for them, no less than for us, to diminish the number of that class which by reason of its lack of intelligence, is slowest to appreciate the value of organization, and furnishes the easiest victims of the padrones and the unscrupulous employer.[19]

Demands for a literacy test were repeated by the AFL on various occasions then and after as it became increasingly clear that the AFL's demand for a literacy test was in line with the tide in Congress, and had a very good chance of being enacted into law. For example, the Executive Council Report to the AFL Convention in 1905 explicated support for the measure, along with a recommendation to exclude physically unfit people; a resolution favoring what was termed the illiteracy test was approved at the AFL Convention in 1908; and a resolution "demand[ing] the enactment of the illiteracy test, the money test, and increased head tax ..." was adopted at the Convention in 1909.[20] When the literacy test was approved in Congress in 1913, Gompers participated in a conference with President Taft, unsuccessfully attempting to discourage a presidential veto.[21] When a bill including the literacy test was again defeated by a presidential veto in 1915, the subject was described by the AFL's Executive Council as "one of the most vital issues to the interest of the workers of the United States ..."[22]

Support among the AFL leadership for a literacy test became widespread, as can be seen by the large margin of votes against one delegate's attempt to have a clause favoring the literacy test removed from a resolution on immigration at the AFL Convention in 1913. His request was denied by 190 to 5 votes.[23] When the literacy test was finally enacted in 1917, the AFL regarded the measure as a major success.

AFL support for a literacy test brought the Federation into an "odd-couple coalition" with the nativist movement and its "scientific collaborators" the eugenicists, who received funds from, among others, the Russell Sage Foundation, the Rockefellers, and the Guggenheims to pursue their studies on heredity.[24] Prominent leaders of the nativist coalition included Henry Cabot Lodge, a leading Republican senator, who played a major role in blocking immigration from the new source countries of Eastern and Southern Europe. As noted by John Higham, there was a "strange alliance of patricians with union labor, an alliance which linked A.F.L. President Samuel Gompers and Henry Cabot Lodge in the only common endeavor of their two careers."[25] It was Lodge who first introduced the bill for a literacy test, and for him and his colleagues it was clearly a racial issue. Lodge considered that the new immigration threatened "a great and perilous change in the very fabric of our race."[26] As noted by another prominent advocate of the literacy test, Senator William Chandler, "No one has suggested a race distinction. We are confronted with the fact, however, that the poorest immigrants do come from certain races."[27]

Key organizations in the coalition fighting for a literacy test included the Immigration Restriction League, which was run by a small Harvard-educated group from well-established Boston families. The League was an important actor in conducting a successful campaign to sway public opinion in favor of the literacy test.[28] The AFL sat on the same side of the fence as the Immigration Restriction League in the statements that they submitted to the Commission on Immigration Reform. The AFL's statement pointed to its support for the enactment of what it termed the illiteracy test, and the money test, and an increase in the head tax. The Immigration Restriction League's statement pointed to its support for a reading test, an increase in the head tax, and a requirement that immigrants be in possession of money for their support while securing employment, among other measures.[29]

While the AFL was clearly in coalition with these nativist groups, it should be noted that union newspapers and convention proceedings, while at times implying that the immigrants from the new source countries of Eastern and Southern Europe were "inferior" to the old stock immigrants, rarely made overt references to the genetic theories of the eugenicists.

After World War I the AFL favored the enactment of measures that would *completely* prohibit *all* immigration in general for several years. This preference again placed the AFL in an "odd-couple coalition" with organizations such as the American Defense Society, that on other issues had no concern for organized labor.[30]

For the most part, as would be expected by the conventional view on unions' immigration policy preferences, the reason that the AFL articulated a preference for a *complete* suspension of immigration was that immigration contributed to unemployment, and would undermine employment opportunities for American workers. This concern was heightened at the end of World War I, when it was feared that demobilization would generate unemployment and immigrants would compete for scarce jobs. The concern was further exacerbated when unemployment rose in late 1920 and 1921, reaching 11.7 percent.

The rationale for a complete prohibition on all immigration focused on the economic issues laid out by the conventional wisdom when the subject was discussed at the AFL Convention in 1919. For example, as one delegate stated:

> The exclusion of immigrants for a short period of time may be selfish in nature and character, and yet I say I am heartily in accordance with that sort of selfishness if it will give employment to our returning soldiers and sailors, and all unemployed workers who are looking to you for an opportunity to be employed ... .[31]

Likewise, reports at the AFL's Conventions the following two years again reiterated this view that immigration would contribute to unemployment. A report in 1920 noted that the AFL's Executive Council had been vigilant in blocking attempts to open the gates to: "... unskilled workers who might be attracted hither by the high rate of pay and whose presence might in a short time result in such a congestion of the labor market as would result in great confusion and produce a most unfavorable situation."[32]

A report in 1921 noted that: "The AFL has urged the complete restriction of immigration for at least two years .... The great increase in unemployment, there being at least 5,000,000 out of work during the early part of 1921, made it imperative that immigration should be restricted as much as possible."[33] While the main focus was clearly economic issues, at times the reasons given for this demand also addressed concerns about assimilation.

Bills that provided for a complete prohibition on immigration for a temporary period of time were considered but not approved by Congress. Instead, Congress initially approved the temporary Emergency Quota Law in 1921, and then the permanent National Origins Act in 1924.

The AFL supported these laws, but articulated that they were insufficiently restrictionist. The 1921 temporary Emergency Quota Law was regarded as "not entirely satisfactory" as it did not meet the AFL's demand for a law that would temporarily prohibit *all* immigration.[34] After passage of the 1921 Law, the AFL continued to urge that more restrictionist measures be adopted that would reduce immigration below the present quotas.[35] When the Emergency Quota Law of 1921 was replaced by the National Origins Act of 1924, the AFL's Executive Council supported the 1924 Act as a second-best alternative to their preferred outcome of "total suspension of immigration for a period of five years or longer."[36] The AFL continued to favor more complete suspension of immigration, and the Executive Council expressed support for a bill introduced in Congress in 1927 that provided for the almost complete restriction of immigration (the bill was not approved by Congress).[37]

The focus of the AFL shifted to immigration from the Western Hemisphere, particularly Mexico, in the mid-1920s. The National Origins Act of 1924 had completely barred all migration from Asia, and had sharply curtailed migration from the new source countries of Eastern and Southern Europe, leaving the Western Hemisphere as a main source of migrants to the United States.

The subject of immigration from Western Hemisphere countries (particularly Mexico and Canada) initially generated differences of views within the AFL in the mid-1920s. However, those in favor of restricting Western Hemisphere immigration gained the upper hand by 1928. The AFL's official policy, beginning in 1928, favored enacting legislation that would incorporate Mexico and other Latin American countries into the quota system that was applied to European countries under the National Origins Act of 1924.[38] As would be expected by the conventional approach, the reasons given for incorporating Mexico into the quota system focused on issues pertaining to job competition and reflected the view that immigrants generate unemployment. The reasons articulated did not refer to racial issues. Given the lack of inhibition about referring to racial issues with regard to Asians, the absence of such references with regard to immigration from Mexico makes it quite convincing that economic issues were indeed a real motivating factor behind the drive to bring Mexico into the quota system.[39]

When hard times hit and unemployment rose to 8.7 percent in 1930, the AFL increased its calls for restrictionism against immigrants from both the Western Hemisphere and from Europe. The perceived link between immigration and unemployment was summarized in a letter by William Green, President of the AFL, sent to all labor organizations in 1930. The letter urged union members to pressure their members of Congress to vote for a bill under consideration in Congress that would bring Western Hemisphere countries into the quota system. Green noted that: "Most of the immigration is assisted and its purpose is to break down the wage standards in our country. This has added to the acute unemployment situation ..."[40]

Similarly a report included in the Proceedings of the AFL Convention in October 1930 argued that:

> The problem of unemployment is in many respects closely allied to that of immigration. Employment conditions as they are now and as they are likely to continue for some time are such as to call for not only the utmost restriction of immigration possible under existing law, but also the enactment of additional legislation to provide for further restrictions. In times like the present there should be almost complete exclusion.[41]

The same reasoning was reflected in another report in the Proceedings of the AFL Convention the following year, when unemployment increased to 15.9 percent. The report noted that:

> Resolutions were introduced in both Houses to suspend general immigration for two years, as applicable to all countries. The need for such action, under present conditions of unemployment, is so obvious as to need no argument. We heartily concur in the declaration that there is no more important question than the protection of the wage earners of the United States and Canada from excess immigration. As to future activities in relation to this subject the Executive Council reports that "It is our purpose to continue a most vigorous campaign to bring about as great restriction of immigration as possible." We urge the strict enforcement of the deportation laws as applicable to persons illegally in the country.[42]

The AFL noted that bills of particular interest that were approved that year included the appropriation of an additional $500,000 to increase the border immigration patrol, and extra compensation for over-time service performed by immigration inspectors.[43] In 1933, when unemployment reached 24.9 percent, the Executive Council noted "that there has never been a time when restricted immigration is more necessary than now."[44]

The AFL's pressure for restrictionist legislation suggests that union leaders considered that the government had the capacity to exert control over migration flows. One may be less likely to devote time to pressuring for laws if one thought that the laws would be ineffective. The AFL gave much more attention to the subject of legal immigration than to the subject of illegal immigration, which suggests that it considered that flows could be largely halted by focusing on legal immigration issues.

Nonetheless the subject of illegal immigration was at times addressed in the early twentieth century. Proceedings of AFL Conventions at times included references to illegal immigration and smuggling of migrants, and the record shows that there was an awareness of the problems of implementing laws then. However, at that time AFL reports tended to attribute the failure of implementation to lack of commitment of funds on the part of the government. There was no mention of *economic internationalization* (and scarce reference to *human rights* concerns) as imposing constraints on the effectiveness of government policy. In contrast there were explicit calls for devoting more resources to border patrol.

The concern to ensure implementation of restrictionist laws was emphasized in quite a few reports that called for "beefing up the border." As stated in a report in the AFL Convention Proceedings in 1920: "Owing to the failure of Congress to appropriate money to pay the patrol on the Mexican border, many Mexicans, Japanese and Chinese, as well as undesirable natives of other countries, were able to gain illegal entry into the United States."[45] Another report noted that:

> Congress should be called upon to make sufficient appropriation to permit the Immigration Bureau of the Department of Labor to function. The Secretary of Labor has claimed 100 foreigners enter the United States every day in violation of immigration laws. This could not occur if sufficient funds were available for carrying out our immigration laws.[46]

An Executive Council report pointed out that: "Another matter of great moment is the necessity of increasing the border patrol. The few hundred men who are now engaged in that duty are insufficient, as they cover thousands of miles. Many aliens are smuggled across the Mexican border."[47]

Opposition within the AFL

There were a few opponents of restrictionism within the AFL in the early twentieth century, but they were a small minority. For example, as noted above, one delegate's attempt to have a clause favoring the literacy test removed from a resolution on immigration at the AFL Convention in 1915 was opposed by a vote of 190 to 5.

The main opponents of restrictionism were the two needletrade unions, the International Ladies Garment Workers Union (ILGWU) and the Amalgamated Clothing Workers of America (ACWA). These unions favored a liberal immigration policy. Demands for the absolute restriction of immigration received some opposition during a lengthy discussion of the issue at the AFL Convention in 1919. For example, the delegate from the ILGWU suggested that the AFL should instead consider other measures to prevent unemployment. And another delegate opposed the restrictionist proposal on the grounds that it would be an obstacle to relations between workers of the various nations of the world. However, these delegates were in a clear minority. They were outvoted by the advocates for the complete restriction of immigration for a given period of time, which became the official policy preference of the AFL.[48]

The ILGWU continued to oppose the AFL's position on immigration policy on several occasions throughout the 1920s. For example, a delegate from the ILGWU, at the AFL Convention in 1922, said that he opposed any measure that in any way restricted immigration. Delegates of the ILGWU submitted a resolution in 1923 advocating that the United States keep its doors open to victims of racial, religious, and political persecution; and they submitted a similar resolution advocating that restrictionist measures be lifted or modified. Neither resolution was adopted.[49] The ILGWU and ACWA themselves approved liberal resolutions at that time.

Despite opposition by a small minority, on the whole, as shown above, the AFL clearly sat in the restrictionist coalition during the early decades of the twentieth century and pressured for laws, and for the implementation of laws that would limit or, more often, completely prohibit legal immigration.

The AFL avoids organizing

The AFL unions, with certain exceptions such as the United Mine Workers, made little effort to organize immigrants and bring them into the union as an alternative strategy for raising wages and work conditions. In contrast, many of the AFL unions used various measures to block immigrant workers from joining the craft unions. For example, preconditions for membership included criteria such as U.S. citizenship, or declaration of intention to become a citizen; particularly high initiation fees for immigrants; approval of the national unions' officers; and special evidence of competency.[50]

AFL President Gompers himself discouraged local unions from organizing Asian workers, arguing that organizing these workers would be inconsistent with the AFL's position of fighting to exclude these workers from entering the United States. For example, upon learning from the Hotel and Restaurant Employees' Union that one of their locals was organizing Chinese restaurants, Gompers, in 1904, replied that:

> I am inclined to believe that it would be unwise and impracticable to unionize a Chinese restaurant ... the American labor movement has set its face against the Chinese coming to this country, and upon our demands the law has been passed for the exclusion of Chinese from the United States ... it would be the height of inconsistency of our movement to unionize the Chinese against whom we have declared.[51]

The AFL's approach to organizing immigrant workers from Southern and Eastern Europe was not much more favorable. At the local level in New York City, immigrant workers received little support from the local AFL central labor body, the New York Central Federated Union. When the immigrants formed their own unions in New York, the AFL showed little support for these socialist-oriented unions. The Amalgamated Clothing Workers of America was refused membership in the AFL, and the Cloth Hat and Cap Makers' Union was suspended from the AFL, and all AFL affiliates were required to cut ties with the United Hebrew Trades.[52] On those rare occasions when the AFL did concede to organize immigrants, primarily those from Southern and Eastern Europe, the efforts were half-hearted. For example, the AFL sent English-speaking organizers who could not communicate with the immigrant workers in a foreign language.[53]

The Construction Craft Unions

The U.S. construction craft unions in the early twentieth century serve as a case study to assess union immigration policy preferences under conditions where the central themes that this study proposes to explain defection from restrictionism are all absent. The construction unions then were craft unions with an exclusionary approach that opposed organizing immigrants and sought to limit union membership, at a time when there was less likelihood that union officials questioned the ability and/or right of the state to control migration. One would thus expect these unions (which dominated the AFL) to closely observe restrictionist immigration policy preferences. They did do so.

However, the rationale given by these unions for their restrictionist posture really did not have much to do with the conventional wisdom that unions seek to restrict immigration so as to reduce the labor supply and raise wages. The statements of the construction unions, as can be seen below, were an example of unrestricted racism (with the occasional reference to economic issues). As to the real reason for the posture of the construction unions, Alexander Saxton has suggested that the anti-Asian approach of these unions, particularly in San Francisco, provided a means for the skilled craftsmen to gain support from the broader working population and to thereby retain their monopoly on the labor movement. Saxton notes that "it may be suggested that the Chinese, and the factor of anti-Orientalism which their presence occasioned, furthered the dominance of the skilled trades by enabling those trades to control and direct the energies of the entire white labor force."[54]

The primary target of the construction unions were immigrants from Asia, and the primary source of restrictionism was the San Francisco Building Trades Council (SFBTC). The restrictionist posture of the construction unions at the national level (which, in turn, contributed to the restrictionist posture of the AFL) originated in San Francisco.

The SFBTC was an unusually powerful labor organization that maintained a closed shop on building sites in San Francisco at the beginning of the century, and obtained high wages and an eight-hour day. The SFBTC was also a major actor in broadening anti-Japanese sentiments among the population at large in San Francisco.[55]

The San Francisco Building Trades Council forged strong links with nativist organizations. In this case, rather than point to an "odd-couple coalition," it would be more accurate to say that they merged with each other and became one and the same entity. The Asiatic Exclusion League (AEL), which was formed in San Francisco in 1905, was largely formed by officials from organized labor with the goal of extending the Chinese Exclusion Act to include all immigrants from Asia, particularly Japanese. The AEL was the main organization responsible for coordinating anti-Japanese activities. It claimed a membership of over 100,000 members.[56] There was a very strong overlap at the leadership level between the Building Trades Council and the Asiatic Exclusion League. The SFBTC was the major source of the AEL's executive board, staff, and financial resources.[57] The President and a founder of the Asiatic Exclusion League, Olaf Tveitmoe, was recording and corresponding secretary of the SFBTC, editor of its weekly journal, *Organized Labor,* and general secretary treasurer of the California Building Trades Council.[58] Abraham Yoell, the recording secretary of International Brotherhood of Electrical Workers, was appointed to the position of financial secretary in the Asiatic Exclusion League—the only full-time salaried position in the League.[59]

At the national level the Building Trades Department of the AFL, in 1909, approved a resolution by unanimous vote that endorsed the goals of the San Francisco Building Trades Council-Asiatic Exclusion League. The resolution called for extending the coverage of the Chinese Exclusion Act to Japanese and Koreans. The resolution urged all the unions affiliated with the AFL's Building Trades Department, and their locals and members, to grant financial and moral support to this goal. The resolution stated that:

> Whereas this country and especially the Pacific Coast and the intermountain states are threatened by an Asiatic invasion of cheap coolie labor, and
>
> Whereas, it is a biological fact, historically demonstrated, that the Mongolian and Caucasian races can never assimilate, and
>
> Whereas, the presence of these Mongolian-Malay and Hindoo peons in any great number among us, will deteriorate the American standard of living...[60]

This call for extending the coverage of the Chinese Exclusion Act to other immigrants from Asia was reiterated in a resolution approved in 1920. This resolution demanded, among other things, the complete exclusion of Japanese, with other "Asiatics", as immigrants, and that "Asiatics" shall forever be barred from American citizenship.[61]

Unions affiliated with the Building Trades Department expressed similar immigration policy preferences. Some examples follow.

The Brotherhood of Painters, Decorators and Paperhangers of America approved a resolution at its 1901 Convention urging Congress to re-enact the Chinese Exclusion Law, which was due to expire in 1902. The grounds given were that:

> Unrestricted Chinese immigration means the actual competition of American with Oriental labor, and in that context white labor must either go to the wall or wink to the Oriental level.
>
> That the act should be extended there can be no doubt. With it out of the way, China would easily find opportunity for disgorging her altogether undesirable millions upon the Pacific coast, to work from there eastward, until the entire land would be flooded with the yellow peril ...[62]

The United Brotherhood of Carpenters and Joiners of America (UBC) approved a resolution at its General Convention in 1906 advocating that the terms of the Chinese Exclusion Act be expanded to cover Japanese and Koreans. The grounds given for this demand were:

> (1) that the wage and living standards of such labor are dangerous to, and must, if granted recognition in the United States, prove destructive of the American standards in these essential respects; (2) that the racial incompatibility, as between the peoples of the Orient and the United States, presents a problem of race preservation which is our imperative duty to solve in our own favor ...[63]

A similar resolution was again approved by the UBC at its Convention two years later, in 1908, and then in 1920 and 1924.[64]

The UBC in the early twentieth century sat in clear coalition with the Asiatic Exclusion League, and the UBC published letters by the latter in the union newspaper, known as *The Carpenter*.[65] The letters, which demanded that the Chinese Exclusion Act be expanded to cover all people from Asia, included both economic and racial concerns. For example, one letter published in 1909 argued that: "Almost every occupation, enterprise and industry on the Pacific Coast is invaded by Japanese, and we have no tangible protection against them ...."[66]

Another letter, entitled "The Menace of Asia" and written by the Secretary of the Asiatic Exclusion League, included a statement that: "Within the limits of the Asiatic continent are included all the five great races of man … of these races the yellow—the most typical Asiatic of them all—is the one with which the people of the Pacific Coast are most concerned."[67]

The UBC also called for increasing restrictionism against immigration from other areas. The union published an article in its newspaper favoring the establishment of a literacy test,[68] and another article that favored making the temporary Emergency Quota Law of 1921 permanent and more restrictive. The article mentioned that it was estimated that 557,000 immigrants could be expected in the current year, and that this was: "… a number equal to more than twenty-seven army divisions … and, according to army intelligence tests made in administering the Selective Draft Law during the war, nearly one-half of the influx would be of very inferior mentality."[69]

Another article in February 1924, which discussed the imminent expiration of the Emergency Quota Law, urged further tightening up of present immigration regulations.[70]

United Mine Workers

The case study of the United Mine Workers (UMW) is more interesting for testing the argument of this study than that of the construction unions. All the key factors presented to explain defection from restrictionism were absent in the case of the construction craft unions in the early twentieth century. In contrast, the UMW is an example of a union that was faced with conflicting pressures in the early twentieth century because it was a union that covered a sector where many immigrants worked and it had an inclusive approach and seriously sought to organize the workforce. On the one hand this presented an incentive to refrain from a restrictionist posture that could alienate immigrants from the union. But on the other hand this presented an incentive to pressure for restrictionist measures so as to limit the labor supply at a time when unions more likely considered that government control measures would be effective than their counterparts in the late twentieth century. How did the UMW handle this?

It will be seen that the UMW adopted a restrictionist posture in the early twentieth century, but this was vocally aimed at Asians. In addition, at times of high unemployment the UMW occasionally articulated restrictionist views, but its proposals in hard times were to block all immigration in general. In contrast, the UMW was not vocal on questions pertaining to immigration from South and East European countries specifically—the source countries of its members or potential members. The union was for the most part silent on issues pertaining to immigration from these source countries.

Background
The United Mine Workers, formed in 1890, was the largest union in the United States in the early twentieth century. A large portion of mine workers were immigrants. Coal operators began recruiting immigrants, often as strikebreakers, from Italy and Eastern Europe in the 1870s. Many of the immigrants from Eastern and Southern Europe who came to the United States in the late nineteenth and early twentieth century worked in the coal mining sector. The 1920 census reported that 52.7 percent of mine workers were foreign born. Of the foreign born, 18 percent were born in Poland, 10.5 percent were born in Russia, and 6.5 percent in Italy. Of the foreign born, 18.4 percent had been in the United States for 5 to 10 years at the time of the 1920 census, 22.3 percent for 10 to 15 years, 20.6 percent for 15 to 20 years, 35.5 percent for over 20 years, and the remainder were more recent arrivals. 40.4 percent had become naturalized by 1920.[71]

The initial reaction of mine workers to the new immigrants from Italy and Eastern Europe in the 1870s and 1880s was harsh and quite often violent.[72] However, this changed with the formation of the UMW.

The UMW organizes immigrants
The UMW, under the leadership of John Mitchell, who served as the union's President from 1898 to 1908, made serious efforts to organize these new immigrants at the turn of the century. The efforts to organize immigrants were not due to a particularly progressive ideology toward immigrants per se. Mitchell's personal record, as well as the approach of miners who had migrated from England, at times reflected a condescending approach toward the new immigrants from Eastern and Southern Europe. For Mitchell, the new immigrant workers were "a drove of cattle, ready to stampede" at the cries of any misleader.[73] Instead the organizing efforts reflected a pragmatic response to the nature of the industry, which required an inclusive approach to raise wages and work conditions.[74]

The UMW at the leadership level recognized that, contrary to conventional wisdom at that time, immigrants could be a source of unionization rather than a barrier to unionization. As argued by Victor

Greene, immigrants had been blamed by workers, and later by scholars and authors, for problems of organization in the mining sector in the 1880s.[75] But, as Greene demonstrated, there were other causes for the failures in organization in the 1880s.

The UMW took practical measures to unionize immigrants, such as using organizers who were fluent speakers in the languages of the workers, printing parts of the union newspaper in foreign languages, and forging links with the immigrants' religious leaders. In addition, at the local level the new immigrants of Eastern and Southern Europe were quickly elected to leadership positions.[76]

The organizing efforts at the turn of the century brought results. From 1900 to 1901 the membership of the three anthracite districts of the UMW increased by 53,000 members, which was a 600 percent growth rate.[77] In 1892 the UMW had less than 20,000 members.[78] The UMW's membership rose to 263,000 by 1908, and 377,688 in 1914. This figure almost doubled after World War I, when the union's membership exceeded half a million people.[79]

The UMW's immigration policy preferences
Although the UMW made major efforts to bring immigrants into the union, its stance toward immigration policy was restrictionist and in line with that of the AFL.

In the first decade of the century the UMW, under the leadership of President John Mitchell, was a vocal advocate of barring immigration from Asia. At the beginning of the century the union made clear its support for the re-enactment of the Chinese Exclusion Act, which was due to expire in 1902. The UMW's President sent a circular to locals advising them to do everything possible to ensure re-enactment of the Act, such as petitioning members of Congress, holding public meetings, and adopting and publishing in local papers resolutions favoring re-enactment. In turn, a number of locals adopted resolutions calling for the re-enactment of the Chinese Exclusion Act.[80]

The UMW's newspaper ran a major campaign to drum up support for renewal of the Act. A number of issues of the newspaper devoted a lot of space to articles articulating the need for renewal. The articles pointed to racial considerations and a fear of economic competition. For example, one article stated that "the abandonment of the exclusion act would be followed by an invasion of the heathen Chinese to the detriment of American labor."[81] Another article was entitled "The Yellow Danger."[82] The newspaper published an article by the Mayor of San Francisco, entitled "The Case Against the Chinaman," with subtitles such as "The Menace of Coolie Invasions," "The Perils of Cheap Coolie Labor," "The Impossibility of Americanizing the Mongol," "Why Yellow Citizens Are Undesirable."[83]

Following the re-enactment of the Chinese Exclusion Act in 1902, the UMW turned its attention to gaining support for expanding the coverage of the Act to include all immigrants from Asia, particularly those from Japan. The anti-Japanese campaign in the *United Mine Workers Journal* was cast as a racial issue and as an issue of job competition. The paper published an appeal by labor's coalition partner, the anti-Chinese and Japanese Agitation League of San Francisco.[84] Examples of the many articles published include one entitled "Another Race Problem," stating that "The Jap is on level and allied with all that is antagonistic to Christian morals, ideas and teachings .... The Jap fully answers the trite description which an Englishman gave of the natives of Madagascar. When asked what the morals and habits of the people were, he replied: 'They have no morals and their habits are disgusting.'"[85] Another article considered that "At the present rate of immigration the Emperor of Japan will soon be able to count more Japanese soldiers on American soil than there are men in the United States regular army ...."[86]

In contrast with this vocally restrictionist stance to immigrants from Asia, the UMW for the most part did not articulate support for restrictionist measures against immigrants from Southern and Eastern Europe in the early twentieth century, although, before the UMW began serious organizing, its newspaper did publish some articles that were antagonistic to the new immigrants from Eastern and Southern Europe in the 1890s.[87] In addition, a few articles in 1904 complained that reduced steamship rates had dramatically increased the immigration rate of "undesirables" (referred to as "human refuse" in one article and as the "dregs of southeastern Europe" in another); and expressed support for the law that compelled steamships to take back those people refused permission to enter the United States at ports.[88] However, for the most part the union's newspaper articles made a clear distinction between Asians and Europeans. For example, one article written in 1905, referring to a forthcoming discussion on immigration to be held by the Civic Federation, stated that:

> The exclusion act will be discussed in all of its forms and from that discussion the friends of exclusion have nothing to fear as they have the arguments, the facts and the truth on their side. The educational test for an European immigrant accords a wide latitude for difference of opinion ... it would exclude many a worthy man ....[89]

Another union newspaper article, written in 1907, was very brief when it noted regret that an "education test" had been dropped from a bill before Congress.[90]

Beginning in the second decade of the twentieth century immigration policy was addressed more rarely by the UMW. Documents in the union's archives and convention proceedings hardly include any references to immigration policy. For example, Convention Proceedings for the UMW District One and for the UMW Tri-District (District 1, 7, and 9) are almost completely void of references to immigration policy in the first twenty-five years of the twentieth century. These Districts covered the anthracite coal region in Pennsylvania, where many of the immigrants from the new source countries of Southern and Eastern Europe worked.

The union's newspaper also included few references to immigration issues after the first decade of the twentieth century. Articles that were antagonistic to the new immigrants from Eastern and Southern Europe almost disappeared from the newspaper. By contrast, a few articles praising (European) foreigners appeared.[91] The material that did refer to immigration issues, however, placed the UMW in the restrictionist coalition. As noted in a resolution approved at the union's convention in 1924, "We continue our efforts to have immigration restricted to the lowest possible minimum … ."[92]

As would be expected by the conventional view, when unemployment in the mining sector increased, a few articles on immigration did appear in the union newspaper. This was evident in 1919, when the mines were producing 60 percent in excess of peacetime needs and a substantial number of miners were laid off.[93] The reasons given for restrictionism at this time did not focus on racial issues but instead reflected the conventional view's focus on economic issues. Immigrants were seen to increase the labor supply and undermine wages and job opportunities of workers in the United States. This can be seen by the UMW's support for the AFL's position of completely barring immigration after World War I. For example, an article in the union's newspaper, entitled "Stop Immigration," argued that:

There is no room in America for immigrants at this time. … Employment must be found for millions of American citizens within the next few months … without being compelled to meet the competition of immigrants who would be used as a club to batter down American wage standards … .[94]

Another article, entitled "Keep Out Cheap Labor," argued that:

> The standards of living, the standards of labor, the standards of education, and the standards of society in America are higher than those of the countries from which have come most of the immigrants in the past ... in order to safeguard this right and this privilege it is necessary that immigration be controlled. Better still, immigration of cheap foreign labor should be absolutely prohibited for a period of years, and the period should be long enough to make it certain that a final lowering of the bars would not unbalance labor conditions in America.
> There is no likelihood of a shortage of mine labor in this country. Therefore, there is no need for the importation of foreign labor to work in the mines. ...
> Heavy, unrestricted immigration would inevitably mean lower wages and lower working and living conditions for American labor. Let's stand opposed to any such plan. Let's tell Congress that the gates should be closed against the cheap labor of foreign lands, until the workers of those countries are elevated to something near the standards of American labor.[95]

Pragmatic reasons were also given for the UMW's particular concern to restrict immigration from Mexico. The UMW, with John Lewis as leader, was among the more vocal advocates within the AFL for restricting immigration from Mexico. It was Lewis who raised the issue of restricting Mexican migration at the AFL Convention in 1919. And a delegate from the UMW again spoke in favor of restricting Mexican migration, by incorporating Mexico into the quota system, at the AFL Convention in 1927. The reasons articulated for this position did not refer to racial issues, but instead focused on employers' use of Mexican migrants as strikebreakers, and a concern that Mexican immigration was threatening wage levels and standards of living.[96]

In summary, the UMW, a major inclusive organizing union in the early twentieth century when officials were less likely to be influenced by economic internationalization concerns or by the internationalization of human rights concerns, held immigration policy preferences that were in sync with the AFL. However, its vocal support for restrictionism focused on Asian immigrants or, at times of rising unemployment, on all immigrants in general. In contrast, the UMW said little when it came to measures that would discriminate against immigrants from the new source countries of Southern and Eastern Europe, which was the main source of its members and potential members. This silence indicates that in the early twentieth century, like the late twentieth century, there were tensions between the strategies of organizing and restrictionism. However, the cost-benefit ratio of these alternative strategies changed in the late twentieth century, pushing major organizing unions, such as the SEIU, to go beyond silence and to instead vocally oppose some restrictionist measures. This is the subject of the next chapter.

Conclusion

It has traditionally been thought that unions would pressure for protectionist measures in immigration policy debates, so as to reduce the labor supply and increase wages. These economic considerations are said to push unions into an "odd-couple coalition" with nativist groups. This analysis helps to explain unions' immigration policy preferences in the United States in the early twentieth century. Organized labor at that time sat in the restrictionist coalition. Unions often urged *complete* restrictionism, either against specific groups (when the motivations stated were often racial), or against immigration in general for a specified period of time (when the motivations stated had more to do with the economic considerations pointed to by the conventional wisdom). Even the UMW, which actively sought to organize immigrants, failed to oppose restrictionism.

This presents a baseline for comparing with unions' immigration policy preferences in the late twentieth century, which constitutes the subject of the next chapter.

CHAPTER 4

Pragmatic Adaptation: Labor Unions and U.S. Immigration Policy in the Late Twentieth Century

Controversies over immigration policy resurfaced later in the twentieth century, when restrictionists fought to reduce legal immigration and to halt illegal immigration.

The AFL-CIO, following the lead of unions such as the SEIU, had clearly changed coalitions by the end of the twentieth century, when it sat with liberal groups on many immigration policy issues. The AFL-CIO was a member of the National Immigration Forum throughout the late twentieth century; and the Director of the Immigration Project of the International Ladies Garment Workers Union (ILGWU) was the Chairperson of the National Immigration Forum for a number of years. The Forum, established in 1982 and based in Washington, D.C., coordinates strategies of the liberal-labor coalition on immigration issues. Its membership includes liberal, ethnic, religious, and immigrant rights organizations. For example, members include the American Civil Liberties Union, the National Council of La Raza, the Organization of Chinese Americans, the AFL-CIO, the National Association for the Advancement of Colored People, the Council of Jewish Federations, Church World Service, and many others. The Forum engages in advocacy, media work, research, and public education. It distributes frequent updates on legislative developments to its members, and organizes numerous visits with congressional staff members.

By contrast, the AFL-CIO firmly rejected any approaches from the Federation for American Immigration Reform, which is the main restrictionist organization in the United States, established in 1978 with headquarters in Washington, D.C. and an office in Los Angeles. Its staff conducts activities such as research, media work, and advocacy. There was a wide gulf between the immigration policy preferences of the AFL-CIO and the Federation for American Immigration Reform on an increasingly broad range of issues in the late twentieth century.

This chapter first discusses the liberalization of union policy preferences on legal immigration, which took place in the 1950s and has remained constant since then. The chapter then considers at greater length union policy preferences on illegal immigration. A few unions began to depart from the restrictionist coalition on illegal immigration issues in the 1980s. But it was only in the 1990s that a more widespread change occurred in organized labor's policy preferences toward illegal immigration issues. The case studies analyzed in this chapter show that this change in coalitions reflected the comparatively pragmatic identity of U.S. unions, which served as a lens through which they filtered and reacted to broader changes. Practical concerns drove the change in their immigration policies. On the one hand, unions came to see support for certain non-restrictionist immigration measures as a way to advance the organizing agenda, which had recently been rejuvenated so as to tackle the declining union density that itself may have been partly caused by the increasing mobility and internationalization of capital. And on the other hand unions saw little to lose by opposing certain restrictionist measures that were deemed ineffective in blocking migration in an era of economic internationalization.

Before turning to an analysis of unions' immigration policy preferences, this chapter first provides background material on immigration flows and U.S. immigration policy in the late twentieth century. Those readers who are already familiar with this material might omit this first section and move directly to the case studies.

Immigration into the United States: Background

Migration Flows

Immigration into the United States was quite low in the 1950s and 1960s. Most of the immigrants were from Europe at that time. Immigration began to increase in the 1970s. Since 1980 more than a half million legal permanent immigrants have entered the United States each year, with sharp increases from countries in Asia and the Americas. The number exceeded 1 million each year in the early 1990s, as happened in the early years of the twentieth century. The figures in the

Table 4.1 Legal permanent immigration flows into the United States: 1951–1998

Year	Legal permanent immigrants	Year	Legal permanent immigrants
1951	205,717	1975	386,194
1952	265,520	1976	502,289
1953	170,434	1977	462,315
1954	208,177	1978	601,442
1955	237,790	1979	460,348
1956	321,625	1980	530,639
1957	326,867	1981	596,600
1958	253,265	1982	594,131
1959	260,686	1983	559,763
1960	265,398	1984	543,903
1961	271,344	1985	570,009
1962	283,763	1986	601,708
1963	306,260	1987	601,516
1964	292,248	1988	643,025
1965	296,697	1989	1,090,924
1966	323,040	1990	1,536,483
1967	361,972	1991	1,827,167
1968	454,448	1992	973,977
1969	358,579	1993	904,292
1970	373,326	1994	804,416
1971	370,478	1995	720,461
1972	384,685	1996	915,900
1973	400,063	1997	798,378
1974	394,861	1998	660,477

Source: U.S. Immigration and Naturalization Service, *Statistical Yearbook of the Immigration and Naturalization Service*, 1998 (Washington, D.C.: U.S. Government Printing Office, 1999, p. 7.

Note: Since 1989, approximately 2.9 million people obtained permanent residence status through the legalization program of the 1986 Immigration Reform and Control Act. Of these 2.9 million, approximately 478,800 were legalized in 1989; 880,400 in 1990; 1,123,200 in 1991; 163,342 in 1992, and others since then.

early 1990s were inflated by the amnesty program, which legalized nearly 3 million immigrants.

The INS estimated that there were approximately 5 million undocumented immigrants in the U.S. in 1996, about 40 percent of whom are considered to be visa overstayers. Undocumented immigrants come from a diverse source of countries. Mexicans constitute the largest undocumented immigrant population in the United States. Of the approximately 3 million people legalized through the amnesty program enacted in 1986, 70 percent of those who could prove that they had been in the United States since 1982 were from Mexico, and 81 percent of those who gained amnesty through the special provisions for agricultural workers originated in Mexico.[1]

Economic Sectors

Today's immigrants display a far greater degree of socio-economic diversity than was the case in the early twentieth century. A greater proportion of legal immigrants today have higher education levels than then, and they also work in a larger variety of occupations.[2] Legal immigrants today include a greater mixture of skilled and unskilled workers. Many immigrants today work as pharmacists, engineers, and computer specialists; and many work as janitors and dishwashers. By contrast, in the early twentieth century most immigrants were concentrated in jobs at the bottom of the ladder.[3]

Temporary "nonimmigrant" workers who are granted visas to work in the United States for a limited period of time are concentrated in the agricultural sector, and in highly skilled professions such as information technology, engineering, arts and entertainment, and nursing.

Undocumented workers are concentrated in the service sector (such as building cleaning, hotels and restaurants, private households); garments, construction, food manufacturing (meat packing and poultry processing); and agriculture.[4]

Immigration Policy

The national origins quota system of 1924 formed the basis of U.S. immigration law until 1965.[5] It was finally abolished at the time of the civil rights movement, with the passage of the Immigration and Nationality Act of 1965. Under the new law each country in the Eastern Hemisphere was assigned the same quota size (20,000 per year). Access by individuals to the quotas was determined by a preference system that prioritized family reunification, but also gave some allowance for employer sponsored immigration. Western Hemisphere countries were not subject to the 20,000 quota limit until 1978.

National debates on immigration policy have re-emerged many times since then. Some of the proposals for immigration reform have been blocked, whereas others have resulted in new laws, most notably the Immigration Reform and Control Act (IRCA) of 1986, the Immigration Act of 1990, and the Illegal Immigration Reform and Immigrant Responsibility Act of 1996.

The *Immigration Reform and Control Act of 1986*, known as IRCA, focused on undocumented workers (illegal aliens). IRCA had two key elements. One measure was intended to be restrictionist—the enactment of employer sanctions, which was intended to restrict illegal immigration. The new measure made it illegal for employers to knowingly hire illegal immigrants. This measure had been proposed at various times in previous years, and had previously been discussed in Congress on a number of occasions. The second measure was non-restrictionist—the enactment of an amnesty program that granted legal permanent resident status to those undocumented workers who could prove that they had resided in the United States since 1982 or who had worked for a specified period of time in agriculture. Nearly 3 million people obtained permanent resident status under the amnesty program. IRCA has been subject to a number of oversight hearings since then.

The *Immigration Act of 1990* focused on temporary workers and legal permanent immigrants. First, it included some restrictionist measures to tighten the procedures for foreigners seeking temporary work permits. Second, it maintained admissions for permanent immigrants entering through family reunion provisions at fairly constant levels. Third, it increased admissions for high-skilled workers entering as permanent residents through employer sponsorship.

Subsequent debates on reforming immigration policy in the early 1990s covered both legal and illegal migration issues. Restrictionist proposals to reduce legal immigration were for the most part defeated. The chief Republican sponsors of the original bills in the House and Senate, Representative Lamar Smith and Senator Alan Simpson, failed in their efforts to reduce legal migration. Instead the new legislation that was adopted, in the *Illegal Immigration Reform and Immigrant Responsibility Act of 1996,* focused on measures that were designed to deter and restrict illegal migration.

This 1996 Act increased the penalties against alien smugglers and document fraud. Penalties against the illegal migrants were also increased. For example, the act specified that illegal aliens who had resided in the United States for a period of 180 days to one year were barred from gaining legal status for three years, and illegal aliens who had resided in the United States for over one year were barred for ten years. An expedited removal process for deporting illegal aliens was introduced.[6]

There were also a number of changes with regard to *implementation* of U.S. immigration policy in the 1990s. These changes focused on the enforcement of restrictionist aspects of U.S. immigration law. Various new strategies were adopted along the southern territorial border, giving the appearance of attempts to restrict illegal immigration. For example a ten-foot-high steel wall was constructed south of San Diego, and a fifteen-foot-fence was constructed along a five-mile stretch at Nogales.

New technological equipment, such as portable telescopic light units, low-light television monitors, night vision equipment, and sensors were deployed at the border.

Resources allocated to the INS were increased for enforcement both at the territorial border and for interior enforcement. The INS received a budget of $3.8 billion for the fiscal year 1998. This represented a 19.5 percent increase over the previous year, and a 153 percent increase over the previous five years. A substantial portion of this increase was used for enforcement measures, such as the hiring of new Border Patrol agents.[7]

The pattern of increasing resources for implementation was also evident in the Illegal Immigration Reform and Immigrant Responsibility Act of 1996, discussed above. The act authorized funding to increase the number of Border Patrol agents by 1,000 each year for five years. The act also addressed interior patrol by authorizing funding for hiring 900 new INS agents to investigate smuggling, harboring or employing illegal immigrants, and for 300 new INS agents to investigate visa-overstayers. It also authorized $12 million to add two additional fences and road construction at a fourteen-mile segment of the U.S.-Mexico border near San Diego; and required the INS to establish preinspection stations at 5 of the 10 foreign airports from where the greatest number of inadmissible aliens come, in order to screen those aliens with improper documentation.[8]

Finally, so as to further improve implementation of measures designed to restrict illegal immigration, the INS changed its strategy of interior enforcement to one that used other federal agencies (such as the Department of Labor) to provide information and help INS enforcement. This strategy was strongly opposed by unions and will be discussed in more detail later in this chapter.

Unions' Immigration Policy Preferences to Legal Permanent Immigration

The AFL-CIO's position toward *legal* permanent immigration in the late twentieth century had its roots in the 1950s/60s, when it changed and liberalized its position from that held by the AFL in the early twentieth century. The AFL-CIO has sat in the liberal coalition on policy toward legal permanent immigration since that time. It has resisted restrictionist proposals to reduce legal permanent immigration and has advocated family reunion as the main criteria for legal immigration, reflecting the liberal view that people with family ties to a member of U.S. society have moral claims to enter. Thus to comprehend the sources of the AFL-CIO's policy toward legal permanent immigration today, one needs to consider the policy shift that took place shortly after World War II.

Ideational issues help to explain this policy shift, which began shortly after human rights gained some small space on the agenda of global politics following World War II, and occurred at a time when people who held liberal values gained greater strength in the labor movement as the CIO (which was formed in 1936 and advocated inclusive industrial unionism), became more powerful and merged with the exclusive craft union-dominated AFL in the 1950s. This norm liberalization was further consolidated with the experience of the civil rights movement. The associated ideational changes broke with the racist discourse and exclusive norms of the AFL, and filtered into the labor movement's policy toward legal immigration as discussed further below.

Having pointed to this norm liberalization, one also needs to note that the internationalization of human rights concerns among the AFL-CIO leadership in practice did not extend far beyond advocating immigration rights for those who had some claim by virtue of family ties to a member of U.S. society. The AFL-CIO then, as today, opposed open borders. Moreover, in those early post-war years the AFL-CIO continued to adopt a protectionist posture on other immigration policy issues. For example it lobbied for an end to the Bracero Program (a program that allowed Mexicans to work temporarily as "guestworkers" in the United States, primarily in agriculture), which was terminated in 1964. And it maintained a restrictionist posture toward illegal immigrants at that time. More generally, the AFL-CIO's policy in the international arena showed little concern for human rights issues at that time, and was instead heavily caught up in Cold War politics. Nevertheless, the AFL-CIO upheld the rights of those with relatives in the United States, and never repeated the early twentieth century AFL demands for a complete suspension of immigration, nor did it clamor for an Asian Exclusion Act as did its counterparts in the early twentieth century.

Given that the labor movement's shift toward legal immigration in the 1950s carried through for the remainder of the century, the policy change at that time warrants further review here.

The AFL and the CIO initially had different immigration policy preferences toward *legal* immigration in the 1950s (a trend that was to re-emerge with regard to *illegal* immigration later in the twentieth century).

The AFL

In the 1950s the AFL's position for the most part replicated its restrictionist position of the early twentieth century. After World War II the AFL, while favoring the repeal of laws that excluded Asian immigration, remained in the restrictionist coalition with regard to retaining the national origins quota system of 1924. The AFL representative presenting testimony at congressional hearings in 1951 noted the AFL's opposition to a proposal that would weaken the national origins quota system by distributing the unused portions of the annual quotas for countries with large quotas to aspiring immigrants from countries with small quotas. He mentioned both the normative and the economic considerations that had dominated the AFL's policy in the early twentieth century, as discussed in the previous chapter. He explained that the AFL: "... is opposed to this change because it would be in direct contravention to the spirit of the quota act of 1924 and would have a tendency to disturb the ethnic equilibrium of this country." He went on to note that the AFL also called for bringing the Western Hemisphere (which had been exempted from quotas in 1924) into the quota system because, among other things, Mexicans: "... have accepted wages much lower than the native American and have been displacing American agricultural labor and railroad labor."[9]

The AFL subsequently modified its position, and in November 1955, just before the formal merging with the CIO, it pointed to the need to revise, but not abolish, the national origins quota system. It avoided taking a definite position on certain issues such as numbers, noting that:

> We cannot permit such a tidal wave of immigration as would threaten the employment opportunities of American workers or undermine established standards of wages and working conditions. It is possible, however, that we can absorb a reasonable increase in the number of immigrants ....[10]

The CIO

In clear contrast, the CIO adopted a liberal position that was in line with the principles laid out in its constitution, which stated that one of its main goals was "to bring about the effective organization of the working men and women of America without regard to race, color, creed or nationality."[11]

The CIO's explanation for its immigration policy position pointed to the normative (rather than the pragmatic) considerations behind an inclusive approach. As noted by the CIO representative presenting testimony at congressional hearings in November 1955:

> The CIO is in favor of a liberal immigration policy. By that we mean, to begin with, that we favor permitting the entrance of substantial numbers of immigrants annually. We favor a policy of generosity in this regard, firstly, because of humanitarian considerations.

The representative went on to note the CIO's support for abolition of the national origins quota system. He explained the CIO's opposition to the quota system, noting that: "Our unions are open to all, and all are accorded equal treatment, equal rights, and equal opportunity."[12]

The differences between the AFL and the CIO resulted in an ambiguous resolution on immigration being approved at the AFL-CIO's founding convention in December 1955. The resolution was so ambiguous that it left the AFL-CIO's Legislative Department with little guidance on how to proceed. A memorandum for the AFL-CIO's Executive Committee on Immigration, noting these differences, stated that the U.S. President's proposals on immigration:

> ...go beyond any specific commitments made previously by the AFL but not as far as the specific position taken by the CIO in its earlier pronouncements. The official AFL-CIO position on immigration, as reflected in the convention resolution, does not provide clear guidance for the Legislative Department.[13]

Over the next decade the civil rights movement brought further changes to the labor movement as civil rights and union activists joined ranks to demand racial and economic justice at the workplace and beyond.[14] At the same time the CIO's position on legal immigration policy gained the upper hand in the labor movement, and the AFL-CIO came to adopt a liberal position toward legal immigration. It was to maintain this position throughout the late twentieth century.

The AFL-CIO's policy to legal permanent immigration thereafter remained influenced by the liberal norms that the CIO brought to the AFL-CIO upon the merging of the labor confederations in December 1955. The AFL-CIO's position to legal immigration has been constant since the 1950s-60s, regardless of the fluctuations in unemployment levels, which can be seen on table 4.2.

The AFL-CIO favored retaining family reunion as the main category of admission for legal immigrants. Within the AFL-CIO there were no significant advocates for reducing admissions of legal permanent

Table 4.2 Unemployment levels in the United States: 1970–1999

Year	Unemployed percentage of labor force	Year	Unemployed percentage of labor force	Year	Unemployed percentage of labor force
1970	4.9	1980	7.1	1990	5.4
1971	6.0	1981	7.6	1991	6.6
1972	5.6	1982	9.7	1992	7.3
1973	4.9	1983	9.6	1993	6.7
1974	5.6	1984	7.5	1994	6.0
1975	8.5	1985	7.2	1995	5.6
1976	7.7	1986	7.0	1996	5.4
1977	7.1	1987	6.2	1997	4.9
1978	6.1	1988	5.5	1998	4.5
1979	5.8	1989	5.2	1999	4.2
				2000	4.0

Sources: For 1970–1988, OECD, *Main Economic Indicators: Historical Statistics, 1969–1988* (Paris: OECD, 1990), p. 74. For 1989–1991, OECD, *Main Economic Indicators, December 1992* (Paris: OECD, 1992), p. 22. For 1992–1994, OECD, *Main Economic Indicators, December 1995* (Paris: OECD, 1995), p. 22. For 1995–1997, OECD, *Main Economic Indicators, December 1998* (Paris: OECD, 1998), p. 40. For 1998–2000, OECD, *Main Economic Indicators, April 2001* (Paris: OECD, 2001), p. 26.

immigrants. Few individual unions took an active stance. Those few unions that took a position opposed new restrictionist measures that were proposed.[15]

The AFL-CIO joined liberal groups and actively opposed restrictionists' proposals to reduce the number of admissions for immigrants entering through family reunion provisions in the negotiations and debates leading up to the Immigration Act of 1990.[16] The AFL-CIO continued to adopt an open and inclusive approach toward legal immigrants during the recession of the early 1990s. The resolution passed at the AFL-CIO's convention in the fall of 1993 noted: "Immigrants are not the cause of our nation's problems.... The AFL-CIO calls on the nation's political, civic and religious leadership to refute and speak out against those who seek to blame immigrants for the country's economic and social problems." The resolution went on to urge unions "to develop programs to address the special needs of immigrant members and potential members."[17]

The restrictionists' attempts to reduce legal immigration in the mid-1990s were defeated by the liberal-labor coalition (coordinated by the National Immigration Forum), together with business organizations. The AFL-CIO was an active supporter of the National Immigration Forum's goal of defeating proposals to reduce legal immigration.

The chief Republican sponsors of the original bills in the debates leading to the Illegal Immigration Reform and Immigrant Responsibility Act of 1996, had originally included proposals to sharply curtail legal immigration along with measures pertaining to illegal immigration. The AFL-CIO supported the National Immigration Forum's strategy of trying to "split the bill" and separate legal and illegal immigration issues and removing proposals to curtail legal immigration and refugee admissions from the bills. The Forum's approach was based on the view that it would be difficult for them to defeat restrictionist proposals on both legal and illegal immigration, and that if legal immigration was considered separately from illegal immigration, there would be inadequate support for passage of restrictionist measures on legal immigration alone. While some immigrant rights groups considered that this strategy amounted to selling out on undocumented workers and thus split from the coalition, for the most part a cohesive approach was maintained between the labor, liberal, ethnic, and immigrants rights organizations within the National Immigration Forum, which, in conjunction with business organizations, thereby defeated major proposals to curtail legal immigration in the mid-1990s.

This liberal-labor coalition, in conjunction with business, left restrictionists isolated in their attempts to restrict legal immigration in the late twentieth century. This change in coalitions resulted in a very different outcome from the early twentieth century discussed in the previous chapter.

Unions' Immigration Policy Preferences to Illegal Immigration

Interests over Norms

The divisions and changes in the immigration policy preferences of U.S. labor unions in the late twentieth century have been in regard to illegal immigration, and on this issue positions have been more heavily driven by interests and pragmatic considerations than by ideational or humanitarian concerns for the human rights of the migrants per se. Union statements often explain their positions by pointing to pragmatic issues such as organizing and the ineffectiveness of certain restrictionist measures in controlling illegal migration flows. There is no particular reason why unions would stress pragmatic concerns if such concerns were not driving their policy preferences. Normative concerns underlie this pragmatism and are thus *in*directly influential. The underlying normative goal is to raise wages and work conditions for native workers (as well as immigrant workers). But for analytical purposes it is useful to separate this from the *direct* normative or "humanitarian" concern influencing unions' policy preferences to legal immigration (and, even more so, to refugees). In contrast, the immediate factors driving U.S. unions' policy preferences to illegal immigrants have been pragmatic and self-interest based.

The variation in intensity of preference between those unions that cover sectors where immigrants are concentrated and those unions that cover sectors where there are few immigrants also suggests that one needs to go beyond norms and focus on interests and pragmatism to explain the policy preferences of U.S. unions to illegal immigration. If interests are an important consideration, one would expect more intense preferences from unions covering sectors where foreign-born workers are concentrated. Intensity of preference is indicated by whether the union presented testimony at public hearings such as those conducted in 1979 and 1980 by the Select Commission on Immigration and Refugee Policy (SCIRP) and at congressional hearings; by whether the union considers resolutions on immigration issues; and by whether the union devotes resources to providing immigration services to current and potential members.

Those unions that cover sectors where immigrants do not constitute a large share of the workforce have devoted little time or resources to immigration issues and have delegated responsibility to the AFL-CIO.[18] For example, the American Federation of Government Employees, which covers a sector where non-U.S. citizen immigrants do not work because employees are required to be U.S. citizens, did not adopt resolutions on immigration policy and did not send representatives to public hearings.[19] The American Federation of State, County, and Municipal Employees, a growing union with over one million members, historically covered the public sector—a sector that includes some legal immigrants but is unlikely to include a high share of undocumented immigrants, as it seems unlikely that such people will be employed by governments. The union did not pass resolutions on immigration prior to the passage of IRCA and did not send representatives to congressional hearings or the SCIRP hearings.[20]

Specific Issues

The logic of the conventional wisdom and that of the argument presented in this study yield different expectations regarding union preferences on specific issues toward illegal immigration that caused controversies in the late twentieth century, such as amnesty, employer sanctions, and inspections of worksites. Examples of the different expectations yielded by the conventional wisdom and the argument presented in this study follow and are then tested on a range of unions.

Amnesty

The conventional wisdom that unions pressure for restrictionist measures so as to reduce the labor supply leads one to expect that unions will oppose granting amnesty to a large number of workers. Opponents of amnesty programs consider that such programs undermine the government's credibility and ability to deter illegal immigration and encourage illegal immigration by setting precedents. Moreover, amnesty applicants, after legalization, may remain permanently in the United States with assurance and, with green cards, may increase the labor supply and competition with American workers for the more desirable jobs in the legal sector of the economy.

In contrast, this study's argument leads one to expect that unions will support non-restrictionist measures such as amnesty programs. First, if one questions the government's ability to fully control migration in an era of economic internationalization, one would expect migration flows to continue and undocumented immigrants to stay for socio-economic reasons, regardless of whether or not there is an amnesty program. Second, these measures are facilitators of effective organization. Amnesty enables undocumented workers to gain legal permanent resident status. Permanent resident status increases the legal protection available to workers who may be illegally fired for engaging in union activities; it thus reduces the risk in joining unions. Permanent resident status increases the shadow of the future in the country of work, raising incentives to join unions to gain advantages, such as retirement benefits. Supporting amnesty programs and giving help with amnesty applications is a service that unions can provide to attract potential members.

Employer sanctions

The conventional wisdom leads one to expect that unions will support penalties against employers of illegal aliens, and that they will support INS strategies to implement employer sanctions legislation, such as INS cooperation with other federal agencies to gather information on the whereabouts of illegal aliens. The goal of such measures is stated to be to enforce exit of illegal aliens and deter further illegal immigration.

In contrast, this study's argument leads one to expect that unions will oppose employer sanctions and that they will oppose those INS implementation strategies that impede organization such as INS cooperation with other federal agencies to gather information to enforce sanctions legislation. First, if one doubts the effectiveness of such measures that are intended to control undocumented migration, these measures would be seen as serving no useful purpose in an era of economic internationalization. Second, employer sanctions impede organization. With sanctions, employees are required to show documentation of eligibility to work in the United States to the employer. During a union organizing drive, employers can impede unionization by asking employees to fill out new forms, by questioning documents, and by requesting new documents.[21]

Inspections

The conventional wisdom leads one to expect that unions will call in the INS to inspect a site where illegal aliens are thought to be working so as to enforce exit and deter entrance.

In contrast, this study's argument leads one to expect unions to oppose INS raids of worksites. If unions doubt the ability of the government to effectively conduct internal patrol at reasonable cost, one would not expect such actions to substantially reduce the number of undocumented workers, and one would expect other undocumented workers to quickly emerge as replacements for those who are forced to exit. Meanwhile union support for such actions would alienate immigrants from unions, making organization more difficult.

These different expectations stemming from the alternative approaches are tested below on a range of unions in the late twentieth century. The inclusive organizing unions, most of which changed their policy preferences to illegal immigration gradually over the course of the late twentieth century, are discussed first (UFCWU, UNITE, the growing SEIU, which has become increasingly influential in the labor movement, and the UFW). The material then turns to the construction craft unions, which displayed a highly restrictionist posture toward illegal immigration issues in the 1970s and 1980s, but came around to adopting a silent approach later in the 1990s. Finally, the material considers the AFL-CIO, which likewise initially displayed a restrictionist posture, but came around to opposing certain restrictionist measures toward the end of the twentieth century.

In the early twentieth century, as shown in the previous chapter, the inclusive United Mine Workers was highly restrictionist on immigration policy to Asia and was often silent on immigration policy to Eastern and

Southern Europe, from where most of its members and potential members came. On those occasions that it did speak out on immigration policy to European countries, such as when unemployment rose after World War I, the UMW was clearly in the restrictionist camp. In contrast, as shown below, most inclusive unions, such as the major Service Employees International Union, in the late twentieth century changed coalitions and came to actively resist certain restrictionist measures that they deemed to be ineffective in controlling migration and impediments to effective organization in an era of economic internationalization.

United Food and Commercial Workers Union (UFCWU)

The UFCWU includes 1.4 million members, many of whom work in retail food, meatpacking, poultry, and other food processing industries. Much of the workforce in these industries is Latino.

Contrary to the expectation of this study's argument, the UFCWU did not take an official position on immigration issues during much of the late twentieth century. It is an inclusive union that covers a sector (food processing) in which a large share of the workforce is foreign. But it has straddled the fence and thus this case does not support the argument presented in this book.

The UFCWU did not pass a resolution on either employer sanctions or amnesty and did not attend relevant public hearings in the 1970s and 1980s. The UFCWU, with no official position, chaired the AFL-CIO immigration committee in the mid-1990s.[22]

The UFCWU continued to straddle the fence on immigration policy issues at the end of the 1990s, when, as discussed below, the AFL-CIO reconsidered and revised its long-standing position on employer sanctions along with calling for a new amnesty program. The UFCWU did produce a statement on immigration at that time. The statement called for a new amnesty program, but it did not call for the repeal of employer sanctions. However, the statement did note that the INS should refrain from workplace enforcement action when there was other action in progress to enforce labor laws.[23]

Union of Needletrades, Industrial and Textile Employees (UNITE)

UNITE emerged from a merger between the International Ladies Garment Workers Union (ILGWU) and the Amalgamated Clothing and Textile Workers Union (ACTWU) in 1995. UNITE approved a non-restrictionist resolution on immigration policy at its first convention in 1999, which, among other things, called for the repeal of employer sanctions because "in recent years we have witnessed too many cases where employers have succeeded in thwarting unionizing efforts by using the sanctions provision."[24]

The ILGWU and ACTWU's positions on immigration policy were quite similar in the 1980s and 1990s, before their merger, as seen below.

ILGWU

The ILGWU's goal in the immigration debates of the late twentieth century was to obtain what it considered to be both "a humane and workable" immigration policy.[25]

Amnesty   The ILGWU was a strong advocate of a generous amnesty program when the subject was considered by U.S. legislators in the late 1970s and 1980s, prior to the enactment of the amnesty program in the IRCA of 1986. This position fit with the union's new policy that began to emerge in the late 1970s, when some union officials, recognizing the reality of undocumented workers' integration into the American economy, moved away from organized labor's traditional hostility toward undocumented immigrants and actively sought to organize such workers.[26] When discussing undocumented immigrants, Jay Mazur, at that time a vice-president of the ILGWU, noted in 1980 that: "Proposals to round up and return these workers to their original countries is both inhumane and impossible ..."[27]

Instead he, along with other ILGWU officials, advocated a generous amnesty program. Legalization of status through amnesty provided a means to reduce employers' ability to break strikes by threatening to call in the INS and a means to increase the opportunities for workers to join the union without fear of employer reprisal.[28] ILGWU officials presenting testimony at the SCIRP hearings and at congressional hearings in the early 1980s advocated a total amnesty for all undocumented workers, regardless of their arrival date in the United States.[29]

After IRCA was enacted in 1986 and the amnesty program was approved, the ILGWU devoted substantial efforts and financial resources to help amnesty applicants, and the union established an Immigration Project to coordinate the work and provide immigration related services to members. The union first engaged in an outreach program through mailing letters and distributing leaflets so as to inform undocumented workers of their rights, and of the union's services for its members. ILGWU staff then helped applicants prepare their files.

The ILGWU's Immigration Project offices in New York, Los Angeles, and Chicago fielded 4,200 phone calls during the first three months of the program; and the union provided English and civics classes so that the applicants could complete the legalization process.[30]

Employer sanctions　Employer sanctions were omitted from the policy prescriptions of ILGWU officials presenting testimony at the SCIRP hearings in 1979–80, but were included in testimony at congressional hearings at that time. The union officially supported the AFL-CIO's efforts to enact employer sanctions then, before the enactment of employer sanctions in the IRCA of 1986. The ILGWU's support for sanctions was given on the condition that a liberal amnesty program be simultaneously enacted.[31] At that time some ILGWU union officials seemed to consider that sanctions might be an effective means to control migration flows. Most notably, the ILGWU's President in 1986, Sol Chaikin, when discussing sanctions and a non-forgeable Social Security card, stated then that:

> If word got back to their home countries that you would not be able to get a job, maybe the flood of undocumented workers would slow down. You will never be able to stop a human being from aspiring to a better life, from wanting to live in freedom, from wanting to live in a community not at war. But at least we could slow down the flood of undocumented workers which provides the exploited labor for unscrupulous employers.[32]

The ILGWU's approach no longer reflects this position. After 1990 the ILGWU, seeking to organize undocumented immigrants, actively sought to repeal the law on employer sanctions that had been instituted in 1986. As explained by the Director of the ILGWU's Immigration Project in 1990: "In the past, undocumented workers could seek the membership and protection of unions. Unfortunately, the new law [employer sanctions] adversely influences the ability of unions to organize and protect undocumented workers."[33] Likewise, a resolution approved at the union's 1992 convention noted that: "The ability of unions to organize undocumented workers, or otherwise defend their rights, has been strongly undermined by the enactment of employer sanctions. The same employers who defy the immigration law with impunity are quick to use the law as a convenient weapon when confronted with an organizing campaign ... ."[34]

The ILGWU's support for repeal of sanctions was also influenced by a concern about the discriminatory consequences of the legislation for certain minorities. A GOP report issued in 1990 concluded that employer sanctions had caused "widespread discrimination" in hiring practices against those of Hispanic or Asian origin (an outcome that many liberal groups had predicted). Employers, fearful of inadvertently hiring undocumented workers, became increasingly unwilling to hire those U.S. citizens or legal permanent residents who may look "foreign" or who have a foreign accent.[35]

INS inspections The ILGWU strongly denounced INS raids, which may break strikes or organizing drives. The union filed a lawsuit against the INS in the early 1980s for conducting raids without appropriate search warrants.[36] The ILGWU, with active backing from the AFL-CIO, sought to change the INS' approach to raids at the worksite. It seems that, upon discussions with the AFL-CIO (supporting UNITE) in the late 1990s, the INS apparently agreed to change its operating procedures so as to avoid raids during times of an organizing drive or labor dispute at the workplace. At these times, caution was to be applied before raiding, and clearance was to be obtained from higher level staff. If implemented, the union considers that this procedural change will reduce the power of employers to kill organizing drives by threatening to call, or actually calling, the INS to conduct a search.[37]

ACTWU
ACTWU's position was similar to that of the ILGWU.

Amnesty ACTWU was a strong advocate of a generous amnesty program. The ACTWU official testifying at the SCIRP hearings in 1979 urged the adoption of a program that would legalize all undocumented workers residing in the United States at that time. As in the case of the ILGWU, the ACTWU's support for a generous amnesty program stemmed from a desire to facilitate unionization. As noted by the ACTWU official testifying at the SCIRP hearings: "If they [undocumented workers] seek to join with their fellow employees to organize for collective bargaining to improve their condition, they suddenly find Immigration waiting to check their papers one afternoon as they leave work."[38]

This position was reiterated in the question and answer period:

Ms. Meissner [who became the commissioner of the INS in 1993]: You indicated in your testimony that you do believe a certain proportion of your members in this area are undocumented. Is it correct to assume that your objection to the undocumented aliens, vis a vis labor standards, has to do with their being unorganized and, therefore, a factor for depressing working conditions, or do you object—but you do not object to them, if there is a possibility of unionizing them, therefore negating that?

Ms. Suarez [ACTWU]: I think you've said it for me, yes.[39]

ACTWU's commitment to legalize undocumented workers continued after the passage of IRCA, when ACTWU locals in areas such as Chicago, Los Angeles, and New York engaged in outreach programs designed to give guidance to amnesty applicants and to provide referral services to appropriate attorneys and community organizations. The union also provided free courses in the English language to assist applicants in fulfilling the language requirements of the legalization program.[40]

Employer sanctions ACTWU, like the ILGWU, officially supported the enactment of employer sanctions in the early 1980s. However, ACTWU officials did not advocate employer sanctions at the SCIRP hearings, and the subject of sanctions was omitted from a resolution on immigration approved at ACTWU's convention in 1984.[41] ACTWU passed a resolution favoring repeal of employer sanctions in 1993 to facilitate organization as sanctions appeared to be channeling undocumented workers into the sweatshop sector and undercutting the union. ACTWU's support for repeal was also influenced by a concern to avoid the discriminatory consequences of employer sanctions.[42]

Service Employees International Union (SEIU)

The SEIU, which represents workers in the growing service sector, became the largest union resisting certain restrictionist immigration policy measures in the 1990s. Pragmatism drove its policy. It took a very active approach on immigration issues so as to facilitate organizing in an era of economic internationalization.

Background

The SEIU originated in the building service sector in Chicago in the 1920s. In its initial years the SEIU was an AFL-affiliated craft union, although it was unusual for a craft union as it represented low-income workers.[43] But the union has since changed and expanded to a diverse range of occupations—public employees, healthcare workers (for example, hospital and homecare), building service workers (for example, window cleaners), and office workers. Some of the occupations that the union covers today are still the low-wage jobs in building service, where the union began in the 1920s. In these low-wage jobs the union's constituents may be the first workers to be affected by competition from new immigrants. For example, 32 percent of the SEIU's members worked in service occupations with positions such as custodians and nurse aides in 1991.[44] The union has a relatively diverse membership, which at the end of the century was 19 percent black, 10 percent Hispanic, 3 percent Asian, 5 percent other, and 63 percent white.[45]

Many of the SEIU's potential and current members are immigrants, as was the case for the United Mine Workers in the early twentieth century. This is particularly evident in California. Latino immigrants comprised 33 percent of service workers in Los Angeles in 1990, and 36 percent in California. Asian immigrants comprised 8 percent of service workers in Los Angeles, and 9 percent in all of California.[46]

The SEIU stood out as an exception among U.S. unions when it introduced various internal managerial reforms, beginning in the 1980s under John Sweeney's presidency (before he became President of the AFL-CIO). Union officials and academics labeled the SEIU as the most innovative union.[47] The innovations went hand in hand with some normative changes when the union, under the leadership of Sweeney, increased the size of its national staff, hiring many people who were what Michael Piore labels "new left radicals." A fair number of them were college educated and read the *Harvard Business Review,* giving them sources for what became unusually successful managerial reform within the union.[48] However, one should not place too much emphasis on norm change as an explanation for the subsequent shift in immigration policy preferences, because it begs the question of why union statements did not focus on norm change as the explanation, and it does not help us to understand why other unions that did not experience this infusion of "new left radicals" nonetheless did come around to changing their immigration policy preferences in the late twentieth century.

The SEIU's membership about doubled in size in the 1980s and 1990s. It increased from approximately 650,000 in 1980 to approximately 1.4 million in 2001.[49] This growth is reminiscent of the growth experienced by the United Mine Workers in the early twentieth century.

The SEIU has perhaps been the most active of all unions with regard to organizing since the mid-1980s, and it has focused on native and immigrant workers alike. As written by John Sweeney in 1986, when the union began to step up its efforts to organize immigrants:

> SEIU is organizing a new wave of immigrants .... For them and for us, it's a matter of survival .... To defend themselves, these immigrant workers

must form unions.... That's true for the rest of us, too. To defend ourselves, SEIU *must* bring the new immigrants in the industries we represent into the union. Otherwise, we cannot defend ourselves against the employers' demand to lower wages.[50] (emphasis in the original)

This statement was for real, not rhetoric. The SEIU devoted substantial resources to organizing and to hiring new staff and organizers who were fluent in Spanish. For example, the SEIU increased resources for Local 399, which was responsible for coordinating the Justice for Janitors campaign in Los Angeles, apparently enabling the local to hire approximately seven new organizers in the late 1980s/early 1990s, almost all of whom were Latino and all of whom were bilingual, or monolingual in Spanish.[51] The SEIU engaged in a number of successful campaigns in sectors where many immigrants work, such as the nationwide Justice for Janitors campaign, which began in the late 1980s; and the successful organizing drive among home health-care workers in Los Angeles, which resulted in the unionization of about 74,000 workers in 1999, and which increased the unionized workforce in LA by over 10 percent and was labeled as labor's biggest success in many years.[52]

Immigration policy preferences
Before the SEIU seriously upgraded its organizing efforts later in the 1980s, the union had not taken a particularly active approach to immigration issues. The SEIU was not an active participant in public hearings (such as the SCIRP hearings and congressional hearings) prior to the 1990s, and it apparently did not devote many resources to such things as helping amnesty applicants prepare for the IRCA legalization program. Convention discussions and resolutions in the 1970s barely addressed immigration issues, although there were some resolutions in the 1980s. The resolutions on immigration that the SEIU approved in the 1980s stressed a relationship between effective organizing and immigration issues. They were comparatively "non-restrictionist", in line with the ILGWU and ACTWU, and advocated a generous amnesty program and opposed INS raids so as to facilitate organizing.

The SEIU, like the ILGWU and ACTWU, officially supported employer sanctions legislation in the 1980s, although at that time the subject was apparently low on the priority list for the SEIU, and the union's support for sanctions showed a lack of enthusiasm.[53] Two resolutions that explicitly stated opposition to employer sanctions were submitted to the SEIU's Convention in 1988, but they were not discussed at that time and were instead replaced by a resolution that was otherwise non-restrictionist on immigration policy and was approved at the convention.

Since that time the SEIU has taken an increasingly active stance on immigration issues. SEIU explanations for its active approach since then occasionally referred to humanitarian concerns, or the rights of immigrants, although couched in terms of the interests of "All Americans". For example, an SEIU resolution in 1992 noted that "All Americans benefit from immigration policies that guarantee equal treatment for all workers, prevent exploitation of the foreign born, and are based on respect for civil and human rights."[54] But the overwhelming amount of SEIU statements focus on pragmatic reasons for its immigration policy preferences.

An Immigration Assistance and Education Program was created in accordance with a resolution approved at the union's convention in 1988. Organizing considerations were behind the program's creation. This linkage between organizing and immigration policy actions was explained by a speaker at the convention who introduced his support for the resolution by saying that: "We that are faced with the responsibility of representing and organizing our undocumented brothers and sisters in the workforce know that the people are burdened with very special problems which surrounds their immigration status."

The resolution itself noted that as:

> the flow of undocumented and immigrant workers into the service sector workforce represented by the SEIU continues to increase ... be it ... Resolved, that the SEIU develop an immigration assistance and education program to assist local unions in servicing their immigrant membership as well as organizing efforts.[55]

The SEIU established an immigration committee in May 1991 to review and make recommendations on SEIU policy.[56]

The union came around to clearly favoring the repeal of employer sanctions, and the subject was pushed up to a higher level of priorities on the SEIU's agenda. A resolution stating opposition to employer sanctions was approved at the union's convention in 1992, stating that the "SEIU will support efforts to repeal the employer sanctions provisions of IRCA,"[57] and the President of the SEIU submitted a statement that strongly advocated repeal of sanctions at congressional hearings held in June 1993.[58]

Organizational considerations, in conjunction with the difficulties of effectively controlling migration, were the driving force behind the

SEIU's increasingly active stance and its related decision to oppose employer sanctions.[59]

On the one hand, sanctions were seen to be an ineffective means for controlling migration flows and the impact of sanctions on illegal border crossing was seen as minimal or non-existent.[60] Thus there was little to lose by repealing employer sanctions legislation. As noted by the union's President in congressional hearings in 1993:

> The intent of the employer sanctions law was to deny employment opportunities to undocumented workers so that they would return home and discourage others from coming. While employer sanctions have indeed succeeded in forcing undocumented workers deeper into economic desperation, it is unlikely to make them more miserable than they were in the economic and political catastrophes from whence they migrated. The basic logic of employer sanctions is fatally flawed ... .
>
> Employer sanctions has done nothing to improve the lot of low-wage workers in the building service industry. Rather, their principal effect is to prevent a union from organizing workers employed by nonunion contractors. This dramatically increases the value of undocumented workers to contractors and building owners ... .[61]

More generally, the SEIU's skepticism regarding the state's ability to completely control migration was articulated in a resolution approved in 1992, which noted that:

> Push factors will continue to encourage people to seek a better life in the United States—no matter how punitive U.S. immigration policy becomes. It is clear that under any scenario, undocumented workers will continue to be a major part of the low-wage service work force in many areas.[62]

On the other hand, sanctions were impeding organization. Thus there was something to gain by repealing employer sanctions legislation. This was particularly clear in Los Angeles, where there was a serious effort to organize workers, at that time particularly in the building service sector. The SEIU's Local 399, which covered janitors in LA, had experienced large absolute losses in membership in the 1980s.[63] The SEIU responded to this de-unionization by taking its Justice for Janitors Campaign to Los Angeles in 1988. The union engaged in a serious organizing campaign, devoting significant financial resources to hiring new organizers who were bilingual, or monolingual in Spanish. The campaign attained significant successes.[64] But the SEIU also encountered some real obstacles due to the existence of sanctions, which gave employers a tool to dismiss undocumented immigrant activists during an organizing drive.[65] (Immigrants accounted for 61 percent of janitors in Los Angeles in 1990.) For example, shortly after a successful organizing campaign in 1990 in the Century City section of Los Angeles among workers who were employed by International Service System, a multi-national Danish cleaning contractor, many employees were asked to present new evidence of work authorization. Consequently, not only did some undocumented workers lose their jobs but others were discouraged from participating in further union activity.[66]

Pragmatic organizing considerations likewise led the SEIU to actively oppose certain aspects of the INS' strategy for *implementing* employer sanctions legislation. The SEIU, along with other organized unions and the AFL-CIO, firmly opposed the INS's strategy of obtaining cooperation from other federal agencies (such as the Department of Labor) to increase the availability of information on undocumented workers so as to facilitate the implementation of employer sanctions legislation. The SEIU opposed this strategy in general, but was particularly concerned by the entrance of the Social Security Administration (SSA) onto the scene of U.S. immigration policy in the late 1990s. The SSA stepped up its efforts to send out "mismatch letters" to employers and employees informing them when the names of workers did not match the SSA's database for employees' accounts. This coincidentally or otherwise served as an indirect means of implementing employer sanctions. Some employers who received these letters took this as a sign that the employee was an illegal immigrant (although quite often the cause of the mismatch was a name change resulting from marriage or divorce). The receipt of the letter would make it difficult for the employer to claim ignorance in the future if subjected to an INS audit on compliance with employer sanctions legislation, which only applies to those who *knowingly* hire illegals. Upon receipt of these letters some employers told the employees that they would again have to prove that they were legal immigrants or leave their jobs. These messages from the employers at times were conveyed to the employees, coincidentally or otherwise, during or shortly after a successful organizing drive.[67]

The SEIU and some other unions received support from the AFL-CIO on this issue, and AFL-CIO representatives met with officials in the SSA in 1999 and successfully obtained a change in the SSA mismatch letters. The SSA agreed to insert a section in the letters that clarified that receipt of the letter alone was not grounds for firing an employee. The new letters also explained how the employer could help the employee clear up the issue.

The SEIU's position on this issue was motivated by pragmatic organizing issues. There was a concern that the turnover in the workforce resulting from the mismatch letters and consequent firings would create a never-ending cycle of re-organizing workers who would be fired and replaced by new workers. Some undocumented immigrants who were fired when employers received the mismatch letters were union members. They would be replaced by new workers, who the union would have to again organize. Moreover, many of the SEIU's contracts with employers were scheduled to be re-negotiated in the year 2000, and the union was concerned that its bargaining power in these re-negotiations would be hindered if some union activists who happened to be undocumented immigrants were the subject of mismatch letters and may thus be fired.[68]

Pragmatic concerns also contributed to the SEIU's (and AFL-CIO's) decision in 2000 to begin to call for the enactment of a new amnesty program for the several million undocumented immigrants who had come to the United States since the previous amnesty program. The SEIU took a number of measures to pressure for a legalization program. For example, the SEIU posted a notice on its website with a direct mailing link to Washington so that people could email a letter to their Representative in Congress to pressure for a legalization program; and Andrew Stern, SEIU President, together with some other union presidents, met with the Mexican Foreign Minister in the summer of 2001 to discuss support for a legalization program, shortly before the Bush Administration's announcement in July 2001 that a form of legalization program might be advisable for some Mexican undocumented immigrants.[69]

As shown, the SEIU's immigration policy preferences in recent years were driven by organizing considerations in conjunction with some skepticism about the government's ability to completely control migration. But it was also influenced by broader dynamics on coalition politics. The SEIU wanted to maintain a cohesive coalition with other organizations in the liberal-labor coalition, such as the increasingly important Latino community in California. The SEIU expanded efforts to build community coalitions, and devoted significant time and resources to fighting Proposition 187 in California, to gain support from Latinos for Labor's agenda particularly in local politics in California. Community groups such as immigrant organizations and students gave indirect background support in organizing efforts by attending demonstrations, for example the Justice for Janitors demonstration in Century City, Los Angeles, in 1990. Broader political considerations also contributed to the SEIU's decision to favor repeal of employer sanctions. For immigrant organizations within the liberal-labor coalition, as well as for some legal immigrants and citizens who are members or potential members of the SEIU, repeal of employer sanctions was crucial due to the discriminatory consequences of sanctions for permanent residents and for American citizens who look or sound "foreign" or have "foreign-sounding" last names.[70]

United Farm Workers (UFW)

Sixty-two percent of agricultural workers in California were Latino immigrants in 1996.[71]

The union in earlier times did occasionally adopt a restrictionist posture and apparently sometimes used the INS against undocumented workers who were brought in to break strikes.[72] But after passage of California's Agricultural Labor Relations Act in 1975 (which allowed secret ballot recognition elections in which undocumented workers could vote),[73] the UFW for the most part joined with the groups resisting restrictionism or straddled the fence.

Amnesty

The UFW favored a generous amnesty program in the 1980s.[74] During the implementation phase of the IRCA amnesty program, the UFW filed a lawsuit against the INS in an attempt to liberalize the filing procedures for agricultural workers. While the lawsuit was unsuccessful, over 1 million people obtained amnesty under the special program enacted for farmworkers.[75]

At the turn of the millennium the UFW tried to reach a compromise with agri-business that would permit a new legalization program for farmworkers, and the UFW President went to Mexico in the summer of 2001, along with several other union presidents, to meet with the Mexican Foreign Minister so as to discuss support for a new legalization program and concerns about a guestworker program.[76]

Employer sanctions

The UFW in earlier times changed its policy toward employer sanctions. It initially took an ambiguous position in the national debate on employer sanctions in the early 1970s. But in the mid-1970s the union noted its opposition to employer sanctions.[77] As in the case of ACTWU and the ILGWU, the subject of employer sanctions was absent from the UFW's policy recommendations submitted at the SCIRP hearings but, like the garment unions, the UFW officially supported the enactment of employer sanctions in the early 1980s.[78]

In the early 1990s, Dolores Huerta, first Vice-President of the union, conveyed her agreement with others favoring the repeal of employer sanctions and argued against further enforcement measures along the U.S.–Mexican border.[79] The President of the UFW, Arturo Rodriguez, spoke in favor of removing sanctions legislation when the subject was discussed at the AFL-CIO's convention in 1999, noting the debilitating impact of sanctions on organizing campaigns.

Construction Craft Unions

The construction craft unions, with a unique identity that included an exclusionary approach to union membership, adopted a restrictionist position to illegal immigration in the late twentieth century, and often sat on the same side of the fence as the main restrictionist organization, the Federation for American Immigration Reform. This was particularly evident in the 1970s and 1980s. But by the late 1990s, when some construction unions began to adopt a more inclusive approach to union membership in general and took organizing more seriously after a sharp decline in union density, they in turn began to change their immigration policy positions.

Employer sanctions

Construction unions were an important force behind the AFL-CIO's support for the enactment of employer sanctions in the 1980s. Unlike organizing unions, the construction unions did not actively push for the enactment of an amnesty program.[80]

The resolutions approved by construction unions at the time of the congressional debates in the 1980s were very much in line with what the conventional wisdom leads one to expect. They blamed immigrants for increasing unemployment and lowering wages, and favored the enactment of employer sanctions.

The Bricklayers, Masons and Plasterers International Union approved several resolutions pertaining to immigration at its convention in 1985. One was a general resolution that noted "the persistence of high unemployment" and called on the government to make every effort to put all Americans back to work. One of the resolution's several suggestions for dealing with the unemployment problem was the need to stop the "flood of illegal immigrants" into the United States through the enactment of strong "sanctions against employers who knowingly hire illegal immigrants." The union also approved two resolutions that were devoted to immigration policy. One favored the enactment of sanctions, and also called for an amnesty program. The other condemned the practice of bringing in temporary non-immigrant workers to do construction work when qualified American workers were available.[81] The United Brotherhood of Carpenters (UBC) approved a resolution favoring the enactment of sanctions at its convention in 1986.[82] The resolution did not mention an amnesty program.

The Building and Construction Trades Department, AFL-CIO, approved a resolution on immigration policy at its 1983 convention, which noted that: "Illegal aliens were taking jobs away from Americans; and ... illegal aliens curtail the ability to improve wages and working conditions of legal workers."[83] The resolution listed a number of proposals, including the enactment of employer sanctions and increasing funds for the Border Patrol and the INS. Another resolution on immigration policy that was approved at the 1985 convention noted that: "The increasing use of illegal aliens in construction jobs nationwide has driven down wage scales for both union and non-union workers, and has increased unemployment among legal workers."[84] The resolution, in line with the compromise position within the AFL-CIO, called for the enactment of employer sanctions and a generous amnesty program.

After the enactment of sanctions in 1986, construction union officials at the leadership level displayed little hesitation to call in the INS to inspect worksites where undocumented immigrants were thought to be employed, and they sought to retain and tighten the laws on employer sanctions in the early 1990s.[85]

In contrast to this actively restrictionist position, the construction unions adopted non-positions in the debates in the 1990s. There were no discussions or resolutions on immigration at the two conventions of the Building and Construction Trades Department, AFL-CIO, held in 1990 and 1995. Likewise there were no discussions or resolutions on immigration at the two conventions of the United Brotherhood of Carpenters held in 1991 and 1995. The construction unions did not oppose the change in the AFL-CIO's position toward employer sanctions in early 2000, allowing a consensus and unity within the labor movement. This silence itself marks a shift from the previous actively restrictionist posture.

Some understanding of why there were these signs of change in the immigration policy preferences of construction unions can be seen by focusing on the local level in Los Angeles and New York. Construction unions, upon seeing union density nationwide shrink from about 42 percent in 1970 to 22 percent in 1990,[86] had begun to take organizing more seriously.

Los Angeles

Immigrants constitute a significant portion of the workforce in the construction sector in California. In 1996, 62 percent of the workforce was white, 4 percent black, 9 percent native Latino, 20 percent foreign born Latino, and 4 percent foreign born Asian.[87] Immigrant workers were concentrated in residential construction. For example, by 1990 almost all residential drywall workers in the region were immigrant Latinos.[88]

Unions had been very strong in the construction sector in California, with a union membership rate of 100 percent of the workforce in the 1950s and 1960s. This declined to 74 percent by 1979, it then rose to 85 percent in 1983, and then fell sharply to 54 percent in 1987 following an open shop offensive, led by the Associated Builders and Contractors.[89]

Immigration into the construction sector elicited two different reactions from union officials in California prior to the late 1990s. As discussed below, some officials sought to bring the immigrant workers into the union; whereas others responded in a highly restrictionist manner in accordance with the conventional wisdom. The former response gained the upper hand by the end of the 1990s.

In the late 1980s and early 1990s some officials, particularly in the Carpenters union, responded in a manner somewhat similar to that of the organizing unions discussed previously. Representatives of the Los Angeles District Council of Carpenters and its affiliated local unions put some effort into helping applicants for the amnesty program that was enacted in 1986. These efforts to provide a service on immigration were conducted so as to encourage immigrants to join the union. As explained by the Los Angeles District Council Administrative Assistant:

> We believe that this legislation has given us one of the most powerful organizing tools imaginable. These workers have come here for the same reasons that most of our parents or grandparents did. They want a better life for themselves and their families. If the union helps them achieve that goal, first by legalizing their residency status and then by organizing their workplace and getting them the benefits of a union contract, we will have their loyalty and their membership.[90]

Likewise Douglas McCarron, then Secretary Treasurer of the UBC's regional District Council (he later became President of the UBC), explained that by helping applicants gain legal status, the fear of deportation would be removed and: "We will take away the club that the non-union contractor has held over their heads for years. Once that is done we will be able to make great strides in organizing."[91]

The lukewarm efforts of the Carpenters to organize immigrant workers became more real in the early 1990s, when the UBC gave crucial support to the drywallers' strike, which closed down residential construction in Southern California for a period in 1992. The strike itself was a grass-roots effort initiated by the workers, almost all of whom were Mexican and were not affiliated with any union. However, the successful conclusion of the strike (an agreement was reached that improved pay and benefits), was in part attributable to the UBC's crucial financial support and other backing such as loaning its offices for meetings, along with crucial legal aid received from the AFL-CIO sponsored California Immigrant Workers' Association. About 2,400 drywallers, in turn, became affiliated with the UBC.[92] The UBC received the "Labor Award for Social Responsibility" from the Martin Luther King, Jr., Center for Nonviolent Social Change, for its support for the striking immigrant drywallers.[93]

However, apart from the Carpenters, there were some highly restrictionist responses to illegal immigrants in Los Angeles at the time. In the early 1990s high-ranking local officials, in line with the expectations of the conventional wisdom, considered that illegal immigrants increased the labor supply and job competition, and lowered wages and work conditions. For example, the Executive Secretary at the Los Angeles County Building and Construction Trades Council wrote that:

> Over the past 12 years we from labor have watched the influx of illegal aliens grow at such an alarming rate that we feel we must speak out. Our job markets have been flooded with people who will work for wages that even they could not survive on .... With almost 20,000 skilled craftsmen unemployed in the Los Angeles County Building & Construction Trades Council we feel that enough is enough. It is time for our elected officials to take a stand to stop the flood of illegals into Los Angeles County.[94]

Elsewhere he wrote that: "The steady flow of illegal immigrants into this country is forcing exploitation onto the legal immigrants with regards to low paying jobs (wages) that no one person can live decently or survive on."[95]

Officials at the Los Angeles County Building and Construction Trades Council actively sought to convey their position to local level politicians, and tried to gain support for ending the Day Labor Programs, such as those in Harbor City and North Hollywood, where many illegal immigrants were hired. This brought the LA building trades unions into coalition with cultural conservatives, and elicited a letter of congratulations and request for a meeting from Alan Nelson, a former INS Commissioner and a consultant to the principal restrictionist organization, the Federation for American Immigration Reform.[96]

This restrictionist response began to be replaced by an approach that emphasized organizing at the end of the 1990s. As one interviewee explained: "There's been a real change in our situation due to the increased portion of non-union contractors. Our initial reaction to this was that we demonstrated and picketed. But we've changed our reaction to increase our organizing efforts and to shift our attention to construction contractors use of non-union workers."[97]

The effort to increase organizing filtered down from the level of the national unions, which had for a number of years been contributing to slowly changing the approach of construction union officials and members through the Construction Organizing Membership Education Training (COMET) program, which was designed to prepare members to be active organizers by explaining why it was necessary to bring all the workers in a sector into the union. This slow change was sped up in June 1999, when a two-day conference on "Organizing in the Building Trades" was organized, sponsored by the UCLA Labor Center, in coordination with the California State and LA-Orange County Building and Construction Trades Councils. Eighty union organizers attended. Speakers included an attorney who spoke on immigrant rights;[98] and an AFL-CIO Project Coordinator who had previously worked for the SEIU's Local 399, which had organized the successful Justice for Janitors campaign in Los Angeles.

As the Los Angeles Building Trades Unions became more open to the rationale for bringing immigrants into unions, they simultaneously became less restrictionist on immigration policy. In the last years of the twentieth century building trades union officials apparently avoided calling in the INS to check on worksites where undocumented immigrants were thought to be working; immigration issues apparently became rarely discussed in meetings; and the Los Angeles County Building and Construction Trades Council adopted a non-position on the subject of employer sanctions. (This non-position was apparently also attributable to a desire to maintain cohesion within the labor movement and to not block unions, such as the SEIU, that strongly wanted the change.)[99] These moves in the direction of "silence" mark a real shift from the actively restrictionist response of the exclusive construction unions in earlier years, beginning in the late nineteenth/early twentieth century (when West Coast construction unions sought to exclude immigration from Asia), and continuing through to the mid-1990s, when some local officials considered that denouncing illegal immigrants was preferable to organizing them.

New York

The building and construction unions in New York, as elsewhere, previously adopted a restrictionist posture to illegal immigrants. For example, as noted by the AFL-CIO's representative in congressional hearings in 1975, in New York the painters' union policed jobs, picketing sites where illegal aliens worked and getting them thrown off the job.[100] In the mid-1970s the Building and Construction Trades Council of Greater New York notified all affiliates to write to their Congressman or Congresswoman to urge passage of a bill being considered that would impose immediate criminal penalties against employers who knowingly hired illegal aliens.[101] By the end of the 1990s, at the level of the Building and Construction Trades Council of Greater New York, immigration issues were apparently low on the agenda of concerns, and rarely discussed in comparison with other issues such as employer violation of health and safety regulations.[102]

Some building and construction unions at the local level in New York, as in Los Angeles, began to replace a restrictionist response with an organizing response in the 1990s. This was most clear in the Laborers Union. For example, the Laborers in New York made serious efforts to organize asbestos removal workers, many of whom were immigrants. The workers, most of whom were from Poland and Latin America, were successfully organized into what became Local 78, with approximately 2,000 members. The locals of the Laborers Union took the immigration concerns of their members and potential members seriously. Northeast locals of the Laborers Union, along with some SEIU locals, showed up with a very strong presence to a march in Washington, D.C., to demand amnesty for undocumented workers in October 1999. The march was organized by grass-roots Latino, religious, and immigrant rights organizations.[103] The President of the Laborers Union attended and spoke at another rally organized in Washington, D.C., in July 2000 to promote amnesty for undocumented workers. The rally was sponsored by the national Coalition for the Dignity and Amnesty of Undocumented Workers, and was attended by some 4,000 Latinos.[104] The President of the Laborer's Union joined the presidents of several other unions on a trip to Mexico where they met with the Mexican Foreign Minister to discuss the subject of amnesty for undocumented immigrants and concerns about a guestworker program.[105]

AFL-CIO

The AFL-CIO's position to illegal immigrants changed in the late twentieth century. But before then, in the early 1970s, the AFL-CIO's position was in line with the conventional wisdom that unions oppose foreign workers due to a fear that this increases the labor supply and job competition and reduces wages.

In 1971, the AFL-CIO approved a resolution that noted:

> ... the rising number of persons who illegally enter this country to work at substandard wages paid by exploiting employers. This intolerable process is robbing large numbers of American citizens and legal immigrants of their jobs, and it threatens an indirect undermining of fair wage levels in other industries.[106]

Similar hostility and a concern about job competition from illegal immigrants was displayed in a resolution approved in 1975, which noted that: "Their presence takes jobs from American citizens and legal aliens and undermines the movement toward fair wages and working conditions."[107] The AFL-CIO took an active stance on issues related to illegal immigrants in the 1970s and 1980s, sending a representative to all relevant congressional hearings.

Amnesty

The AFL-CIO, having initially shown little enthusiasm for amnesty in 1975 due to a concern about "sweep[ing] into legalization for employment large numbers of aliens who came here illegally in the first place," soon came to support a generous legalization program.[108] The federation took a clearly supportive position toward amnesty by the late 1970s. The President of the AFL-CIO, Lane Kirkland, when presenting testimony in congressional hearings held in 1982, noted that the federation favored giving immediate permanent resident status to illegal aliens who had resided in the United States since 1 January 1980.[109] This position was reiterated in an AFL-CIO Executive Council statement issued in 1983, which noted, "We support the most generous, practical amnesty for these people."[110] By 1986, the AFL-CIO supported amnesty for all undocumented workers who had lived in the United States for one year prior to enactment of the new law.[111]

The AFL-CIO came to view support for amnesty as an organizing tool, and it adopted a resolution at its 1987 Convention that stated, "We urge vigorous efforts to legalize as many eligible undocumented immigrants as possible."[112] The AFL-CIO and its constituent parts embarked on an outreach campaign to assist undocumented workers with the legalization process. For example, Spanish-language radio and television stations in Los Angeles broadcast public service announcements produced by the AFL-CIO. In addition, the California Immigrant Workers Association was developed and funded by the AFL-CIO. The Association, which provided benefits such as free courses in the English language to assist amnesty applicants and low-cost health care insurance, was designed to facilitate organizing undocumented and documented immigrant workers in Southern California.[113]

A few years later, at the turn of the millennium, the AFL-CIO became a firm advocate of setting up another amnesty program. Members of the AFL-CIO Executive Council joined a march sponsored by the Massachusetts General Amnesty Coalition in Boston, in May 2001, where they were gathered for an Executive Council meeting; and the AFL-CIO posted a section on immigration on its website, which included several short articles on subjects such as why people move, and immigration in the United States. The Executive Council issued a statement on immigration policy in July 2001, which noted that:

> The AFL-CIO and its affiliated unions will work vigilantly with our coalition partners representing the immigrant, ethnic, faith, and civil rights communities to ensure that comprehensive legislation providing for legalization and the enforcement of workplace rights for all workers is introduced in Congress and ultimately signed into law.[114]

At the same time, the Executive Council statement reflected the view that restricting legal immigration serves to increase illegal immigration in an era of economic internationalization. The statement noted that: "We should recognize that one of the reasons for undocumented immigration is that our current legal immigration system for family members and for workers is in shamefully bad shape." It went on to urge the government to devote adequate resources to INS benefits and services, so as to address the family reunification backlogs or to process applications of those seeking to adjust their status. This tone was quite different from the AFL in the early twentieth century, when it called on the government to devote more resources to beefing up the border.

Employer sanctions

The AFL-CIO, sitting together with other restrictionists, consistently sought the enactment of employer sanctions and pressured for sanctions prior to the enactment of IRCA in 1986. For example, in 1973 the AFL-CIO wrote a letter to the Chair of the House Committee on the Judiciary with regard to a bill to repeal the exemption of employers from the prohibition against "harboring" illegal aliens. The letter noted that the AFL-CIO "has long supported legislation along this line." The reason given reflected the conventional view that the net effect of the employment of illegal aliens: "... has been to reduce job opportunities needed by the unemployed in our own country and to depress and maintain low-wage levels and substandard living conditions for both American citizens and non-citizens. The effectiveness of collective bargaining is also being seriously undermined."[115]

Until the year 2000, the AFL-CIO did not join the growing coalition favoring repeal of sanctions. The AFL-CIO continued to support sanctions. However, the AFL-CIO's support for sanctions in the 1990s was muted, reflecting conflicting pressures from the construction craft unions on the one hand and, on the other, the inclusive organizing unions such as the SEIU, ILGWU, and ACTWU, which, in conjunction with the Industrial Union Department at the AFL-CIO, favored repeal of sanctions.[116] The AFL-CIO refrained from pressuring for a tightening of the legislation in the 1990s. Having sent a representative to all the congressional hearings on immigration issues in the 1970s and 1980s, it evaded presenting testimony at congressional hearings held to consider the repeal (or tightening) of employer sanctions in the early 1990s.[117] This silence itself marked a break with restrictionism.

Moreover, the AFL-CIO adopted a resolution at its convention in the fall of 1993, at a time of economic recession, that urged resisting restrictionism. But in this instance the resolution pointed to normative concerns for the human rights of the migrants, noting the AFL-CIO's commitment to: "... immigration policies and laws that protect the rights of all workers, provide fair opportunities for legal immigration, and insure compassionate and humane treatment and due process of law for all people who enter, or attempt to enter, the United States illegally."[118]

The following year, in August 1994, the AFL-CIO Executive Council stated that "Illegal immigration affects many states and communities. Its impact has been grossly and unfairly exaggerated. This scapegoating of immigrant workers is a calculated political ploy."[119]

The AFL-CIO changed its policy on employer sanctions at the turn of the millennium. It became evident at the AFL-CIO Convention in

October 1999 that change was likely to occur. The convention was held in Los Angeles, a city where there were active organizing efforts with a focus on immigrant workers, and a city where the County Federation of Labor, AFL-CIO, committed to shifting 30 percent of its resources to organizing.[120] For the Immigration Committee of the Los Angeles County Federation of Labor: "We are living in an era where the movement of labor, like capital, is increasingly common and difficult to regulate. The world has become a smaller place and organized labor is adjusting."[121] The Los Angeles County Federation of Labor, AFL-CIO itself had already approved a resolution calling for the repeal of employer sanctions and the enactment of an amnesty program, following the California Labor Federation, AFL-CIO, which approved a resolution on these issues in 1994.

The Executive Council announced the AFL-CIO's policy shift in February 2000. The Executive Council statement, among other things, called for a new amnesty program, and the repeal of the current I-9 system of employment eligibility verification as a tool of workplace immigration enforcement.[122]

This policy shift brought the AFL-CIO into a firmer coalition with liberal/immigrants rights groups, and deepened the conflict with the main restrictionist organization, the Federation for American Immigration Reform, which criticized the AFL-CIO's policy shift.[123] The Federation for American Immigration Reform strongly denounced any kind of amnesty or legalization program, arguing in numerous news releases and action alerts on its website that amnesty encourages illegal immigration by rewarding those who break immigration laws and by sending a message that the United States does not take its immigration laws seriously, among other things; and it favored beefing up employer sanctions by developing a federal system for verifying worker identification and eligibility.

The change in AFL-CIO policy was driven by the organizing agenda. The AFL-CIO had come to take organizing more seriously (devoting 30 percent of its budget to organizing) since the former President of the SEIU, John Sweeney, became President of the AFL-CIO in 1995. The change in the AFL-CIO policy was actively pushed for by the organized unions, such as the SEIU, UNITE, and the Hotel Employees and Restaurant Employees International Union (HERE). Other unions such as the construction unions did not oppose the change. As unions and their locals had engaged in more organizing in recent years, an increasing number of locals had encountered the debilitating impact of sanctions on organizing. As noted by John Wilhelm, who in 1998 had become President of the 300,000 member HERE: "Anyone who is trying to organize workers in America today has got to grapple with the fact that employers are abusing the immigration system to terrorize workers."[124]

One of the numerous examples that HERE had encountered was the case of the Holiday Inn Express in downtown Minneapolis. Workers there voted to join Local 17 of HERE in August 1999. Shortly after this, three weeks before contract negotiations were scheduled to begin, the manager called in the INS to check on the immigration status of some workers, who were then arrested.[125]

The organizing concern was emphasized by delegates speaking at the AFL-CIO Convention in October 1999.[126] It was organizing considerations that brought immigration onto the agenda.

In conjunction with this concern to remove an organizing obstacle, statements expressed that sanctions were ineffective in controlling migration flows. Thus there was little to lose by repealing a measure that had been enacted with the goal of restricting illegal migration. As the President of HERE noted in his capacity as a delegate to the AFL-CIO Convention in 1999: "The facts and the reality are, as we observe them in our workplaces, that employer sanctions don't contribute to controlling illegal immigration."[127]

He expressed similar views on the need to be realistic elsewhere. For example, in the summer of 2001, he noted that "Immigrants are in every workplace in the United States, and they're not leaving."[128] At the same time HERE invited the Mexican Foreign Minister to speak at the union's convention, held in Los Angeles, and gave him a rousing ovation when he stated that illegal Mexican immigrants should be given legal status to prevent their exploitation.[129]

Another delegate at the 1999 AFL-CIO Convention placed the subject more broadly in the context of economic globalization, noting that:

> It is time to revisit the immigration debate. With the economy more than ever global, workers more than ever mobile, and the economic despair and disparities deepening worldwide, more and more immigrants come to our shores and cross our borders for the simplest of reasons: They need to work.[130]

A similar view was expressed in a short background article on the causes of migration written for and posted on the AFL-CIO's website. The article, while noting that only a small percentage of the world's population lives outside their home country, pointed to the changing nature of migration in the era of internationalization at the turn of the millennium. It noted that:

> Technological advances have erased barriers to job creation and information flow, and rapid changes in transportation and communication technology have made it possible for greater numbers of people to move beyond the country of their birth. Global marketing of the image of the "American Dream" serves as a powerful attraction to people who immigrate to the United States.[131]

Interior patrol

The AFL-CIO and the organized affiliated unions such as the SEIU and UNITE strongly opposed those aspects of the INS' strategy of interior patrol that undermined organizing. The AFL-CIO opposed INS raids of worksites when organizing campaigns were in progress, and opposed collaboration between the INS and other federal agencies to gather information for *implementing* employer sanctions legislation. A lengthy resolution approved at the AFL-CIO convention in 1999, which included one section on immigration, called on the INS to:

> ... recognize and respect the federally protected rights of workers to organize, bargain collectively and act in concert .... We call upon all federal agencies to recognize and respect the federally protected rights of unions to represent their members and to organize workers. The AFL-CIO opposes immigration enforcement programs that undermine unionized workforces ... .[132]

As explained above, the AFL-CIO supported the organized unions such as the SEIU in opposing the content of the SSA's mismatch letters, which served as an indirect means for implementing employer sanctions and could be used by employers to hinder organizing drives. AFL-CIO negotiations with the SSA resulted in some changes in the letters.

The AFL-CIO likewise actively opposed the Memorandum of Understanding between the INS and the Department of Labor, which was written in the first Bush Administration. The Understanding called for the Department of Labor to inform the INS when it discovered illegal immigrants during its investigations on compliance with issues such as wage and hour regulations. The AFL-CIO explained that "this practice, which is not required by law, has been distorted by some employers to frighten workers, thwart union organizing drives and hinder investigations of other labor law violations."[133] Union officials were concerned that this collaboration between the INS and DOL deterred workers from filing legitimate complaints about employers who were breaking the law on workplace conditions, wages, and hours; thereby increasing the vulnerability of undocumented workers and dragging down standards for all.[134]

The AFL-CIO, apparently with the benefit of a new, very talented General Counsel, who (like the AFL-CIO President Sweeney), had moved to the AFL-CIO from the SEIU, succeeded in obtaining a new Memorandum of Understanding between the INS and the Department of Labor that clarified the enforcement roles and responsibilities of each agency, and conditions for communication and coordination between them. The key paragraph in the memorandum that resulted from negotiations with the AFL-CIO stated that the Department of Labor would not review the I-9 employment eligibility forms in those cases where the investigation resulted from a complaint brought by a worker.[135]

Territorial border patrol

The AFL-CIO, and its affiliated unions including the SEIU and the ILGWU, favored the increased resources authorized for border patrol at territorial boundaries in the Illegal Immigration Reform and Immigrant Responsibility Act of 1996, and in the 1990s more generally. On this issue the AFL-CIO and its affiliates departed from some of the immigrant rights organizations in the liberal-labor coalition. Patrol of the border at territorial boundaries, unlike internal patrol, has no direct detrimental impact on workplace issues. As one interviewee phrased it, "if we didn't advocate increasing resources for border patrol that would be equivalent to advocating open borders, which we're not for."[136]

Union Immigration Policy Preferences to Temporary Non-Immigrant Workers

The subject of temporary non-immigrant work permits generated clear conflict between business organizations and labor unions at the turn of the millennium. Business organizations pushed for removing restrictions, and labor unions pressured for protectionism on this issue.

Temporary non-immigrant workers who are granted visas to work in the United States for a limited period of time are often skilled workers employed in desirable jobs that American workers want, such as academia, engineering, arts, and entertainment. In recent years information technology has been the crucial sector where business has sought to increase hirings of temporary, non-immigrant workers. In addition to these skilled sectors, agriculture has also for many years been a sector where business has pressured for temporary workers.

The AFL-CIO and many individual unions adopted an actively restrictionist posture toward temporary non-immigrant worker admissions and consistently opposed the enactment of guestworker programs. Unions' positions toward this issue have been in line with the conventional expectation that they seek to restrict foreign workers so as to limit the labor supply. The AFL-CIO's concern about job competition on this issue was expressed in a resolution approved at the AFL-CIO Convention in 1999, which noted that:

> Far too many employers have sought to exploit the H-2B (other skilled worker) and H-2A (agricultural guest worker) programs in order to depress the wages and working conditions of U.S. workers.... The U.S. Department of Labor in 1998 approved more than 99 percent of all agricultural guest worker applications—even though many rural areas suffer from double-digit unemployment.[137]

The AFL-CIO's Executive Council statement on immigration in July 2001 reiterated this message, noting that: "The upshot of every guestworker program in the United States to-date has been to further depress wages for all workers, foreign and U.S.-born, to cause greater exploitation, and to reduce overall employment opportunities."[138]

The United Farm Workers and unions covering professions such as engineering and arts and entertainment sought to restrict the admissions of temporary non-immigrant workers, sending representatives to SCIRP hearings and congressional hearings. The AFL-CIO backed those unions, sending representatives to relevant public hearings.

The AFL-CIO pressured to tighten the criteria for admission of temporary non-immigrant workers in immigration debates. Some restrictionist measures on this issue were enacted in the Nursing Relief Act of 1989, and similar although more diluted measures were applied to other professions in the Immigration Act of 1990. Agribusiness' attempts to enact a new guestworker program in agriculture in the late 1990s met with clear opposition from organized labor, which was backed by the National Immigration Forum. Businesses, particularly those hiring information technology workers, did succeed in obtaining a large increase in the admissions for temporary non-immigrant workers (H-1B specialty visas) at the turn of the millennium. This increase in the admissions cap was clearly criticized by the AFL-CIO, which argued that instead the credentials of applicants for temporary non-immigrant visas should be more thoroughly reviewed, and that there should be more focus on (re)training American workers.[139]

Conclusion

U.S. unions in the late twentieth century have been most clearly restrictionist with regard to high-skilled jobs (for example in engineering and information technology). Foreign workers in these sectors often enter the United States on temporary non-immigrant visas, and the AFL-CIO and its affiliates have been restrictionist on issues pertaining to temporary non-immigrant visas. In contrast, the evidence presented in this chapter shows that the AFL-CIO and its affiliates have changed their approaches on issues pertaining to illegal immigration, and most undocumented immigrants work in the least desirable jobs. Unions have not favored open borders. But they have come to favor certain non-restrictionist measures.

However, one needs to get beyond a sectoral approach to explain the *change* in immigration policy preferences of the AFL-CIO and its affiliates in the late twentieth century. These are sectors (such as janitors, restaurant workers) where there have always been a lot of immigrant workers since the early twentieth century. The jobs did not suddenly become undesirable in the late twentieth century. Why was it that unions covering such sectors opposed certain restrictionist measures in the late twentieth century, unlike their counterparts in the UMW in the early twentieth century, which was the largest union representing unskilled workers then?

Reflecting back to the pragmatic identity of U.S. unions helps to explain the policy shift. What did change in the late twentieth century was a rejuvenation in the organizing agenda of certain unions such as the SEIU, and of the AFL-CIO, in conjunction with, on the one hand, a recognition of a deepening tension between support for restrictionist measures and effective organizing in an era of economic internationalization and, on the other hand, a growing skepticism about the ability of certain restrictionist measures to effectively control migration flows in an era of economic internationalization. U.S. unions adopted a pragmatic approach and adapted.

This elicited a coalition pattern that was quite different from the situation in the early twentieth century, when there was a "strange alliance" between the AFL and nativist groups, and when the AFL at times demanded a *complete* halt to all immigration for a period of time. The AFL-CIO's position in 2000 showed little resemblance with then.

CHAPTER 5

French First: Labor Unions and French Immigration Policy in the Early Twentieth Century

France, like the United States, experienced substantial immigration in the early twentieth century, and many of the immigrants came from the same region of Eastern and Southern Europe.

This chapter reviews the immigration policy preferences of unions then, so as to give a baseline for comparison with unions' immigration policy preferences in later times. The documents and newspapers of French unions at that time were more or less void of the numerous racial comments that were articulated by U.S. unions then, and French unions did not embark on a crusade in the manner that the AFL did, for example with regard to Asians. Nonetheless, the majority of French unions then pressured for protectionism, and the conventional wisdom that focuses on economic issues helps us to understand why.

Immigration into France: Background

Migration Flows

France had a higher rate of immigration, proportional to the number of inhabitants, than any other country in the mid-1920s (when immigration to the United States was sharply cut).[1] Foreigners constituted 2.5 percent of the total population in 1906; 3.9 percent in 1921; 6.1 percent in 1926; and 7 percent in 1931.[2]

By 1930 immigrants made up 15 percent of the working class in France.[3] They were concentrated in sectors such as mining, heavy metallurgy, construction work, the chemical industry, and domestic service.

In the mines, immigrants were 42 percent of the labor force in 1931, up from 6.5 percent of the labor force in 1906. And in heavy metal industries immigrants constituted 38.2 percent of the labor force in 1931, up from 18.4 percent in 1906.[4]

Migration to France in the late nineteenth century had been from the neighboring countries of Belgium, Italy, and Spain. After World War I, migration increased from the new source countries of East-Central Europe, particularly Poland. Poles constituted 4 percent of foreigners in France in 1911, 18 percent in 1926, and over 20 percent at the beginning of the 1930s.[5]

Different immigrant groups dominated different sectors, reflecting the timing of the wave of migration of the particular group. Immigrants from Belgium, who had been coming to France in significant numbers since the nineteenth century, tended to work in agriculture, textiles, and metalworking. Italians were concentrated in the building and construction sector, and also in agriculture and heavy metalworking. The newest wave of immigrants (Poles) were concentrated in the least desirable jobs in the mining sector.[6]

The Causes of Migration

French government restrictions on migration flows (primarily restrictions against emigration) were removed in the nineteenth century, when movement to and from France became essentially free and subject to no controls.[7] During much of the nineteenth century migrants came on their own initiative from neighboring countries in search of work. By the late nineteenth century thousands of workers commuted across the French–Belgium border on a daily basis to work in the French textile factories or metal works.[8] Active recruitment of migrants by employers began in the late nineteenth century and was at that time oriented to workers from Belgium and Italy. After World War I both the French government and French private employers intensified their recruitment efforts for migrant workers.

The *demand* for immigrant labor in the early twentieth century stemmed from several particular factors. France had experienced a low birthrate since the nineteenth century (lower than any other European country). In conjunction with this demographic fact, France faced a shortage of workers in the 1920s as a result of World War I, in which many French men of working age had been killed or seriously injured. The war had also increased the demand for labor to reconstruct those parts of the country that had been destroyed in the fighting.

Along with this overall labor shortage, there was a demand for workers who were immigrants to take up the least desirable jobs that French workers shunned. Changes in the economy and the industrial dynamism in France in the early twentieth century, along with technological developments, increased the portion of unskilled, undesirable jobs, and thus generated a demand for immigrant workers in particular to fill this gap. In many sectors it was clear that immigrants worked in the least desirable jobs and, as the portion of these jobs increased with technological developments, French workers moved out and up to other professions. Examples of the division of labor between French and immigrant workers include the Lorraine iron-ore workers, in which most of the underground laborers were immigrants; and the Nord-Pas-de-Calais region, where immigrants made up 46 percent of the underground workers and only 17 percent of the surface workers.[9] In the steel manufacturing region of Longwy in the North-East of France, French (and Belgium) workers monopolized the more skilled factory jobs, whereas the Italian (and later Polish) immigrants were employed in the mines.[10]

In sum, demography, war, and technological developments generated a demand for immigrant workers to take the growing portion of undesirable jobs.

The *supply* of immigrant workers was initiated largely through active recruitment by employers and the French government—a process that began during World War I when the government actively intervened to bring in workers, primarily from French colonies.[11] After World War I the French government and employers recruited abroad to bring immigrants to France to fill the least desirable jobs. The government negotiated bilateral treaties with foreign countries such as Poland, Italy, Czechoslovakia, and Belgium. The treaties allowed French recruitment in these countries. France, in turn, committed to treat the immigrant workers in a similar manner to French workers on such issues as salaries (a commitment that rarely moved from paper to practice). The specifics of bilateral treaties at times varied. For example, Poland allowed French recruitment agents to set up anywhere in Poland. In contrast, the Italian government sought to retain some control over the process, and thus stationed recruiting agents in towns on the country's border.[12]

Private companies also directly recruited abroad, outside this governmental structure. The Société Générale d'Immigration (SGI) (General Society of Immigration), an anonymous society created in 1924, functioned as a recruitment agent working on behalf of employers. The SGI set up recruitment centers in many countries, particularly in Poland, Yugoslavia, and Czechoslovakia. The most famous recruitment center was at Myslowice in Poland, where there was a French government mission and through which 276,969 foreigners were recruited between 1919 and 1929.[13] The SGI agents at these recruitment centers served as major advertisers for employers in the "land of opportunity." At the recruitment centers the workers were submitted to a medical and professional exam. Quite a few were rejected for failing the medical exam. The centers were busy. About 500 or 600 potential emigrants were inspected on average in a day and the process was completed quickly. The workers who were approved were then photographed, showered, disinfected, and vaccinated. They spent the night in huge dormitories, often with insufficient heat, and the next day they were put in special trains (or, in some locations, placed on boats), and transported to a reception center in France. The largest reception center was at Toul in the North-East of France, which opened for business in December 1919 and became the French version of Ellis Island for Polish immigrants. There the newcomers were welcomed by a four-kilometer walk with their baggage from the train to the center, which made use of former military barracks for housing. The immigrants were then handed over to their future employers. The SGI brought half a million workers to France from 1924 to 1931.[14]

The French government maintained significant control over this supply of foreign labor, manipulating the quantity of the supply according to the economic situation in France. When recessions set in and unemployment rose, the government cut the foreign labor supply by halting entrances and inducing or enforcing exits. The government had various measures at its disposal to do this. First, to reduce entrances, the government could turn down requests for workers. Employers, to obtain foreign workers, had to submit a request to placement offices in France, which, in turn, forwarded the request to the Ministry of Labor or Ministry of Agriculture. In times of prosperity, requests were largely automatically approved, but this process gave the government an opportunity to decline requests at those times when unemployment rose.[15] Second, to increase exits, it declined to renew work permits and identity cards, it engaged in voluntary repatriation, and it enforced expulsions. As noted by Gary Cross, the "state opened and closed the frontier to labor immigration as if it were a faucet."[16]

The impact of government policy on manipulating the supply of labor is suggested in tables 5.1 and 5.2, which show a strong correlation between unemployment levels and sharp shifts in the quantities of controlled entrances and exits. While one cannot prove that the shifts can be fully accounted for by government policy, it is likely that

Table 5.1   Unemployment indicators in France: 1925–1935

Year	Unemployed in receipt of public relief	Applications for work at employment exchanges
1925	1,271	20,027
1926	17,562	29,433
1927	33,590	46,778
1928	4,949	14,982
1929	928	9,710
1930	2,514	13,774
1931	55,781	74,845
1932	266,456	305,380
1933	275,316	306,718
1934	342,165	376,359
1935	426,879	465,796

Sources: International Labor Organization, *The ILO Year Book, 1932* (Geneva: ILO, 1933); and International Labor Organization, *Yearbook of Labour Statistics 1935–36* (Geneva: ILO, 1936).

Table 5.2   Controlled entrances and exits of foreigners, 1920–1935

Year	Entrances		Total	Exits	Balance
	Industry	Agriculture			
1920	N.A.	N.A.	201,925	12,151	+189,774
1921	25,998	54,414	80,412	62,536	+17,876
1922	107,787	73,865	181,652	50,309	+131,343
1923	184,255	78,622	262,877	59,951	+202,926
1924	173,170	90,185	263,355	47,752	+215,603
1925	104,477	71,784	176,261	54,393	+121,868
1926	98,949	63,160	162,109	48,683	+113,426
1927	18,778	45,547	64,325	89,982	−25,657
1928	36,055	61,687	97,742	53,759	+43,983
1929	110,871	68,450	179,321	38,870	+140,451
1930	128,791	92,828	221,619	43,789	+177,830
1931	25,804	76,463	102,267	92,916	+9,351
1932	12,817	56,675	69,492	108,513	−39,021
1933	12,260	62,375	74,635	49,047	+25,588
1934	11,188	60,350	71,538	40,004	+31,534
1935	9,989	46,517	56,506	67,215	−10,709

Source: Ralph Schor *Histoire de l'Immigration en France* (Paris: Armand Colin, 1996), pp. 58 and 124.

there is a causal connection to the correlation. For example, when unemployment began to rise in 1931, the government initially declined applications for new entrances. In the following years of the Great Depression the government focused on measures to induce or enforce exit. Foreign workers who were laid off often did not qualify for unemployment aid, or were denied such aid by local authorities even if they did qualify. Work permits and then identity cards were not renewed, applications for regularization of status were rejected, and the government offered foreigners free transportation to the frontier.[17] Expulsions increased. For example, 140,000 Polish workers were expelled from the North of France in 1934.[18] Measures at the level of local governments also appear to have had some influence over migration flows. For example, a local government report in Meurthe-et-Moselle in 1932 stated clearly that lay-offs were first geared at unmarried foreign workers, then at married foreign workers, and only subsequent to this were French workers laid off. The report noted that the administration obliged those foreigners whose work permit had expired to depart to the frontier. A later report written by the same region's prefect noted that Meurthe-et-Moselle was one of the most industrialized regions in France, but in 1934 it was one of the regions that experienced the least victims of unemployment due to various measures, including that of repatriation of foreign workers who were laid off before French workers.[19]

It is very likely that the sharp shifts in migration flows at times of unemployment would have been different if government policy had been different. The large number of exits that occurred would have likely been less if the government had ensured all immigrants full access to unemployment aid, or automatically renewed work permits and identity cards, or granted requests for regularization of status, or avoided expulsions.

French government control in the early twentieth century, while showing a good deal of ability to manipulate migration flows, was nonetheless imperfect. France has thousands of kilometers of frontiers. Then, as today, there were also quite a lot of immigrants who entered the country illegally, often crossing the frontier in the mountains. Others came as "tourists" and, once in France, stayed and looked for work. Those migrants who came irregularly applied for regularization of status once in France, and the government often approved these requests except in times of economic recession and unemployment.[20]

French Immigration Policy

Immigration laws in France developed in an ad hoc manner in the early twentieth century, and were often changed through decree. This was evident, for example, with regard to the issue of identity cards. A decree issued during World War I, in April 1917, required foreigners to have identity cards.[21] But the administrative rules on the criteria for obtaining and renewing identity cards, and the period of time for which identity cards were valid, often changed (sometimes twice in one year).[22]

The main new laws approved in the inter-war years were minor in comparison with developments in U.S. immigration law in the early 1920s. There was no equivalent of the National Origins Act. In France, the main developments were with regard to laws that, to use Tomas Hammer's definition of immigration policy, "control foreign citizens (aliens) once they visit or take residence in the receiving country, including control over their employment."[23]

One such law, enacted on 11 August 1926, aimed to halt the practice whereby foreigners who were brought in to work in agriculture, once there, moved quickly to instead work in industry. The law placed certain restrictions on this practice. Henceforth immigrants were to be required to work in the sector for which they had been granted a work permit, with certain exceptions, at least for the first year of employment in France; and the immigrant could not change the place of work until the expiration of the work contract for which the immigrant had received a permit. Another such law, enacted on 10 August 1932, gave the government the right to limit the proportion of foreign workers in certain branches or certain regions of an economic sector (except agriculture). The new law extended to the private sector a law that had existed for the state sector since 1899. The precise quota limiting the number of foreigners in a particular profession was to be set on a case by case basis, with input from labor unions and employer organizations. Relatively few quotas were established until 1935, when there was a rapid increase in the number of professions with quotas, particularly in the building and construction sector. The effectiveness of both of these laws was limited by the very small number of labor inspectors.[24]

Brief Background on Unions

The Confédération Générale du Travail (CGT), which had been created in 1895, was the main union confederation in France at the beginning of the twentieth century. In its early years the CGT, like the Left in France in general, included a variety of approaches but it was dominated by those who upheld the doctrine of revolutionary syndicalism, which aimed to eliminate the state. The main belief of revolutionary syndicalism was that unionism was sufficient to bring the working class to a social revolution, and to then install a classless society where the union would be the main cell.[25] It stressed that economic rather than political means should be used to attack the existing system. Direct action in the workplace, particularly through strikes, was seen as the main avenue to overturn the system. Revolutionary syndicalists distrusted parliamentary democracy, intellectuals, and politicians and opposed union affiliation with political parties and class reconciliation through reform.[26]

The French labor movement went through major changes and divisions after the Russian Revolution of 1917. By the end of the First World War revolutionary syndicalism had lost some of its appeal and the reformists gained control of the CGT. However, struggles among various radical and reformist factions continued during the next few years and culminated in the official split of the confederation. The communists, anarchists, and remaining revolutionary syndicalists split from what had become the reformist, majority CGT and then, in 1922, they formed the revolutionary, minority Confédération Générale du Travail Unitaire (CGTU). Within a year communists came to dominate the CGTU. After further struggles between what Annie Kriegel has pointed to as the two opposed traditions of, on the one hand, French revolutionary syndicalism (which stressed economic means and union autonomy from political parties) and, on the other hand, Russian bolshevism (which stressed the subordination of the union to the party), the CGTU became dominated by the French Communist Party, which itself had become "bolshevized" and subordinate to the Soviet Communist Party by 1924–25.[27] Federations that were dominated by the remaining syndicalists, most prominently the Building Trades Federation, left the CGTU. Meanwhile the older CGT reacted against Soviet communism and revolution and became increasingly reformist.[28]

The two confederations (the majority, reformist CGT and the minority, revolutionary CGTU) dominated the French labor movement during the inter-war period, and officially reunified in 1936.

Unions' Immigration Policy Preferences

The CGT

The reformist CGT accepted immigration as a means to facilitate post-war reconstruction and economic growth in France. However, this acceptance was conditional upon the introduction of measures that would regulate and direct migration flows so as to protect French workers. The CGT gave priority to French workers. The CGT's support for French first was noted in a report published in the CGT journal in 1923 and adopted by the Congress: "We have to say that we are not hostile to foreign workers coming to France, but we equally have to say that our social union mission is to first protect the interests of national labor."[29]

The CGT's approach in the inter-war years reflected its general view that the government was not necessarily hostile to labor but rather, through lobbying, labor could use the state to advance its interests.[30] The CGT generally pressured for measures to regulate the entrance of foreign workers into the country and into specific sectors of the economy.

The CGT, focusing on the economic concerns pointed to by the conventional wisdom and reasoning that immigrants increase the labor supply, reduce wages, and cause unemployment, called for the creation of an institutional mechanism to control the introduction of foreign labor in the early 1920s. The CGT advocated the creation of a national office linked to local placement offices that, between them, would compile a database and provide a network to first move and place workers already in France rather than bring in workers from outside the country. The office, known as the National Council of Labor, was created by a government decree in 1925 and included employer and worker representatives and government members. CGT officials took the time to participate in the Council, which suggests that they did not think that it would be an ineffective institution.[31] The CGT likewise supported the local placement offices that channeled immigrant workers to less desirable jobs and regions when issuing work permits, and it urged local unions to participate in the administration of placement offices in those localities where they existed, or to actively pressure for creating placement offices in localities where they were absent.[32]

Unions did not need to protest loudly for restrictionism. As mentioned by Cross, the "state in fact controlled immigration in order to minimize potential French labor unrest...."[33] For example, in December of 1920 the government, anticipating the recession of 1921, blocked most new labor immigration, and the Minister of the Interior deported immigrants who lacked work papers. The restrictions were lifted in March of 1922 when the economy showed signs of recovery.

When unemployment began to increase in December 1926 and January 1927, as would be expected by the conventional wisdom, the CGT advocated immigration restrictions and a halt to immigration except for absolutely justifiable employment.[34] The CGT received an obliging response from the Minister of Labor, who said that unemployed foreigners would be channeled to jobs in the provinces where there was little unemployment among French workers. The Foreign Labor Service's placement office in Paris sent 85 percent of the 9,486 immigrant job applicants at least 100 kilometers from the capital.[35] As in the recession of 1921, the government again suspended labor immigration in early 1927.[36] The CGT, in its journal in 1927, included a report by the head of the service of foreign labor, which noted that the authorities had modified their approach considerably and had participated in the protection of the French labor market, which would have been profoundly disrupted by new labor immigration.[37]

CGT unions openly upheld the principle of national priority with the onset of the Great Depression in the early 1930s, placing them in coalition with the extreme Right. Numerous CGT unions at the departmental and regional level, in conjunction with some federations, displayed sharp hostility toward immigrants and clamored for restrictionist measures.[38] For example, CGT hotel and restaurant unions urged that recruitment of foreigners by private employers be banned. Entertainment unions demanded priority for French workers. The CGT construction and garment unions urged the Confederation to pressure for further restrictions. As noted by Cross, the CGT accordingly sent a delegation to the Ministry of Labor in late 1930 and "it demanded that immigration be controlled and that foreign work permits be shortened."[39]

As in the recessions of the 1920s, the government restricted immigration flows when unemployment increased in the 1930s. In 1931, the government began to restrict immigration by increasing the portion of rejections for work permit applications. In the following years the government encouraged repatriations, and expulsions were increased.[40] Measures to increase exit were also pursued at the level of local government.

The CGT and its constituent parts on the whole found themselves in coalition with the extreme Right, which it opposed on a number of other issues. This was evident, for example, with regard to the 1932 Law for the Protection of National Labor, which permitted unions to petition for a quota specifying the maximum percentage of immigrants allowed to work in a sector. This law was enthusiastically welcomed by both the CGT and the extreme Right. For example, the support for the law in radical right-wing circles was reflected in the newspaper *l'Ami du Peuple* (*The Friend of the People*), a low-priced daily paper with mass circulation and owned by François Coty, a millionaire who was a major financer of a number of radical right-wing groups in the inter-war years and the founder, in 1933, of the radical right-wing group known as Solidarité Française.[41] The paper described the new law as "a new victory for *The Friend of the People*," and thereafter presented itself as the inventor of the 1932 law.[42] The CGT likewise firmly supported the new law and distributed a circular to its unions inviting them to propose quotas for their sectors. Over the next two years CGT unions, in conjunction with the extreme Right, lobbied the government to implement the 1932 law, which was eventually more stringently applied beginning in 1935.[43]

The CGT initially approved the government's policy of repatriation of foreign workers. However, as it became evident that repatriation was doing little to resolve the unemployment situation, the CGT at the confederation level changed its position and noted in 1933 that expulsions would not resolve the crisis. In explaining its opposition to repatriation, the confederation pointed to the moral obligations pertaining to workers who had been called into France in earlier times and who had contributed to the French economy, and it argued that immigrants continued to benefit the economy as consumers and as workers in certain jobs that French workers turned down.[44]

In summary, during the inter-war period the reformist CGT advocated measures to regulate migration flows into the country and into specific sectors of the economy—measures that they perhaps may not have devoted scarce time to pursuing had they not thought that these control measures would be effective. On reading the CGT's press in the inter-war years, one finds only a few exceptions to this approach. Exceptions include: (1) an article in the CGT's journal *La Voix du Peuple* in 1926, which noted that residence permits should not be denied, as this would deter unofficial immigrants from applying for regularization of status—a comment that suggests the limits of the state's capacity to control migration (and a comment out of line with the CGT's proposal in late 1930 to shorten work permits, noted above);[45] and (2) an article in *La Voix du Peuple* in 1925, which discusses the National Origins Act enacted in the United States in 1924, and which argues that this closure of U.S. borders will lead to an increase in clandestine migration into the United States and will also direct more migrants toward France—a comment that suggests the problems of controlling migration flows under conditions of economic interdependence.[46]

The CGTU

The revolutionary, minority CGTU was dominated by the French Communist Party, which itself gained significant power in local government, particularly in the Paris suburbs or the so-called Red Belt.[47]

The CGTU had a quite different approach to immigration policy issues from the CGT. Although the CGTU produced some contradictory policy statements in its initial two or three years, after 1925 it came to favor open borders, a united front between French and foreign workers, and equality of treatment and rights for French and foreign workers.

The CGTU maintained this policy in times of unemployment, when it opposed the increased repression and expulsions, and criticized the CGT's policy of prioritizing French workers.[48] For example, in the unemployment crisis of the Great Depression, the CGTU noted its opposition to the 1932 Law for the Protection of National Labor and criticized the CGT for supporting the law.[49] And the CGTU's Congresses in 1931 and 1933 resolved to favor "Complete freedom of frontiers, an abolition of all police measures and control of immigration, and an end to all expulsions."[50]

What is the explanation for the minority CGTU's policy of resisting restrictionism in the inter-war years? Why did it differ from the majority CGT? This outcome presents a puzzle for the conventional wisdom, and suggests that the CGTU's identity mattered.

The CGTU's policy may be attributable to several factors. The policy fit with the Communist Party's ideology of international class solidarity. For the CGTU, as noted in a resolution approved at its third Congress in 1925: "There is no homeland for workers; there are no foreign workers in France; there are workers of the same country: the proletariat. Capitalism has created differences in languages and differences in exploitation. The CGTU will fight to make them disappear."[51]

However, the policy was not divorced from strategic reasoning. The CGTU's policy reflected its view on the role of the state and its view on organizing workers, and is thus consistent with the two inter-connected themes stressed in this study.

Role of the state

First, the CGTU's policy reflected a skeptical view that it portrayed about the ability to control migration flows. However, the CGTU's skepticism at that time did not refer to the government's inability to block migration due to economic internationalization—a consideration that came to influence French unions' positions in the late twentieth century. Instead, the CGTU then held what amounted to an instrumental Marxist view of the government as the "executive committee of the bourgeoisie." For the CGTU, the government's policy was and would remain determined by business interests. This reflected the logic explained by Gani in his analysis of why the CGT departed from a restrictionist posture in the early 1960s—a sense of inevitability and a notion that both the government and patronat policy toward immigration was motivated by a search for profits. As one person stated at the CGTU Congress in 1931:

> In a capitalist regime there cannot be reglementation of foreign labor in order to protect French labor. Do you imagine that they will close the

frontiers to foreign labor so as to raise the salaries of French workers? Come on! They'll expell militants, and the rest ... will remain in France and work at a lower pay rate.[52]

During the unemployment crisis of 1927, reflecting similar reasoning, the CGTU argued that the CGT was simply playing into the hands of employers by demanding that the frontier be closed. The CGTU considered that entrance would not be limited as employers would continue to bring in other new immigrant workers anyway and that regulations that sought to increase exit would simply be used to enforce exit of select immigrants such as union activists.[53]

The CGTU's doubts that labor interests would be taken into consideration likewise led the CGTU to oppose the National Council of Labor that the CGT, in the hope of controlling migration flows, had favored. In contrast, the CGTU was skeptical that labor's voice would be heard on the National Council, as employers were to have substantially more representatives at the Council than labor. Instead, the CGTU proposed that to change the direction of migration flows so as to better represent workers' interests, international offices of emigration should be created that would be under the guidance of the international union movements. The offices would be responsible for publishing and disseminating information to workers on such things as the state of the labor market, salaries, cost of living, and social laws so as to counter-act the propaganda of employers.[54]

The CGTU's view that the government would simply follow business interests may appear puzzling in light of the government's actions and sharp shifts in migration flows at times of high unemployment in France in the inter-war years, but it fit with the ideological prism that constituted the identity of the CGTU.

Organizing immigrants
Second, and of related concern, the CGTU covered sectors where immigrants were concentrated and it engaged in fairly serious efforts to organize its potential members. Immigrants were concentrated in the private sector, and in 1927 three-fourths of the CGTU's membership was in the private sector, particularly metal and building.[55] The CGTU's organizing efforts placed it apart from other French unions, which, while inclusive, made scant efforts to actively organize at that time or in the post-World War II period. On this issue the CGTU was in a somewhat similar situation to the United Mine Workers in the United States, discussed in chapter three. However, the UMW had a very different

ideological prism from the CGTU and did not display the doubts about the role of the state that permeated the CGTU's views, as discussed above. Only the CGTU showed the dual features of skepticism on the role of the state in controlling migration and organizing concerns.

Organizing concerns gave the CGTU a practical reason for refraining from a restrictionist immigration policy posture that would alienate immigrants from unions; and for opposing restrictionist measures, such as expulsions, that sought to increase exit but would likely impede organization. CGTU statements critiqued the government's policy of expulsions because immigrant union activists were main targets for expulsion, and the CGTU considered that this discouraged immigrants from attending union meetings.[56]

These differences between the CGTU and the CGT reflected their broader divergent approaches. As explained by George Ross, the CGTU in general devoted substantial efforts to "organizing workers into unions which would, in turn, further the aims of the PCF."[57] In contrast, the reformist CGT made comparatively little effort to organize either workers in general or immigrants in particular. It instead focused on lobbying and bargaining in the political arena.

The CGTU's general focus on organizing filtered down into the specific question of foreign workers. To facilitate organization the CGTU created a special Department for Foreign Workers (Bureau de la Main-d'Oeuvre Etrangère). The Department had a central coordinating office in Paris, five intermediary regional offices in the Provinces, and, at the grass-roots level, ethnic sections.[58] This commitment to organizing immigrants was subsequently clarified and reiterated at the CGTU's Congress at Lille in 1925.

The language barrier then, as today, constituted an important issue that needed to be broached for effective organization. It was clear, for example, that few Polish immigrant workers in the North/Pas-de-Calais region attended meetings when only French speakers were scheduled to talk.[59] The CGTU was very conscious of the need to overcome the language barrier to communication between militants and workers so as to facilitate organization. The Federation tried to do this in a number of ways. It created French-language classes for foreign workers in 1925. However, this was not very successful and two years later the CGTU's Congress clarified that French militants should learn foreign languages.[60] Other, more important efforts to bridge the language barrier included printing pamphlets and propaganda in foreign languages (mainly Polish, Italian, and Spanish). Newspapers, or sections of newspapers, were also often printed in foreign languages.

Another way in which the CGTU tried to bridge the language barrier was by encouraging militants who were bilingual to take an active role. One particularly famous example was with regard to Thomas Olszanski, an immigrant from Poland who worked in the mines in the North/ Pas-de-Calais region. Olszanski was able to take on an active role because he had been in France longer than most of the Polish immigrants and had become a naturalized French citizen at an early stage, in 1922. Thus, as a citizen, he did not face the legal prohibition that banned non-citizen immigrants from becoming union officials and, as a citizen, it was thought that he was protected from expulsion. The CGTU promoted Olszanski to the position of Secretary of the Federation of Miners in 1923, where he was responsible for issues pertaining to foreign workers; and he was given a position in the CGTU's Department of Foreign Labor in 1926, which gave him responsibilities of organizing meetings in various economic sectors. Olszanski's linguistic (and oratory) skills enabled him to organize numerous well-attended meetings with workers in both the Polish and French languages, and to write up pamphlets, posters, and propaganda in both languages for distribution.[61]

However, the CGTU's efforts to organize foreign workers were not particularly successful, and only a fairly small percentage of its members were foreigners.[62] The CGTU's limited success can be attributed to a number of factors, some at the level of law and government policy and others resting with the union itself.

French law at that time did not allow immigrant workers to become union officials. The resulting lack of immigrants at the union leadership level could plausibly have reduced the desire of foreign workers to join unions. Of more importance, the CGTU's organizing efforts were often stunted by counter-actions taken by the government and employers. Immigrant workers survived under a constant threat of being fired or expelled from the country if they became too militant, without any possibility for legal recourse.

Olszanski the activist, in his memoirs, gives a number of examples of the ways in which the repression of Polish workers in the North/ Pas-de-Calais region hindered effective organization. For example, police sometimes surrounded the entrance to meetings. There were some police on foot on the sidewalks, and other police mounted on horses in the middle of the road. At times the police checked people's papers at the entrance and exit of meetings. These tactics often deterred workers from attending the meetings as clean records were needed to avoid lay-offs and expulsion from France and to avoid problems for those who planned on applying for French citizenship.[63] One example that

Olszanski points to as particularly severe took place in 1931 when the police, in addition to encircling the meeting room, took documents from the workers and put the workers in trucks, which drove them to the Belgium frontier.[64]

Likewise, Gérard Noiriel, a prominent French scholar, has pointed to similar ways in which foreign workers were made vulnerable by government repression. For example, he notes that the police hindered the CGTU's organization of foreign (primarily Italian) workers in the North-East/Longwy region. There, as in the Pas-de-Calais region, the police surrounded and blocked entrances to meeting places.[65]

The government also counter-acted the CGTU's efforts at spreading its message by banning communist newspapers that were published in foreign languages. For example, *Robotnik Polski* (The Polish Worker), a weekly paper published in Paris, was banned in December 1923. And *Glos Pracy* (The Voice of Work), a bimonthly CGTU paper, was banned in June 1928 after one year in existence.[66]

The tension between restrictionism and organization was shown in the early twentieth century when authorities used expulsions to dampen union activity. These restrictionist immigration policy measures constrained effective organization. For example, more than 1,500 foreign militants were expelled in 1931.[67] In Longwy, as shown by Noiriel, when the CGTU increased its organizing efforts in the summer of 1926, there was a wave of expulsions. This not only deprived the CGTU of committed militants who were expelled from the country, but also made immigrant workers fearful of joining the union or even of being seen talking to the union secretary.[68] Likewise Olszanski pointed to the debilitating effects of expulsions. For example, he notes that there was a wave of expulsions of CGTU activists in 1927, which caused panic among union members, some of whom left the union.[69] Expulsions became more severe at times of unemployment, and Olszanski notes that in 1932 there was another wave of expulsions of Polish CGTU militants. In 1934 lay-offs and expulsions were massive and more general.

The government's use of expulsions to rid France of communist militants was what made Olszanski particularly famous. As a result of his extreme activism throughout the 1920s and early 1930s, the French government stripped him of his citizenship in the early 1930s under the rarely used Article 9 of the nationality law of August 1927, which allowed denaturalization of those who committed acts "contrary to the interior and exterior security of the French state." After his citizenship was removed, Olszanski was expelled from France in 1934, when he went to the Soviet Union and, later, returned to Poland.[70]

Another person, who later became a prominent politician, expelled for his militancy was Edward Gierek. Gierek, when an immigrant worker in France, was also a militant for the French Communist Party in the North/Pas-de-Calais region and was expelled in 1935. He later became the leader of Poland with the formal position of General Secretary of the Polish United Workers Party (the Polish Communist Party).[71]

The CGTU's policy of organizing immigrants, while impeded by these counter-actions of the government, was also impeded by the clear lack of enthusiasm by many of its own militants and members. There was a gap between the approaches at the top leadership level and the militant and grass-roots level, with the result that the CGTU's policy was quite often not put into practice. The Confederation repeatedly acknowledged problems from some unions and militants who showed little enthusiasm for its approach. For example, at the CGTU Congress in 1925 it was noted that the results of organizing immigrants thus far were unsatisfactory and that greater effort needed to be made by all militants and at all levels of the CGTU.[72] At the same Congress the delegate from the woodcutters received applause when, contrary to CGTU policy, he urged thinking about means to prevent the introduction of foreign labor in those areas where it already existed in excess.[73] Olszanski, the union official and militant familiar with grass-roots organizing efforts, was an exception in his activist efforts to organize immigrants. He reported that the language sections lacked real links with the regular organizations, and complained at the lack of solidarity and almost non-existent mobilization when immigrant militants were expelled. In a report to the CGTU in 1927 he stated that "we ask the Congress to see to it that the decisions and resolutions approved for immigrant workers don't remain just pious and token wishes, but that our unions be obliged to fulfill their commitments, under the supervision of the higher bodies of the organization."[74] At the CGTU Congress in 1929, it was noted that there was a "lack of serious reaction by CGTU unions against the expulsions of foreign workers."[75] In 1930 the CGTU criticized some leaders of the Parisian CGTU Union of Bakers for echoing the CGT by speaking about repatriation of foreign workers.[76] The Confederation, in its weekly newspaper *La Vie Ouvrière*, often urged its militants and members to make greater efforts to actively pursue the position of the CGTU (and the Communist Party).[77]

The Construction Unions

Many immigrants, primarily from Italy, worked in the construction sector. The portion of foreigners working in this sector increased during the inter-war years, reaching 24.1 percent in 1931.[78] Construction unions in France, unlike their American counterparts, did have an inclusive organizational structure. But they were among the most restrictionist unions in France in the inter-war period and their views at that time reflected the conventional wisdom that unions seek restrictionist immigration policy measures so as to reduce the labor supply.

When the union movement split into the CGT and the CGTU in 1921–22, the majority of the building trades unions were affiliated with the revolutionary CGTU rather than the reformist CGT. However, the struggles within the CGTU the following year over the relationship between political parties and unions led to a further splintering of the labor movement. The building trades unions had for many years been among the strongest supporters of revolutionary syndicalism and its belief in union autonomy from political parties. Thus the Building Trades Federation left the CGTU in 1924, when the communists came to dominate the CGTU and the union became subordinate to the French/Soviet Communist Party. The Building Trades Federation instead formed what were labeled as "autonomous unions."[79]

CGT

The Construction Federation, CGT included many articles on immigration in its otherwise short newspaper in the 1920s. The articles criticized employers for recruiting foreign workers in a manner that created victims among both immigrant and French workers and argued that immigrant workers increased unemployment, undermined the salaries of French workers, and undermined the implementation of an eight-hour day.[80] An article written by a representative of the Construction Federation for the CGT's confederation newspaper noted that foreign labor was replacing French labor in the fight for work contracts. He urged that the authorities take energetic measures to stop the recruitment of foreign labor by employers so as to avoid the further outbreak of serious conflicts.[81]

The Construction Federation campaigned for the creation of the National Council of Labor (which was supported by the CGT as noted above); and the need to demand "a serious and effective control" of foreign labor was noted at the Construction Federation's Congress in August 1925.[82] When the National Council was created in 1925, the Construction Federation passed a resolution saying that its members must actively participate in the placement offices that, it was hoped, would work with the National Council to effectively control the labor market.[83] When the National Council was discussed at a Federation meeting in April 1926, it was hoped that if unemployed workers register at placement offices, then it would be possible to avoid bringing in foreign workers who were "saturating the labor market," although one person did express skepticism about the likely effectiveness of the National Council.[84]

In those times when unemployment rose, the CGT construction unions sought to control and limit the employment of immigrant workers. In 1927, the Construction Federation, in a meeting with employer organizations at the Labor Ministry, put forward various proposals to deal with the unemployment situation. Among other things, it was considered that there was no reason to bring immigrants to work in the construction sector in Paris and that, in contrast, there was reason to induce exit of those who were there.[85] Articles in the Parisian CGT construction union newspaper in 1931 reflected increasing hostility to immigrant workers at this time of rising unemployment. One article noted that "new recruits are penetrating the metro, thus further aggravating the situation. We say that this is intolerable."[86] Another article noted that it "deplored the ease with which regularization of situation" was conducted for workers in sectors where, contrary to exaggerated reports of prosperity, there were already many French and foreign unemployed people.[87] Another article, seeking to preempt accusations of nationalism by the CGTU, wrote that with regard to the CGTU, "we advise them to go and defend their demagogic thesis in front of the 50,000 unemployed in the Parisian construction sector."[88] As noted above, it was at the request of the construction (and garment) unions that the CGT sent a delegation to the Labor Ministry in 1930 and demanded that immigration be controlled and that foreign work permits be shortened. The CGT construction unions strongly supported the 1932 Law for the Protection of National Labor, and they petitioned for quotas, which were established for the construction sector.[89]

CGTU

When the union movement split into the CGT and the CGTU in 1921–22, the majority of the building trades unions, which had a strong tradition of revolutionary syndicalism, were affiliated with the revolutionary CGTU rather than the reformist CGT. The Construction Federation, CGTU displayed hostility to immigrant workers in the early 1920s. For example, the Building Laborers of the Seine supported the use of violence against non-union immigrant workers, a position that had been approved by the Construction Federation. This approach received a strong protest from the CGTU's Office of Foreign Labor of the Seine region.[90] At a meeting of the CGTU's Comité Confédéral Unitaire in September 1924, a representative from the building trades argued that foreign workers were undermining salaries of French workers and that it was necessary to get the government to do something about the situation. He considered that the government would have to close the frontiers if foreign workers were chased and hunted down. Another representative praised the Construction Federation's actions—such as distributing leaflets calling for class consciousness, inviting immigrants to demand satisfactory salaries and to join unions, warning that if they refused to do so workers would be considered as having placed themselves outside the French labor movement and would expose themselves to the latter's anger. In contrast, some others present at the meeting criticized the Construction Federation and its offshoots for their willingness to use violence and for obstructing the work of the CGTU's Department of Foreign Labor.[91]

Many unions left the CGTU Construction Federation that year, 1924, to form autonomous unions. After this, the CGTU formed a new Building Trades Federation with its remaining members. The portions of the building trades that remained with the CGTU included the strongly organized "Terrassiers" (least-skilled building workers) in the Parisian region.[92] The CGTU's new Federation adopted the same approach as that of the Confederation and remained in line when unemployment rose in the early 1930s.[93]

Autonomous unions

The departure of construction unions from the CGTU in the early 1920s was particularly pronounced in Lyon, a city that was notable for its strong unions in the construction sector—unions that had held a twenty-four hour strike in 1923 to protest salary levels and to protest against the employment of foreign labor.[94]

The newspaper of the autonomous unions in Lyon (which constituted the large majority of the city's construction unions and were organized into what was known as the Cartel) published a number of articles on immigration during what was referred to as the unemployment crisis of 1927. Some of the articles, without providing much by way of commentary, succinctly reviewed new measures pertaining to foreign workers—the kind of measures that were in contrast criticized in the CGTU's press. For example, one article succinctly noted that free transport to the border was to be provided to unemployed foreign workers and gave the address in Lyon where requests could be submitted for this free transport.[95] Other articles argued that foreign workers undermined the salaries of French workers by increasing the labor supply and by accepting work at low wages and that the abundance of labor created unemployment and strengthened employers. This accounted for what was seen to be a "foreign preference" by employers, giving French workers reason to complain.[96] One article reflected the views by noting that: "[we] are internationalists, but on one condition: that it makes us live and not die."[97]

The autonomous unions at times sought to bring the issue to the attention of local authorities and, while they did not publish newspaper articles on immigration in the unemployment crisis of the early 1930s, they apparently supported the restrictionist 1932 law that established quotas on the percentage of foreign workers who could be employed in particular sectors. They simultaneously tried to bring immigrant workers into the union.[98]

In summary, in the inter-war years the Construction Federation of the CGT and, to a lesser extent, the autonomous construction unions, considered that immigration caused unemployment and undermined salaries. They pressured for protectionist government measures and urged participation in placement offices—actions that they presumably would not have devoted time to had they not thought that the measures would be effective means of controlling migration. In contrast, from the late 1920s, the Construction Federation of the CGTU, in line with its Confederation, opposed restrictionism.

Conclusion

The CGT, which constituted the majority of the French labor movement, called for restrictionist immigration policy measures when hard times hit during the inter-war years. In contrast, the minority CGTU, with an instrumentalist view of the state and seeking to organize immigrants, opposed restrictionist measures even when unemployment rose. This division ended with the official reunification of the two confederations in 1936. Upon reunification the CGTU fell into line with the restrictionist posture of the CGT.

The CGT's restrictionist posture in the inter-war years brought it into an "odd-couple coalition" with various groups, including the extreme Right on some issues. People who usually held opposite views were united in their common fight against immigrant workers.[99] In the 1930s there was a broad-based coalition that blamed immigrants for the high unemployment levels and demanded a reduction in foreign labor. "Work for French first" and "France for the French" became the slogans of the day.[100] This coalition was spread across diverse social sectors, professions, and regions. It included prominent members of the Left, the socialists, and one of the leaders of the League of Human Rights.[101] It also included the CGT, and many members of the CGTU at the grass-roots level, although not at the leadership level. As noted by Ralph Schor, "The main remedy appeared to be a reduction in the number of immigrants. This goal would be attained by closing the frontiers, a measure that was very broadly demanded, from the extreme right to the CGT, and by a repatriation of non-citizens."[102]

Immigrants had few supporters when hard times hit in the inter-war years.[103] On the Right, employers, who wanted to retain labor for use after the recessions, spoke out to oppose repatriations and to "justify" the presence of a mass numbers of immigrants in the 1920s and at the beginning of the 1930s. But their voices became more muted as high unemployment persisted in the 1930s. Employers laid off immigrant workers first, before French workers. On the Left even the League of Human Rights was not always a clear defender of immigrants in the inter-war years. While the League did clearly speak out for the rights of refugees and immigrants, it also indicated a need to respect the security of the state and to defend the essential interests of French workers. The League actively opposed some expulsions. But some League leaders considered that expulsions and repatriation were justified if done for economic reasons and if the repatriations prioritized the most recent arrivals and unmarried people.[104] The Communist Party and the minority CGTU at the leadership level did sit on the opposite side of the fence from the restrictionist majority until reunification with the CGT in 1935.

CHAPTER 6

Resisting Restrictionists: Labor Unions and French Immigration Policy in the Late Twentieth Century

Immigration policy was a very contentious subject on the French political agenda in the late twentieth century. The debates took place in the context of high unemployment levels, and at a time when the National Front was a significant actor on the political scene.

Restrictionists put forward numerous proposals that aimed to reach what became known as the slogan of "zero immigration." Some of these proposals were adopted. French governments in the late twentieth century instituted many measures that sought to further restrict immigration. At the same time France also instituted some regularization programs, which were non-restrictionist measures that granted legal status to undocumented immigrants (known as amnesty in the United States).

How did unions react during this period? The conventional wisdom would lead us to expect that unions would join the restrictionist coalition during these times of high unemployment when jobs became scarce. Instead unions resisted restrictionism and stayed in a fragile coalition with liberal groups.

For French unions, immigration policy measures that aimed to reach "zero immigration" inflated both the ability and the right of the state to control migration. French unions, like U.S. unions, questioned the ability of the state to fully control migration in an era of economic internationalization. At the same time the internationalization of human rights discourse contributed to the moderate position of French unions, reflecting their particular identity, which relies more heavily on the

realm of ideas and convictions than that of their pragmatic U.S. counterparts. Organizing concerns, while contributing to French union
support for regularization programs, weighed less heavily for the French
unions, with their inclusive ideals but inactive recruiting agenda.

Immigration into France: Background

Migration Flows

France experienced high immigration flows in the so-called thirty glorious years of economic growth and prosperity after World War II. The
government then officially suspended labor migration in 1974, and
flows have since reduced. But migration flows into France today are still
quite significant (in comparison with years of high unemployment in
the early twentieth century), as can be seen on table 6.1. The percentage
of foreign born in the total population increased steadily from 5 percent
in 1946 to 7.4 percent in 1975, and did not change much in the later
years of the twentieth century.[1]

Italy was the most important source country in the first decade after
the war, and there was also a significant increase in Algerian immigrants
at that time. As happened in the U.S. case, migration flows to France
became much more diverse in the 1960s. There was a sharp increase in
immigrants from Spain, Portugal, Morocco, Tunisia, and Yugoslavia.
Immigration from a broader range of African countries increased in the
later 1960s.[2]

Table 6.1 Inflows of foreign population into
France: 1989–1998 (in thousands)

Year	Inflows of foreign population
1989	53.2
1990	102.4
1991	109.9
1992	116.6
1993	99.2
1994	91.5
1995	77.0
1996	75.5
1997	102.4
1998	138.1

Source: SOPEMI *Trends in International Migration Annual
Report 2000* (Paris: OECD, 2001), p. 304.

Note: The figures for 1997 and 1998 include those people
who were granted legal status in the regularization program.

Table 6.2   Stock of foreign
labor in France: 1990–1999
(in thousands)

Year	Stock of foreign labor
1990	1,549.5
1995	1,573.3
1999	1,593.9

Source: SOPEMI, *Trends in Inter-national Migration Annual Report 2000* (Paris: OECD, 2001), p. 357.

Table 6.3   Unemployment levels in France: 1970–2000

Year	Unemployed percentage of labor force	Year	Unemployed percentage of labor force
1970	2.5	1984	9.9
1972	2.8	1986	10.4
1974	3.0	1988	9.9
1976	4.5	1990	9.0
1978	5.4	1992	10.4
1980	6.4	1994	12.3
1982	8.2	1996	12.4
		1998	11.8
		2000	9.5

Source: For 1970–1988, OECD, *Main Economic Indicators: Historical Statistics, 1969–1988* (Paris: OECD, 1990), p. 334. For 1990, OECD, *Main Economic Indicators, December 1992* (Paris: OECD, 1992), p. 22. For 1992–1994, OECD, *Main Economic Indicators, December 1995* (Paris: OECD, 1995), p. 22. For 1996, OECD, Main Economic Indicators, December 1998 (Paris: OECD, 1998), p. 40. For 1998–2000, OECD, *Main Economic Indicators, April 2001* (Paris: OECD, 2001), p. 26.

Immigrant workers have been concentrated in such sectors as building and construction, industry (for example, automobiles), and domestic service and cleaning service. Immigrants also constitute a disproportionately large percentage of the unemployed in France in recent years. Immigrants from countries other than the European Union had an unemployment rate of 31.4 percent in 1998 (the unemployment rate for French was 11.1 percent that year).[3] They had worked in declining sectors such as automobiles, where factories were closed down, and they were placed on the priority list by employers for lay-offs in the construction sector.

It is not possible to ascertain with full accuracy the sectoral distribution of illegal immigrants, but in France as in the United States, a fairly accurate guide comes from the surveys conducted during the regularization (amnesty) programs. A survey of illegal immigrants who normalized their situation in the French regularization program of 1981–83 showed that 30 percent worked in the building and construction sector; 12 percent in hotels and restaurants; 15 percent in domestic service and cleaning service; 11 percent in agriculture; 8 percent in textiles; and the remainder elsewhere.[4]

Immigration Policy

The initial impetus to encourage immigration after the war came from government officials, rather than business. The government estimated that there would be a high demand for workers given the ambitious plans for modernizing the economy. The supply of labor was limited. France had lost many young men during World War II. 1.4 million young French men were killed or disabled in the war. The size of the immigrant population had also been reduced, from 2,792,000 in 1931 to 2,326,000 in 1936, and was left at 1,986,000 in 1946.[5] Thus the government quickly addressed the subject of immigration after the war.

The government set up a formal system to control and increase labor recruitment and migration immediately after the war. A new department within the Ministry of Labor, known as the Office Nationale d'Immigration (ONI), was set up in 1945 to recruit and regulate migration flows. All recruitment was supposed to pass through the ONI, and private recruitment agencies of the inter-war years, such as the SGI, were banned. Employers who wanted immigrant workers were supposed to submit their requests to departmental labor offices, which, in turn, submitted the requests to the Ministry of Labor. Government officials were supposed to verify that there were no available French workers for the jobs. The ONI set up offices in major capitals abroad, providing an opportunity for foreigners to learn about job opportunities in France. Aspiring migrant workers were given a medical and vocational exam. Migrants were supposed to go through these governmental channels abroad, before entering France, and to arrive with a work contract, which was needed for a work permit and residence permit.[6]

However, this formal interventionist policy was barely implemented. It soon gave way to what amounted to a laissez-faire policy. As in the inter-war years when government recruitment schemes became secondary to private recruitment schemes through the SGI, so in the post-World War II period the formal governmental channels for bringing in immigrants became secondary to informal routes. By the mid-1950s, at a time of rapid economic expansion, many employers began to bypass the bureaucratic procedures for finding workers. And many workers began to enter France as "tourists" without work papers. After obtaining employment in France, they then submitted a request to the ONI for regularization of their status. By 1968, 82 percent of foreign workers entered through these informal channels and regularized their status once in France.[7]

The government decided to bring this laissez-faire policy to an end in the early 1970s. The procedures for regularization were tightened in 1972, and were then made more restrictive in the fall of 1973, after which it was supposed to become impossible to regularize the status of individual workers.[8] Thus the formal procedure became the only channel for entering France if one wanted to work and live legally in France. The formal procedure was also tightened in 1974, when the government announced that all labor immigration was suspended.[9] Family reunion immigration was also halted, but this ban was subsequently lifted. Employer sanctions were reinforced, and attempts were made to improve control at territorial borders.[10]

Since this end of the laissez-faire policy in the mid-1970s, French governments have proposed and/or adopted a series of restrictionist measures in search of more complete control over migration flows. The restrictionist measures proposed included expanded powers for the Minister of the Interior to expel immigrants who threatened the public order or whose visa status was out of order; more stringent criteria for the renewal of work and residence permits and the shortening of the time span of permits granted.[11] As for non-restrictionist measures, French governments have adopted several small regularization programs and two larger ones. A brief review of these measures since the mid-1970s follows here.

The restrictionist trend that began after the laissez-faire policy was halted was introduced by Jacques Chirac in 1976, then Prime Minister. In a television address in 1976, Chirac stated that: "A country that has 900,000 unemployed people but more than 2 million immigrant workers is not a country where the employment problem is insoluble."[12] Unions were not in agreement with Chirac. For example, the Construction Federation, CFDT, described Chirac's statement as "insidious."[13]

In the late 1970s the government sought to move beyond restricting entrances. Much attention was given to the question of how to increase exits, as occurred in the inter-war years. There was an unsuccessful attempt to induce exit by paying money to those who agreed to leave. Policies to enforce exit were also proposed, such as increasing the ease of expulsions and the non-renewal of permits.[14] In contrast to the otherwise restrictionist measures proposed at that time, there were some small regularization programs such as one that was instituted for undocumented immigrants working in the Parisian garment sector in 1980.

Some of the restrictionist measures were eliminated when the socialists initially gained power in 1981. The socialists initially limited expulsions and instituted a major regularization program for immigrants who lacked legal status in 1981–82 (about 135,000 immigrants had their papers normalized through this program). But at the same time the socialist government approved a law, in October 1981, that aimed to restrict illegal immigration by increasing the fines and lengthening the potential prison sentences against employers of undocumented immigrants who lacked work papers.[15] The socialist government then applied further restrictionist measures after 1983 that, for example, made family reunion immigration more difficult.

More restrictionist measures were then instituted by the conservatives in the Pasqua Laws of 1986 and 1993, and subsequently in the Debré Laws of 1997. The measures included more stringent conditions for entrance and for receipt and renewal of residence permits, and less stringent conditions for expulsions.

Subsequently the socialists, under Prime Minister Jospin, instituted the regularization program of 1997–98. This regularization program, however, imposed more stringent criteria for normalization of status than had been imposed in the socialists' regularization program of 1981.[16] Data on the number of applications submitted varies, but figures from 1999 estimate that about 146,000 people formally requested regularization. Nearly half of the applications were rejected, and about 81,000 were accepted by 1999, after the government had slightly liberalized the criteria for regularization following hunger strikes and protests.[17] A few months after deciding on a regularization program, the socialist government's Chevènement Laws of 1998 were adopted. This new immigration law partly modified some of the details of the previous restrictionist measures enacted by the conservatives, but it did not fundamentally break with them.

French government policy appears to have effectively exerted a great deal of control over migration flows. There was a substantial reduction in migration flows in the early 1970s and one can imagine that immigration to France would be much higher absent the restrictionist measures imposed since the early 1970s.

But government policy has clearly failed to reach the "zero immigration" sought by some French government officials such as Charles Pasqua, Minister of the Interior and the architect of French immigration laws in 1986 and 1993, who announced in 1993 that he wanted to "aim towards zero immigration" and instituted many measures that he hoped would accomplish this.

Inflows remained quite significant after the 1970s and did not show the very sharp shifts and net reverse flows apparently induced by government policy at times of rising unemployment in the inter-war period. The limits of effective restrictionism were noted soon after the immigration ban was imposed in 1974. Immigrant workers in France, realizing that it would be more difficult to re-enter in the future, settled in France rather than leave, and encouraged family members to join them. Family reunion immigration continued outside legal channels. Family members did not take the state's new regulations seriously.[18] As noted by a secretary of state in 1975, "From a practical point of view, family immigration occurs through channels that are difficult to control. Many families enter France as false tourists; it is in effect impossible to prohibit a family from joining the 'head of the family' for holidays."[19] (The ban on family reunion immigration was subsequently lifted.)

Brief Background on Unions

In the period after World War II, the Confédération Générale du Travail (CGT) was the largest labor confederation. The CGT quickly became dominated by the Communist Party at the end of World War II and remained so until periestroika set in during the 1990s. The CGT was also the confederation that experienced by far the largest loss of membership in the late twentieth century, in part because it was concentrated in the heavy industrial sectors where many plants were closed down. The Confédération Française Démocratique du Travail (CFDT) has since become another major confederation covering sectors where immigrants work.[20] The CFDT emerged in 1964 from a Catholic union movement, after a period of deconfessionalization. The CFDT has since gone through several ideological changes. After a more radical and militant period, when it upheld the transformative ideology of autogestation (worker self-management) and engaged in attempts with the CGT to pursue a united front, it then changed to a more moderate reorientation.

Immigration issues in the post-World War II period have been primarily addressed by unions at the Confederation level in France.

Below the Confederation level the location of discussion in the union structure has differed from that of unions in the United States. Unlike the United States, immigration issues are rarely addressed at the union Federation level in France but are instead often addressed at the regional level of the union institutional structure (known in France as the Departmental level). For example, the federations covering textiles and services (both sectors where many immigrants work) gave comparatively little attention to immigration policy issues in their newsletters and magazines in the late twentieth century in France and are thus not discussed in this chapter. The chapter does briefly cover the immigration policy preferences of the construction union federations so as to compare their positions with those of their counterparts in the early twentieth century.

Union Immigration Policy Preferences during the "Thirty Glorious Years" in Brief

The CGT, which was the largest union confederation in the period of prosperity after World War II, adopted a restrictionist posture toward immigration in the immediate post-war years. Resolutions approved at CGT Congresses consistently called for a halt to immigration until 1963. The CGT argued that business and the government brought immigrants to France so as to expand the industrial reserve army of labor. This, in turn, would increase competition between workers, and reduce salaries and living standards.[21]

The CGT's policy changed in 1963 when two different trends emerged at the Confederation's Congress. As shown by Léon Gani, "The first continued to demand a stop to immigration, expressed in the resolution on unemployment. The other challenged the validity of such an attitude which did not appear after that in the resolution on immigrant workers."[22] To explain this trend, Gani pointed to a CGT official who stated that "the working class does not have an interest in massive immigration, but practically, it does not have the possibility to thwart the competition and division."[23] As Gani explains, the CGT considered that both the government and the patronat policy toward immigration was motivated by a search for profits, and thus there was little that could be done to block it.[24] The CGT held an instrumentalist view of the state.[25]

The government subsequently sought to restrict immigration in the 1970s, thus undermining the rationale for unions to maintain the reasoning behind the sense of inevitability explained by Gani for an earlier time period. After the government showed that it was serious about restricting immigration in the early 1970s, the CGT then, in the late 1970s, returned to an explicitly restrictionist posture and called for a suspension of all recruitment and introduction of workers, except for cases of family reunion and refugees.[26] For example, a CGT report in 1980 stated that: "The common interest of immigrant and French workers demands that all recruitment and introduction of workers be suspended regardless of their qualifications and their country of origin, except for cases of family reunion and refugees."[27]

Material below explores to what extent and why unions have since refrained from advocating restrictionist immigration policy measures in the 1980s and 1990s—years of high unemployment generating conditions that for theoretical and for historical-empirical reasons might be expected to elicit a restrictionist response from unions.[28]

Union Immigration Policy Preferences in the Late Twentieth Century

In the late twentieth century most union leaders and the official union preferences (which is the focus of this study), have been moderate with regard to immigration policy. They have opposed open borders and a laissez-faire policy or labor recruitment schemes. But they have simultaneously opposed certain restrictionst measures considered or adopted by the government in the high unemployment years of the 1980s and 1990s.

A complete interpretation of the sources of union immigration policy preferences requires considering multiple factors. But much emphasis in union explanations was placed on normative issues and, increasingly in the late twentieth century, the ineffectiveness of certain measures intended to accomplish Pasqua's desired "zero immigration."

Unions' Views on the State's Right and Capacity to Control Migration

Norms

Changes in the power position of union leaders with different norms may help to explain the change in union immigration policy preferences since the early twentieth century. In the U.S. case, liberal norms took on greater prominence in the labor movement's position to legal immigration in the 1950s as the CIO, with more inclusive values, increased in strength and merged with the conservative AFL. In France there were certain changes that could have plausibly reduced the power of those union leaders with conservative norms on immigration issues. Many right-wing union leaders were purged after World War II for having collaborated with the Vichy government during the war, and were excluded from further union activity.[29] This likely freed the labor movement of some leaders who might have sat in the restrictionist coalition on immigration policy issues. More recently, as a result of legal changes in the 1970s, immigrants gained more union rights, and, although still few in number, more union officials at the leadership level were themselves of immigrant background than was the case in the early twentieth century. This likely broadened the forces within the labor movement who opposed some of the restrictionist immigration policy measures proposed in the late twentieth century. For example, the Secretary General of the Construction Federation, CFDT, in the late 1990s had only recently become a naturalized French citizen; and the Head of the Immigration Collective of the CGT's Construction Federation in the 1990s was an immigrant who was also a member of the Federation's Federal Bureau.

At a broader level, the experience with Nazism and the Resistance Movement in World War II contributed to a change in the universe of normative discourse in France. The changes resulting from the wartime experience meant that an illiberal position on immigration issues would immediately place unions in the "wrong" camp, which was not the case before the war.

French unions have affiliated with the human rights institutions and agreements which for the most part began to emerge after World War II and were then developed further in the post-Cold War world of the late twentieth century. For example, the unions (along with various non-governmental organizations, independent experts, and government officials) are members of France's National Consultative Commission on Human Rights. This Commission, which was initially established in 1947, was rejuvenated in the late twentieth century when its mandate and membership were enlarged and it was given formal legal status as an independent institution directly attached to the Prime Minister's office. For its reference texts, the Commission draws on international agreements (with liberal philosophical groundings), such as the European Convention of Human Rights and the Universal Declaration of Human Rights. It has submitted recommendations on a broad range of subjects, such as the creation of an International Criminal Court, human rights situations in other countries, immigration control issues in France, regularization of status for undocumented immigrants (known as "sans-papiers" in France), and racism and discrimination in France.

Union statements at times referred to the Commission's recommendations to support their positions on immigration policy issues.

Unions, beyond referring to the Commission's recommendations, also increasingly referred to the deepening web of international human rights agreements to strengthen their position in domestic debates. Increasingly in the mid-1990s and after they quite often pointed to agreements such as the European Convention of Human Rights and other pertinent international agreements. The increasing frequency of union references to these texts as the 1990s progressed was in line with the broadening internationalization of human rights issues on the global agenda. Likewise, unions gave attention to the Universal Declaration of Human Rights at the time of its fiftieth anniversary in 1998. In recognition of the anniversary, the CGT included a number of articles on the Universal Declaration in an issue of its magazine *La Tribune de l'Immigration,* and the CGT made a statement that began by noting that:

> The universal declaration of human rights is 50 years old.
>
> This anniversary has the merit of highlighting a fundamental text which constitutes a reference and support for all workers and people who aspire and fight for unity, social justice and human dignity. Adopted after the second world war by the United Nations general assembly, the universal declaration recognizes the universality and indivisibility of economic, social and cultural rights, and of civil and political rights. These rights, too often scorned and ignored, still need to be translated into facts and into life for millions of people ....
>
> ... The growing influence of transnational corporations and of the movement of speculative capital on the political economies and societies of States creates new attacks on these fundamental rights ...[30]

Unions have not presented lengthy philosophical discussions of a general nature on normative issues. Instead their views on the right of the state to control migration are intermingled with statements on policy preferences toward specific issues and thus will be discussed in the later section on unions' preferences to specific issues.

This discussion of changing norms and discourse is not meant to imply that unions have become staunch internationalists in practice. They have not, and there has continued to be some coded illiberalism in unions. Nonetheless, one cannot dismiss union statements that point to an internationalization of human rights concerns on immigration issues as entirely irrelevant rhetoric. They quite often backed their normative discourse with concrete actions such as participating in protests, and organizing petitions. Of equal importance, they certainly resisted the restrictionist temptation to sit on the other side of the fence and clamor for protectionism at a time of high unemployment. Unions neither articulated, nor took actions in support of the conservative norms associated with the restrictionist coalition.

Capacity

There are quite a few statements by union officials articulating their views on the changing ability of the state to control migration in the late twentieth-century era of economic internationalization. Union statements place their views on the ability of the state to manage migration between the extremes, and their overall policy preferences are, at a general level, logically consistent with their underlying views.

On the one hand, union statements today point to the decline in immigration flows since the government suspended labor migration in the mid-1970s. Such statements show that they consider that the government has the ability to exert some control over migration. Their policy preferences are consistent with this. Unions today oppose open borders and do not favor labor recruitment schemes. Although in recent years they have avoided explicit statements such as those made by the CGT in 1979 affirming support for the suspension of the introduction of foreign workers (except for family reunion and refugees), it is highly probable that they would pressure for protectionism if the government should return to the laissez-faire policy of the "thirty glorious years." Thus, in one sense unions today clearly remain restrictionist.

On the other hand, union statements quite often show skepticism about the ability to completely control migration and indicate that they consider that French proponents of further restrictionist measures are being unrealistic and inflating the standard of policy that can reasonably be expected of the state in an era of economic internationalization. Their policy preferences are consistent with this—unions today oppose certain measures that have sought to further restrict immigration in recent years. Thus, in another sense, unions today oppose restrictionism.

The CFDT's skepticism regarding the state's ability to fully manage migration due to economic internationalization is shown, for example, in the following argument that it made in 1996:

> The considerable development in information—that one will be able to get henceforth through television programs as a result of satellites— encourages the candidates for departure to go to the countries that appear as Eldorado. All the more so as the means of transportation are more and more accessible and faster .... However, measures such as generalization

of visas, multiplication of obstacles for obtaining the right of asylum or the reinforced control for family reunion will not make these European countries inaccessible....

...despite the immigration restrictions put into place by receiving countries, clandestine immigration still continues.... No country will in effect be able to control migration flows if it simply applies police measures and does not try to treat the question in economic and political terms with the sending countries.[31]

In September 1997, at the time when new proposals for immigration policy were being drawn up by the Jospin government, the CFDT (which generally agreed with the government's proposals) explained its position on the connection between state capacity and appropriate immigration policy, situating itself between those who advocated yet greater restrictionism in recent years and those who advocated open borders. The CFDT pointed to the number of people who had applied for the most recent regularization program and argued that:

This single figure shows the gap with the dishonest publicity of zero immigration ... there is a need to organize and manage the migration flows which constitute a reality, a given that cannot be ignored in our contemporary societies and in French society in particular. This position is opposed to those who favor a complete opening of borders, who do nothing other than promote a 'neoliberal' or 'ultraliberal' conception of the question.[32]

The CFDT also devoted a special issue of its journal, *La Revue de la CFDT,* to the subject of migration in 1997, shortly after the socialist government came into power. The special issue, which was designed to broach the theme of state capacity to control migration flows, was composed of articles by prominent academics.

The CGT favored the government's policy of halting labor migration in 1974, at the onset of the economic recession. As noted above, at an Executive Commission meeting in March 1979, the CGT reaffirmed its position of support for the suspension of all recruitment and introduction of foreign workers, except for family reunification and refugees. Since that time, "The CGT has completely modified its position over the course of a long process," according to the Head of the CGT's Immigration Section writing in an article in the fall of 1997,[33] at the time when new proposals for immigration policy were being considered by the Jospin government—proposals that the CGT critiqued for not breaking sharply enough with previous restrictionist measures.

The article, pointing to multiple considerations, criticized both those who subscribe to a stop on immigration and those who subscribe to completely open borders.

CGT articles and documents in recent years show, on the one hand, a view that the government has had the ability to exert significant control over immigration flows. There are many references to the decline in immigration flows since the implementation of restrictionist measures in the mid-1970s, and detailed data is given to criticize those who argue that France is experiencing an "invasion." They point to the number of applications made for legalization of status in the regularization program of 1997–98—a program that some people lacking documents did not apply for, as they did not meet the criteria for regularization, and submitting an application that was likely to be rejected risked revealing identities to authorities. The CGT suggests that one can thus estimate that there were a total of about 300,000 people without papers since the previous regularization program of 1981–82, some of whom entered without proper papers and some of whom were already in France in a legal status but were transformed into a status of lacking papers by changes in immigration laws. Thus the CGT suggests that about 20,000 people without papers were added each year—a figure that it considers to be far from the notion of an invasion that is put forward by some.[34]

On the other hand, CGT officials have in recent years also displayed the view that French proponents of still further restrictionist immigration policy measures in the 1980s–90s, or "zero immigration," are not realistic. For the CGT, the management of migration flows is a complicated subject. The Head of the Immigration Section at the CGT wrote in 1994: "We know likewise that the question of the 'regulation' or of the 'management' of international migration flows is to say the least difficult or even impossible."[35] The subsequent Head of the Immigration Section at the CGT wrote in 1996: "But let's be clear, a stop to immigration is an illusion except in constructing immense walls ..."[36] A Secretary of the CGT stated that:

> At a time when there is globalization of production and trade, while capital crosses in a fraction of a second from one continent to another, from one bank to another, and from one stock exchange to another, who could still think that it is realistic to surround the country with an electric barrier? Our country takes pride, quite rightly, in welcoming more tourists than any other in the world. How can one envision that it could, by police measures, prohibit all meetings, all contact, all exchange, be it

friendly, professional, cultural, scientific, or sport, with men and women who have come from elsewhere? ...

On the other hand, to demand that borders be "open to all" is neither realistic nor responsible in our opinion. One has to understand that that kind of attitude would generate a situation of extreme exploitation ....[37]

Pointing to economic internationalization and the changing nature of migration flows that complicate control, a member of the CGT's International Department wrote that:

If migration flows have always existed for diverse reasons ... we are now witnessing a globalization of migration flows .... All continents are concerned, the number of countries affected by migration is growing and diversifying, some countries that were previously suppliers of migrant labor have themselves become countries of immigration. A more precise examination indicates that new population movements which, while taking place in the phenomenon of globalization, are marked by region-alization .... One can thus ask the question: 'why an acceleration, or more precisely an increase, or at least, a modification in migration flows?' In less than a quarter of a century the planet has become an economic space that is always more open ....[38]

A member of the CGT's Executive Commission, pointing to the complicated issues involved and criticizing the notion that a liberal commercial policy toward developing countries will reduce migration pressures, wrote that:

Liberalization of trade and financial flows have, on the contrary, exacer-bated [migration pressures] by encouraging the elimination of jobs and social expenditure, and by creating selective and different dynamics of development according to the regions and the countries .... But even with a more favorable development dynamic, it is certain that in the short and medium term a country's development will accelerate mobility and departures abroad ....[39]

The author suggested that one needs to think about migration policy as one dimension of aid and co-development.

The above statements indicate that unions consider that the state's ability to control migration flows has been complicated in the late twen-tieth century due to economic internationalization. Unions' views on the changing nature of migration flows and the associated changes in state capacity—views that were particularly clarified at the time that the Jospin government was drawing up its immigration policy proposals—fit with their policy preferences toward the broad, overall direction of immigration policy.

Unions' Policy Preferences on Specific Issues

This section considers to what extent unions' views on the right and/or ability of the state to control migration have filtered into their positions on more specific and detailed aspects of immigration policy proposals that were considered in the 1980s and 1990s.

Legal Immigration

The rationale for further increasing restrictions on legal immigration and the non-renewal of work and residence permits (measures adopted by the French government in recent years) is that such measures will deter and reduce entrance and increase exit. The conventional wisdom, and the historical experience of the inter-war years, would lead us to expect that unions would support such measures, particularly under conditions of high unemployment, anticipating that the measures would lower the labor supply.

In contrast, if unions consider that it is difficult for the government to fully control migration flows in an era of economic internationalization, one would expect them to oppose measures that make it more difficult to obtain and retain legal permits, as, instead of increasing exit and reducing entrance, they would consider such measures to have the likely effect of increasing the quantity of irregular immigrants without documents who are more difficult to organize than those with legal status.

The CGT and the CFDT have opposed restrictionist measures, such as the Pasqua Laws and the Debré laws, that made it more difficult for legal immigrants to renew permits. This contrasts with the CGT's position in late 1930, when unemployment was rising and, as noted in the previous chapter, it demanded that work permits be shortened. Questioning the state's capacity to further control migration flows, a member of the CFDT's immigration section, discussing the measures under consideration by the government, noted in 1980 that the: "... project, which denies the automatic renewal of residence and work permits, will result in a multiplication of irregular workers: everyone knows that the denial of regular status leads workers to go underground.... Thus the CFDT is preparing to fight against this project."[40] With regard to the restrictionist bill proposed by the Minister of the Interior, Debré, in 1996, a CFDT press release stated that: "The National Assembly, in its first reading, ignored humanitarianism and realism by adopting and toughening the Debré bill on immigration."[41]

The CGT has in recent years opposed measures that seek to restrict legal immigration further by making it more difficult for legal immigrants to renew permits because it considers that the immigrants will remain in an undocumented status. This indicates some skepticism about the ability to increase control over migration flows further. A CGT Declaration noted that: "It is for the repeal of the Pasqua Laws. Because they transform men and women who were previously in status into clandestines."[42] Similarly the CGT has noted that: "The Pasqua Laws of 1993 have weakened immigrants: bolting entrance doors for refugees, restrictive renewals of the ten year permits, complicated criteria for family reunion, thereby making 'clandestines.'"[43]

Unions have also pointed to the normative consequences of attempts to restrict legal immigration. They have placed particular emphasis on the right to family reunification, pointing to international agreements to support their position and reflecting the liberal view that those with family ties to members of French society have moral claims to residence. For example, with reference to the Pasqua Laws, the CGT noted that: "They contradict the right to live as a family embodied in the International Convention and the European Convention of Human Rights."[44] Similarly a member of the CGT's Immigration Collective noted that: "More often than not, the decisions barring family reunification contravene article 8 of the european convention of human rights [sic]."[45] The CGT, in a note to the Prime Minister in 1987, urging support for the automatic renewal of permits among other things, stated that: "France would bring credit to itself by ratifying the ILO's Convention number 143 and in applying the convention's recommendations on the protection of immigrant workers."[46]

To advance the CGT's policy preference, the Confederation gathered 20,000 card petitions demanding the repeal of the Pasqua Laws, which it sent to the government in March 1996.[47] In March 1991 the CGT sent a letter to the Prime Minister saying that it considered that denying work permits to applicants for asylum gave employers non-declared and exploitable workers.[48]

The CFDT published an article about the National Consultative Commission on Human Rights in its newspaper. The article focused on the Commission's criticisms of the Pasqua Laws, noting that "on each point it reviewed, the commission drew up proposals that went in the direction of greater respect for human rights."[49]

The CFDT and the CGT jointly published a press declaration in April 1996 opposing the restrictionist Pasqua Laws and the new restrictionist immigration policy measures under consideration by the government in the spring of 1996. The two labor Confederations participated in a demonstration in Paris in June 1996 to protest restrictionist immigration policy measures. They likewise published a joint declaration opposing Interior Minister Debré's restrictionist immigration policy measures and participated in a demonstration against them in February 1997. Reflecting the multiple causes of union's immigration policy preferences, the CGT considered that the Debré project would create undocumented immigrants and reinforce xenophobia and the National Front.[50]

Illegal immigration
Issues pertaining to illegal immigration may be interlinked with legal immigration policy, but it is useful to separate them here for purposes of clarity.

Expulsions and inspections The rationale for expulsions of those immigrants who lack documents is that such measures will increase exit and deter entrance. In contrast, if unions consider that it is difficult for the government to fully control migration flows in an era of economic internationalization, one would expect them to oppose expulsions for those who lack legal status and to oppose inspections of worksites where undocumented immigrants work as, if one doubts the ability of the government to effectively conduct internal patrol at reasonable cost, such actions would not substantially reduce the number of undocumented workers, and others may emerge as replacements for those who are forced to exit. Meanwhile union support for such actions would alienate immigrants from unions, making incorporation less likely.

French unions have chosen to oppose the government's restrictionist policy of expulsions, many of which result from identity checks by the police outside the workplace. Reflecting skepticism about the state's ability to completely control migration, a Declaration of the Executive Commission of the CFDT written in 1991 noted that: "There will always be more to replace those who are expelled."[51] Likewise a CFDT document written in 1993 observed that: "The impossibility and the absurdity of a massive expulsion of all the clandestines does not need to be demonstrated any more."[52]

The CGT likewise opposes expulsions.[53] However, CGT statements on expulsions do not refer to state capacity to control migration.

Instead, they point to human rights concerns and a desire to avoid divisions among workers and to deter policies that they consider play into the hands of the National Front.[54] For example, a CGT statement discussing expulsions in 1998 noted that: "For the CGT there is no question of moderating our solidarity with these workers. The authorities ... ignore that binding and gagging individuals is an attack on human rights and international law."[55]

French union officials from both the CFDT and the CGT regard the question of inspections of worksites where undocumented immigrants work, to implement sanctions against employers, as "complicated." The unions' official positions on this issue have evolved a bit in the last two decades, although not nearly as sharply as it has for U.S. unions. In the 1980s, French unions urged the use of employer sanctions as a means to control illegal immigration, and at that time they discussed clandestine work and illegal immigrants together. In the late 1990s unions sought to strictly separate these two issues and to cease discussing non-declared work in the context of discussions on immigration issues.

The intermingling of discussions on clandestine work and illegal immigration in the same article or report, in the 1970s and early 1980s, can be seen in the following examples. A joint statement on immigrant workers by the CGT and the CFDT in 1973 called for "severe sanctions against employers who do not live up to their obligations."[56] An internal CFDT report in 1973 on immigration noted, among other things, that it favored severe sanctions against employers and not against workers.[57] An article in the CFDT newspaper in 1983 noted that "the control of migration flows ... occurs through the fight against clandestine work."[58] Another article several months later noted that the CFDT considered that "the most sound means for fighting this phenomenon [clandestine workers] is to constantly attack the very existence of clandestine work. It is after all those who use clandestines who ensure the presence of workers in irregular situations."[59]

In contrast, by the late 1990s unions stressed that clandestine work involves many French workers and immigrants with papers (as well as some who lack papers). Unlike two decades before, by the end of the century the official policy of unions was that the subject of clandestine work should not be considered together with, or in the context of, discussions pertaining to irregular immigration.[60] Thus the kind of quotes noted above that mix the two subjects in earlier years were difficult to find for the late 1990s. Instead, when the two subjects were discussed together in the late 1990s it was so as to criticize others for mixing up the two issues.

Nonetheless, French unions (seeking to avoid employer evasion of government regulations on issues such as health and safety standards, taxation, and union rights), supported employer sanctions in the late 1990s, although officially they saw sanctions as a means to combat broader problems of the informal economy rather than a means to combat illegal immigration. They urged more inspections of worksites in the informal economy to implement sanctions against employers, regardless of whether the undeclared workers are French, legal immigrants, or irregular immigrants. But they stressed that inspections should be conducted by labor inspectors to ensure that the inspections focus on employer violations, and they firmly opposed the provision of the Debré Laws of 1997 that sought to authorize the police to enter enterprises and conduct identity checks of foreigners at the workplace.[61] Union officials interviewed stressed that they do not denounce undocumented workers (some of whom are thought to be union members or sought as potential union members). Union material, such as newsletters and leaflets, stress that their fight is not with the undocumented immigrants, who are seen as the victims rather than the cause of economic problems.

While the unions' battle is with the employers and their goal is to deter the growing informal economy, the by-product of inspections and raids may be expulsions of those undocumented immigrants found working at the site. In addition, union support for inspections (with the by-product of expulsions) could alienate undocumented immigrants from union. Hence, union officials interviewed regarded the question of inspections as "loaded," but, as would be expected by the conventional wisdom, they continued to support inspections to implement provisions for sanctions against employers in the informal economy—measures that they presumably would not pressure for if they did not think that such measures could be effective.

Regularization (Amnesty) Opponents of regularization programs consider that such programs undermine credibility to deter illegal immigration and encourage illegal immigration by setting precedents. If unions consider that it is difficult for the government to fully control migration flows in an era of economic internationalization, one would expect them to instead favor legislation that reduces vulnerability and increases legal security that, in turn, increases these workers' abilities and incentives to join unions. Thus one would expect unions to favor regularization programs that grant undocumented immigrants legal resident status.

France has instituted several regularization programs in the last two decades to legalize the status of undocumented immigrants. Some were for very specific groups; one was the more general program in 1981–82, which had few conditions for eligibility; and the other was the program in 1997–98 that attached significantly more conditions for eligibility. The CFDT and the CGT have supported regularization programs. The support fits with human rights considerations. However, principles were not divorced from strategic reasoning. This was one issue where organizing concerns did weigh into the immigration policy preferences of French unions, like their U.S. counterparts. Recognizing the reality of these irregular immigrant workers, the unions saw regularization as a means to provide a service to potential members who, upon obtaining papers, would be less likely to undercut French workers and who, it was hoped, would be encouraged to join unions that helped them in the regularization process. As noted by the Parisian Department of the CFDT, clandestine work undermines the gains of collective bargaining contracts, leading the union to take actions to regularize the status of undocumented immigrants so that the latter may join unions and defend employment contracts.[62]

The CFDT, in 1980, was a main sponsor of a special program instituted to regularize the status of undocumented immigrants in the Parisian garment district, known as Le Sentier and located near the Stock Exchange. In early 1980 the undocumented workers in Le Sentier undertook various activities to obtain a regularization program. The activities, initiated by workers from Turkey, included hunger strikes, demonstrations, and work strikes. They received support and logistical backing from the CFDT. Many of the immigrants, in turn, joined the union. CFDT representatives met with relevant government officials, and a working group was set up that included officials from the French government and Turkish embassy, and CFDT officials and a delegation of Turkish workers. While French government officials were initially only willing to discuss the regularization of status for a few individual workers, such as those on hunger strike, the final discussions in the working group in the spring resulted in the creation of a regularization program for several thousand garment workers in Paris.[63]

Both the CGT and the CFDT were active participants in the regularization program that was instituted shortly after the socialists were elected to power in 1981. Union representatives had meetings with government officials, enabling them to have some substantive input. In particular, the unions insisted that the condition for regularization (possession of a work contract) be supplemented by an opportunity to use other means (such as testimony of co-workers and neighbors) to prove employment in case the employer failed to cooperate and provide a work contract. Union representatives also urged the government to speed up the procedures by increasing the number of personnel dealing with the issue.[64]

The government, in turn, encouraged the unions to play an active role as intermediaries in the regularization process. Unions were authorized to submit files on a collective basis to reduce congestion in reception areas and to improve the quality of files submitted. Many volunteer militants devoted time to the issue after work and on weekends, seeking out undocumented immigrants in workplaces in, for example, the major Paris cafes and encouraging them to go to the union, where volunteer militants helped the applicants fill in the required forms and prepare their files.[65] About 135,000 immigrants gained legal status through this regularization program.

The CGT joined into a coalition with immigrant associations and liberal groups such as the League of Human Rights to support the "sans-papiers" (without papers, or undocumented) movement that emerged in 1996. The movement called for the regularization of status for immigrants without papers, many of whom had lost legal status following the implementation of the Pasqua Laws. It was initiated by immigrants who occupied churches and went on hunger strike to bring attention to their cause. The CGT gave support to the coalition of organizations supporting the sans-papiers, and made numerous declarations of support for the sans-papiers movement. Louis Viannet, Secretary-General of the CGT, visited the sans-papiers who were occupying the church Saint-Bernard in August 1996. Concerns for human rights were cited as the reason for the CGT support for this movement. For example, one of the numerous CGT declarations in support of the sans-papiers movement noted that: "It is Human Rights that are at stake."[66]

The CFDT also supported the sans-papiers movement and made quite a few declarations articulating its support for a humanitarian issue. For example, a CFDT press release stated that the undocumenteds: "... no longer receive certain fundamental rights that France had committed itself to respect in various international conventions."[67]

The CFDT signed a joint declaration with the CGT, among others, calling on their organizations to mobilize in support of what was described as a humanitarian issue.[68]

There were also some concrete actions taken in quite a few local areas, and some sans-papiers became union members. For example, in Nantes the CGT turned over their area of the Bourse de Travail (Labor

Exchange building) to the sans-papiers movement, inviting the undocumented immigrants to "occupy" the place in July 1998.

A local CFDT union joined the collective supporting the sans-papiers in Seine et Marne. The collective, which pressured for regularizing the status of the sans-papiers, considered that: "The notion of zero immigration is unrealistic, scandalous, and dangerous in the era of globalization and free circulation of goods and capital."[69]

The Parisian Department of the CFDT gave some support to the movement, although it denounced the radicalization of the movement and its methods and the Parisian Department of the CFDT preferred to instead work quietly on its own project of regularizing the status of private household employees—something that it had worked on "behind the scenes" for a number of years.[70]

Both the CGT and the CFDT supported the regularization program instituted by the Jospin government in 1997–98. The CGT sought to liberalize the program further from the outset, and opposed the conditions for eligibility that were attached to the program, which left leeway for alternative interpretations by prefects in the implementation stage.[71] The CFDT was initially supportive of the criteria for regularization, but by the summer of 1998 the CFDT likewise considered that the conditions for regularization had been implemented too restrictively, and the criteria had left too much leeway for arbitrariness by prefects during the implementation phase. The CFDT thus joined into the liberal coalition with organizations such as the League of Human Rights, and stated that a re-examination was needed.[72]

Neither labor confederation played as great a role in helping applicants file forms as they had done in the previous major program of 1981–82, when they were the primary actors. Since that time, immigrant associations had proliferated and grown, following the legal changes of 1981 that allowed immigrants to establish their own associations, and most applicants went to the immigrant associations for practical assistance in the regularization program of 1997–98. Moreover, the perceived incentive to help applicants so as to promote organization was reduced as the number of legalized immigrants who had remained union members after the regularization program of 1981–82 was less than had been previously anticipated.

The CGT also signed a joint declaration with various immigrant rights groups that criticized the more general immigration bill introduced by Jospin's government, a bill that became the Chevènement Laws. The declaration criticized the bill for not breaking with the logic of the previous conservative bills of Pasqua and Debré, and noted that what was needed was a complete re-working of current laws so as to make France into "a country where human rights are fully respected."[73] In contrast, the CFDT, although noting some concerns with certain details of the bill, expressed support for the general orientation of the bill.

Construction Unions

Many immigrants, particularly from Portugal and Algeria, worked in the construction sector in the post-war period. However, immigrants constituted a disproportionately large share of those laid off in the construction sector since the 1970s, and for this and other reasons the portion of French workers employed in the construction sector increased in the late twentieth century.[74]

The construction sector has increasingly fallen into the informal or non-declared sector of the economy in recent decades, and in 1990 more employers in the construction sector than any other economic sector were found guilty of hiring immigrants lacking work permits. 45.6 percent of the total number of employers found guilty of hiring immigrants without appropriate permits were in the construction sector in 1990. The irregular immigrants were primarily from Portugal, Tunisia, and Morocco.

The Construction Federation of the CGT has traditionally been larger than that of the CFDT, although the CFDT's Construction Federation has grown considerably in the 1990s. The CFDT's Construction Federation more than doubled its number of members in the decade from 1988 to 1998.[75]

CGT

The CGT Federation's position was summarized by the material left in a prominent place at the entrance to its offices in recent years, which has included a large poster stating opposition to the restrictionist Pasqua Laws and newsletters on immigration and racism. A similar message was conveyed in the large number of articles on immigration (and racism) in the Federation's monthly newsletter.

The Federation of Construction, CGT, at the leadership level firmly opposed restrictionist immigration policy measures considered or adopted in recent years. CGT construction union officials, in contrast with many construction unions in the inter-war years, tried to convey the message that immigrants are not the cause of the unemployment situation and should not be scapegoated. In the late twentieth century they pointed out in meetings with workers that immigrants had been disproportionately laid off. The data given in one newsletter showed that between 1974 and 1995 the number of immigrants working in construction declined by 59 percent, whereas the number of French working in the construction sector declined by 19 percent.[76]

The Federation's newsletters often explained its opposition to further restrictionism by pointing out that migration is inherently linked to capitalism, immigrants constitute part of the working class, restrictionist policies undermine human rights, and immigrants are not the cause of unemployment.

With regard to the theme of the state's ability to control migration, this was explicitly referred to in the Construction Federation's newsletter in 1996, where an article on the Pasqua Laws and undocumented immigrants noted that: "For some years policies employed have set as their goal a halt of migration flows .... What legal wall or concrete can really keep out people who hope to come and participate in the economic life of Europe[?]"[77]

With regard to the Pasqua Laws that made it more difficult to retain legal permits, the Federation considered that such measures would increase the number of undocumented workers and enlarge the already large portion of the construction sector that is non-declared. For the Construction Federation the Pasqua Laws "create clandestines."[78] One interviewee in 1998 stated that:

> We can't say that we'll stop immigration, and it will stop. As long as there's exploitation, there will be migration. People will circulate. Despite the repressive laws of Pasqua, despite the decline in visas granted to refugees, despite all this, people come clandestinely, but they don't come in such a great number. You can work out the approximate number of clandestines each year by looking at the number who applied for the regularization program of 1997, some of whom were people already in France but made clandestine by the Pasqua Laws, and others of whom were new entrants .... A good and real policy can't be done outside of the economic, social and political realities of the world.[79]

Another interviewee, who was a retired construction union militant in Lyon, when asked what he thought was similar or different about migration today and in earlier times, responded that: "Migration flows have changed. It used to be the employer who actively recruited migrants and who activated migration. Before migration was used by employers to break unions. That's not really what's going on today. Migrants today come on their own in search of work. Before, the employers went in search of workers."[80]

The Construction Federation's position on expulsions, inspections, regularization, and renewal of permits was similar to that of the CGT in the late twentieth century.

The Construction Federation's position, in its broad outline, followed that of the CGT. However, there were nuanced aspects that indicated that the Federation's position was in part determined by its specific interests stemming from a sector where many immigrants are concentrated. As one interviewee responded, "We have no choice but to make an effort on immigration issues."[81]

The CGT Construction Federation engaged in various activities that were neglected by CGT Federations covering sectors where few immigrants worked. For example: (1) The Federation for many years has had a special immigration collective (committee) including ten to fifteen people (two-thirds immigrants and one-third French, and a mixture of salaried federation officials and volunteer militants); (2) The Federation's newsletter includes quite frequent articles on issues pertaining to immigration and racism; (3) The Federation supported literacy and language training for immigrant workers, and apparently forged close contacts with AEFTI, an association for language training for immigrant workers; (4) The Federation apparently sends a disproportionately large number of delegates to the Confederation's immigration conferences, which are held every few years.

CFDT

The CFDT Construction Federation's official position on immigration policy is the same as that of the Confederation. The Federation does not favor open borders, but apparently opposed restrictionist government measures that were put forward in the 1980s and 1990s, arguing that immigrants were the victims rather than the cause of unemployment. The CFDT Construction Federation apparently favors an automatic renewal of permits and has opposed measures that call this into question because non-renewal creates clandestines, and it apparently considers that if the government makes it harder for immigrants to come legally they will come illegally.[82]

However, in recent years the CFDT Construction Federation has been less active than its counterpart in the CGT. Its newsletters include scarcely any references to immigration. Although neither do the newsletters of other CFDT Federations that cover sectors where immigrants are concentrated, such as services (in contrast, newsletters at the CFDT Confederation level and at the CFDT Regional levels include numerous references to immigration). The CFDT Construction

Federation declined to participate in a study on racism coorganized by the CFDT and academics in 1996, unlike the CFDT Federation of Services, which was an active participant in the study. The Construction Federation had an Immigration Collective from the mid-1970s until the 1980s. Unlike the Construction Federation of the CGT, the CFDT Construction Federation's Immigration Collective no longer exists.

Despite these signs of inactivity, a representative from Construction did attend a meeting on immigration issues at the regional Ile de France CFDT Congress in June 1997, reporting to the committee that "all was going well in construction." Moreover, the Construction Federation's Council held a debate on the Debré Laws and the rise of the National Front in April 1997. The meeting condemned the restrictionist Debré Laws.[83] A report of the Federation's Congress in 1998 noted that construction had been a route to integration for immigrants for many years, and the Federation, in its plan of action, stated that, besides demonstrations, it must denounce the National Front's theses at the workplace.[84] The Federation included a couple of articles on racism in its newsletter in 1999, one of which was a published interview with the Secretary of the construction union in Lille, who had initiated debates on racism with militants in his union and then with union members.

In summary, while the CFDT's Construction Federation has been less active than its counterpart in the CGT, the Federation, in line with the CFDT, has officially opposed proponents of further restrictionist immigration policy measures. Moreover, an inactive stance at a time of high unemployment differs from the stance of those construction unions that actively pressured for restrictionism in the inter-war years.

Both Construction Federations (CGT and CFDT) have clearly refrained from the restrictionist statements and demands of French construction unions in the early twentieth century, and it appears that the sources of their policy preferences are similar to those of their respective Confederations

Racism at the Workplace

Both the CFDT and the CGT intensified their actions to fight racism in the workplace in the mid-1990s—a subject that is beyond the scope of this study's focus on immigration policy. Nonetheless, as the CFDT and the CGT have devoted more time and resources to this subject than to immigration policy since the mid-1990s, it is appropriate to briefly digress and address the subject to provide perspective. Changing notions of the role of the state do not explain their actions against racism in the workplace, which have taken place in the context of their campaign against the National Front since the mid-1990s, at a time when the National Front began distributing leaflets in workplaces, attempting to infiltrate existing unions, and setting up its own unions.

The CFDT, in conjunction with academics, conducted a study on racism in the workplace. The goals were to sensitize militants (not all of whom shared the same views) to the problem and to open up a debate on racism at the workplace. Militants organized meetings between academic researchers and workers inside firms to discuss racism. The results of the study were then disseminated in union journals and a book;[85] and researchers reported their findings at local CFDT meetings throughout the country, opening the meetings to debate the subject further. The CGT embarked on a similar campaign to open debates with union leaders, militants, and members, not all of whom shared the same views. The Confederation conducted a "Tour de France" in the spring of 1997, in which it organized debates in towns such as Marseilles, Orange, Toulon, Toulouse, and Paris, and some sharply conflicting views emerged in the debates held in workplaces.[86]

The union confederations also tried to block the National Front's attempts to set up its own unions in such sectors as transport, police, and prison officers. The CFDT, then joined by the CGT, took legal action to ban the National Front in its attempts to establish unions. Some, although not all, of the earlier court rulings banned the National Front unions on the grounds that the pseudo-unions were simply an extension of a political party.[87] After appeals, the Supreme Court (Cour de Cassation) banned the National Front unions in the prison and police sectors in April 1998 on the grounds that they did not meet the criteria for unions as laid out in the Labor Code and that they sought to act against the principles of non-discrimination embedded in the Constitution, labor laws, and the international commitments of France.[88]

Conclusion

French unions in the late twentieth century opposed restrictionist measures that complicated the criteria for renewal of permits or shortened the length of permits, they opposed expulsions, and they favored regularization programs. The main exception to their general policy of resisting many of the restrictionist measures proposed or adopted in the late twentieth century was union support for inspections of work-sites to implement sanctions against employers in the informal sector of the economy. This practice may have the by-product of expulsions of irregular immigrants and is thus restrictionist. However, even on this latter issue, in recent years unions argued that clandestine work and irregular immigration should not be considered together and that inspections are instead aimed at sanctioning the employer and are an issue pertaining to the employment of many non-declared French workers, in addition to legal immigrant workers and irregular immigrant workers.

The unions' overall positions clearly separated them from the restrictionist camp in the late twentieth century. Union statements often denounced restrictionists. Unions likewise kept away from groups that advocated what amounted to open borders. Unions quite often sat in a fragile coalition with "moderate" immigrant associations and human rights groups.

French unions' immigration policy preferences in the late twentieth century in some respects remained fairly constant since World War II, at least by comparison with the clear shift in the AFL-CIO's policy to illegal immigrants since the 1970s. The main changes were the CGT's flip-flops on policy toward legal immigration—it advocated restrictionism in the period of prosperity in the 1950s; and, as would be expected by the conventional wisdom, it again advocated restrictionism for a brief period in the years of rising unemployment in the late 1970s. But the CGT's restrictionist statements, even in the late 1970s, were short and soft by comparison with some statements from the early twentieth century, when construction unions pressured for restrictionist measures and the CGT urged, in late 1930, that permits be shortened. The CGT then liberalized its position a bit toward the end of the twentieth century, at a time of persistently high unemployment when the conventional wisdom would have led us to anticipate the opposite outcome.

Unemployment was consistently high throughout the late twentieth century in France. However, unions did not jump on to the restrictionist bandwagon. Instead, they maintained moderate positions and opposed certain restrictionist measures. Why? The puzzle is heightened by the rise of the National Front as a significant political party in France in the late twentieth century. The rise of the National Front shifted the whole agenda of immigration politics further to the right as other political parties sought to coopt the National Front's agenda so as to retain voters. Why did unions decide to oppose rather than coopt the National Front's agenda? Why did unions react differently from their counterparts in the early twentieth century?

The argument is that French unions sat in coalition with moderate liberal groups because of their views on the ability and the right of the state to control migration in an era of internationalization—views that had changed among French union officials since the early twentieth century. Views on this subject ruled out the restrictionist temptation.

CHAPTER 7

Conclusion

This book presented a puzzle that has been overlooked in the scholarly literature: Why did unions in the United States and France change coalitions between the early and late twentieth century?

Unions' immigration policy preferences in the late twentieth century contrasted with the immigration policy preferences of most of their counterparts in the early twentieth century. To recall, in 1921, the AFL "urged the complete restriction of immigration for at least two years" and in 1924 the AFL stated that its preferred outcome was the "total suspension of immigration for a period of five years or longer." In 1923 the majority CGT noted that it favored French first, stating that "We have to say that we are not hostile to foreign workers coming to France, but we equally have to say that our social union mission is to first protect the interests of national labor."

The argument presented was that unions changed coalitions as they considered the challenges of various forms of internationalization. Many union leaders considered that economic internationalization and/or the internationalization of human rights concerns called into question the ability and/or right of the state to fully control migration. This reduced the rationale for pursuing some restrictionist measures that were deemed ineffective and/or undesirable in controlling migration. Meanwhile many union leaders saw support for certain non-restrictionist measures (or opposition to certain restrictionist measures) as a way to facilitate organization, which is an alternative strategy to restrictionism for improving wages and work conditions for those unions that have an inclusive approach.

This chapter asks to what extent the findings of this study are unique to the specific cases examined, or can be generalized to unions in a broader range of countries. The chapter begins with a review of the role of the variation in union identity on the U.S. and French cases, and a discussion of additional factors that might generate variation in outcome in a range of other countries (such as the level of union density or strength). The chapter then analyzes the British case in the 1990s, so as to explore how union immigration policy preferences played out in a broader range of cases and conditions.

Comparing Unions in the United States and France: The Role of Union Identity

This book went beyond a single country study, so as to begin to assess the generalizability of the argument.

The two countries chosen were liberal democracies with advanced post-industrial economies that experienced immigration in both the early and late twentieth century. Both countries had weak unions in the late twentieth century. Union density in France and the United States is well below that of other post-industrial economies. Union density in France was the lowest, down from 25 percent in 1974 to about 8 percent in 1992.[1] Union density in the United States fell from 21 percent in 1980 to below 15 percent in 1995.[2] Unions in France have had no input into the government policy-making process throughout the post-war era, with some slight exception in the early years of the socialist Mitterand presidency and under the socialist Prime Minister Jospin. Unions in the United States have at times had some input through lobbying Congress, although this input has been quite limited by comparison with a number of European countries.[3]

Although labor movements in both the United States and France are weak, they differ greatly in terms of their identities. American unions are pragmatic and incrementalist, with a focus on immediate interests. In contrast, French unions operate more in the realm of ideas and are more radical in their vision. Their behavior is more ideational than that of their counterparts in the United States. This comparative study thus permits some assessment of the impact of union identity on union policy position.

The book points to some similar trends in terms of union responses to internationalization, regardless of variations in union identities in the United States and France. Unions in both countries are adapting to what they see as changing dynamics in the global arena.

First, union officials in both countries quite often articulated that in their view, while the state still has much control over migration flows, complete control is complicated by economic internationalization.

Second, while some coded illiberalism remains in the union movements in both countries, there has been a certain degree of liberalization and internationalization of the normative discourse (and at times actions) of unions when one considers contemporary positions in historical perspective. French unions today articulate human rights concerns more than did their counterparts in the early twentieth century, and today they often point to international conventions on human rights to support their position. U.S. unions today do not articulate human rights issues as much as do their French counterparts, nor do they refer to international conventions in the way that their French counterparts do. But, when placed in historical perspective, it is clear that there has also been a liberalization of discourse in the U.S. labor movement. As shown in chapter four, the CIO brought liberal norms to the mainstream of the labor movement after World War II at the time of the merger with the AFL, and U.S. unions today refrain from using the openly illiberal discourse of U.S. unions in the early twentieth century.

At the same time the study also points to the importance of unique identities even in the face of global-level changes and challenges. The individual lenses through which events were interpreted mattered. The pragmatic U.S. unions and the ideational French unions filtered the dilemmas posed in somewhat different ways. Certain explanatory factors, while relevant in a range of cases, carried different weight and importance among different unions.

Organizing concerns had greater influence over the immigration policy preferences of the pragmatic U.S. unions than their French counterparts. This reflects their identities and broader approaches. French union identity, while upholding inclusive ideals, does not involve active organizing of anyone, be they native or immigrant.

Unionism in France has been labeled as "ideological unionism."[4] As described by two prominent scholars of French unionism, it "conceived of membership as an act of conviction rather than as a simple commitment linked to immediate interests. In general, it remained devoid of genuine service functions aimed at members."[5] Thus it is not surprising that French unions articulated greater emphasis on normative concerns than did their U.S. counterparts. The French unions' articulation of normative issues fit with this stress on "conviction." French union officials quite often questioned the right of the state when its policies hit on the rights of migrants. Normative concerns were brought to the surface and heightened in the late twentieth century in France as the National Front became implanted on the scene of French politics.

While a stress on norms fits the ideational feature of French unions, it may nonetheless appear to be a bit out of sync for the class-oriented French unions to articulate support for human rights issues and to draw on international human rights conventions to legitimize and strengthen their position given the liberal and individualistic philosophical underpinnings of these conventions.[6] But the positions of French unions in the late twentieth century were quite often in accord with liberal norms, which dictate granting access to citizenship to those people who are members of the society by virtue of living in the community for a period of time (even if in an undocumented status), and to those people with family ties to a member of the society. Unlike the revolutionary CGTU in the inter-war years, French unions in the late twentieth century did not advocate a policy of open borders that may be more consistent with a class-oriented desire to see the "Workers of the World, Unite."

Other Possible Sources of Divergence

Our understanding of the generalizability of the argument presented here, and of the sources of union immigration policy preferences, would be enhanced by exploring a broader range of cases. It would be pertinent for future research work to consider a case that involves strong unions. Several propositions might be made as to why strong unions might react differently than weak unions.

First, unions with a high density (percentage of workforce unionized) may have less sense of need to consider the interests of potential new members so as to expand the union's base. It would already have a large base. The existence of a labor movement with greater union density might reduce incentives for unions to organize immigrants and, in turn, reduce incentives to oppose restrictionist measures that impede organization at a time of economic internationalization.

Second, it might be thought that the incentive for unions to pressure for restrictionism would be increased in the case of a strong labor movement with greater input into the government's immigration policy-making process. A strong labor movement would have an incentive to call for restrictionism because its voice would be heard and restrictionist measures would be imposed. Thus this would factor out skepticism about effective restrictionism that may stem from a concern that the government will ignore union preferences. As noted in earlier chapters, French unions, as weak actors with no input into government policy, abandoned a restrictionist posture in the early 1960s because they were skeptical that the government would listen to their calls for protectionism. Strong unions would presumably not share this view and may have greater incentive to pressure for restrictionism. However, the rationale for this reasoning no longer makes sense. Most European governments, including the French government, imposed restrictionist measures in the 1970s regardless of whether unions were strong or weak. The situation was reversed. The French government pressured for a range of restrictionist measures in the late twentieth century and it was the unions that opposed the protectionist temptation.

To assess whether, and if so in what way union strength matters, pertinent cases for study include Sweden and Austria. Germany would also be a pertinent case for future study and comparative analysis. Both Germany and the United States have a similar percentage of foreign-born residents, and both share borders with less prosperous countries, raising the problems of undocumented migration. Although the U.S. case is unique due to the vast disparities in wealth between Mexico and the United States, Germany's situation is not so different since the liberalization of rules of exit in Eastern Europe. But Germany, unlike the United States, has a relatively large and centralized labor movement and a political system that gives unions some input into the policy-making process, although their input has declined in recent years. Research on Germany could help to assess to what extent the strength and structure of organized labor shape immigration policy preferences. It could also serve to further test the role of the union's identity toward organizing, a theme that has already been explored in this book. German unions have adopted a comparatively conservative approach to recruitment that protects insiders.[7] This orientation may dilute their enthusiasm for pursuing a strategy of organizing immigrants rather than one of restrictionism.

There is some indication that strong labor movements adopted different policies than did weak labor movements in the 1960s and 1970s, before the onset of economic internationalization. The strong Swedish unions accepted labor migration at that time on the condition that it occurred in a way that protected native (and immigrant) workers' rights and they put forward certain demands to ensure this. Given their comparatively weak bargaining position, it would have been futile for French or U.S. unions to make similar demands to those that their strong Swedish counterparts made. The Swedish unions pushed for (and obtained) measures that automatically unionized immigrant workers so as to mitigate competition. The bilateral agreements negotiated by Sweden with other countries in the immediate post-war years included a clause that required foreign workers to join unions. This clause was abolished in 1965, but after that employers were committed to recommend to foreign workers that they join unions. Foreign workers were normally asked to go to the local union office before signing the employment contract, and many gained the impression that it was necessary to join the union to get a job. Foreign workers (like native workers) joined unions at a high rate.[8] Under these conditions there would be less need for unions to refrain from advocating restrictionist immigration policy rules so as to facilitate organization (even if the restrictionist rules came to be seen as less effective with the onset of economic internationalization in later years).

That said, one should be cautious about exaggerating the importance of union strength in explaining responses to immigration in that earlier time period because there was a clear variation in response among strong unions at that time. The strong Austrian unions adopted a quite different approach from their strong Swedish counterparts.[9] The Austrian unions adopted a policy of firm resistance and they sat in coalition with conservative groups at that time and since. They displayed a much more restrictionist posture to both immigration and immigrant policy than did their Swedish counterparts, and they even opposed a liberalization of asylum policy in more recent years in case it would provide a route in for economic migrants. An agreement reached in 1962 ensured business of access to foreign workers on certain conditions demanded by the unions, such as the assurance that foreign workers would be repatriated after the expiration of a contract, and that foreign workers would be laid off before Austrian workers. Organized labor also demanded that work permits be only short-term. The clause that foreign workers be laid off before Austrian workers was subsequently incorporated into a new law in 1975. In contrast to Swedish unions, Austrian unions, in addition to trying to severely restrict the entrance of foreign workers into the country and labor market, also made no effort to change the law that excluded foreign workers from membership in works councils, which is a precondition for becoming a union official.[10] Some parts of Austrian organized labor began to push for change and a liberalization in union policy toward immigrants in the early 1990s, and it remains to be seen to what extent their views were taken into account by the Austrian Trade Union Federation in later years.

An alternative factor that may generate variation in union response is geography. Geographical location may influence views on the state's capacity to control migration. It is possible that unions in more geographically isolated countries, such as Britain as an island, may see the state as more robust than unions in countries that face greater pressures of illegal immigration due to proximity to areas with a major disparity in wealth, such as Spain and Italy—which are close to North Africa—and Germany—which is close to Eastern Europe and the former Soviet Union.

There is currently inadequate available research that is thorough on the immigration policy preferences of unions in a range of countries in the 1990s to test to what extent these, or other factors, may generate different outcomes from the U.S. and French cases. That part of the argument presented in this book that focuses on the role of economic internationalization was published in Haus 1995 and has since been given some preliminary testing on other countries.[11] Gamze Avci and Christopher McDonald tested the argument presented in Haus 1995 on the British case.[12] After reading Haus 1995, Julie Watts decided that for her Ph.D. dissertation she would follow Haus' research questions and test Haus' argument on two new countries of immigration: Spain and Italy.[13] Her findings followed the arguments presented in Haus 1995 and Haus 1998. Unlike Watts, Avci and McDonald go significantly further and they give preliminary data on the British case that points to a need to supplement a focus on economic internationalization with a focus on race issues. Avci and McDonald convincingly suggest that a concern to avoid racial discrimination played an important role in explaining why British unions resisted restrictionism in the late twentieth century. The data that they give is only preliminary, but it is sufficient to suggest a need for more research on the British case. The remainder of this chapter undertakes this task, and, while not as detailed as the material presented on the U.S. and French cases, nonetheless gives primary data that helps to assess the sources of unions' immigration policy preferences at the turn of the millennium.

The British case presents important characteristics that differ from the U.S. and French cases, and thus provides an interesting comparison to consider the conditions under which the argument presented can (or cannot) be generalized. First, as a result of geography one might expect that the British state's capacity to control migration is stronger than that of France and particularly that of the United States, which shares a 2,000-mile border with Mexico. Britain's isolated status as an island, although slightly altered with the building of the channel tunnel, shelters it from some of the pressures of unauthorized border crossings faced by France and particularly the United States. At the same time, foreigners constituted a smaller (although rising) percentage of the total

Table 7.1 Inflows of foreign population
into the U.K.: 1992–1997 (in thousands)

Year	Inflows of foreign population
1992	203.9
1993	190.3
1994	193.6
1995	206.3
1996	216.4
1997	236.9

Source: SOPEMI *Trends in International Migration Annual Report 2000* (Paris: OECD, 2001), p. 304.

Table 7.2 Stock of foreign labor in the
U.K: 1990–1999 (in thousands)

Year	Stock of foreign labor
1990	882
1995	862
1999	1,005

Source: SOPEMI *Trends in International Migration Annual Report 2000* (Paris: OECD, 2001), p. 362.

population in the United Kingdom than in France and the United States. Foreigners constituted 3.8 percent of the total population in 1998, up from 3.1 percent in 1991.[14]

Second, British unions have a stronger membership base than their French or U.S. counterparts, with a union density in the U.K. of about 30 percent in the late 1990s. This figure, although dramatically lower than British union density in the 1970s, was still much higher than in the United States and France.

The British Case

Introduction

The following study of the British case in the 1990s shows that the labor movement there, represented by the Trades Union Congress (TUC), opposed many of the restrictionist immigration policy measures enacted in the late twentieth century, as was the case with the labor movements in the United States and France. However, British unions appear to have devoted less time and resources to immigration issues than their counterparts, particularly by comparison with unions in the United States in the 1990s.

An important part of the explanation for British unions' immigration policy preferences resembles part of the explanation for the U.S. case— a pragmatic rejuvenation of the organizing agenda. Although British unions had a much higher union density than that of U.S. unions in the 1990s, they had nonetheless experienced a dramatic decline in membership. Declining union density, sometimes thought to be partly attributable to economic internationalization, was the common factor, and it elicited a similar response by the traditionally pragmatic unions in both the United Kingdom and the United States. As unions in both countries embarked on new organizing agendas, they took into account the immigration policy preferences of potential members. In the United States, legal and undocumented immigrants were an important target of the unions' new recruitment drive. In the United Kingdom, black British workers were an important target of the unions' new recruitment drive and unions have increasingly accommodated the immigration policy preferences of black British workers. International issues have been intermingled with this. The TUC's Black Workers Conference (a group for non-white workers within the TUC) strongly opposed restrictionism in part for reasons relating to international issues—to protect a route for family reunification of their transnational relatives, and to uphold ideals that protect the rights of the migrants seeking residence in the United Kingdom. Black workers have also opposed restrictionism for domestic reasons—a concern to avoid measures that are seen to increase discrimination against black British workers at home.

Economic internationalization has only played a direct role in British union immigration policy positions in the regional European Union (EU) context. At a broader level, British union officials, unlike their American and French counterparts, do not link immigration policy debates to larger changes in the global political economy and they do not show skepticism about the state's capacity to fully control migration. This is not surprising given the specific geographical circumstances that may have mitigated the amount of unauthorized immigrants in the United Kingdom.

British Immigration Policy: Brief Background

In the later decades of the twentieth century Britain cracked down on immigration more severely than any other advanced industrialized country. Highly restrictive immigration measures were adopted under

Margaret Thatcher's Conservative government and then continued by Tony Blair's Labour government.[15]

Three principal new laws were approved in the 1980s, and they all aimed to increase restrictionism. The British Nationality Act of 1981 revised the nationality code, restricting the definition of U.K. citizenship. The Carrier's Liability Act of 1987 imposed penalties against airlines and shipping companies that brought in people who lacked proper papers. The Immigration Act of 1988 removed certain rights for family reunion migration, and restricted certain rights of appeal against denial of entrance and deportation, among other measures.

Immigration and asylum issues became increasingly intermingled in laws and government discourse in the 1990s, and asylum seekers were often labeled as people seeking to evade immigration control. Subsequent legislation incorporated the two categories in the same acts. The Asylum and Immigration Appeals Act of 1992, among other measures, denied certain rights of appeal to some categories of asylum seekers, and removed the obligation for local authorities to provide housing for asylum seekers. Illegal or unauthorized immigrants were a major target of the next act, the Asylum and Immigration Act of 1996. This act included measures that sought to deter unauthorized immigration. Most notably, it introduced sanctions against employers of illegal immigrants, who were thenceforth obliged to check the immigration status of job applicants and who became subject to fines if caught employing unauthorized migrants.

Many of the restrictionist measures, including the employer sanctions legislation introduced in 1996, were retained by the Labour government, which came to power in 1997. Indeed a further tightening was imposed by the Labour government in the Asylum and Immigration Act of 1999, which among other measures increased the search powers of immigration officers, and sought to deter asylum seekers by providing them with food vouchers instead of cash aid. The Blair government likewise tried to beef up British border control at the channel tunnel, which connected Britain with the European continent, and which was portrayed as a leakage point for the entrance of unauthorized immigrants.

Unlike the United States and France, the restrictionist measures in the United Kingdom were not complemented by the enactment of an amnesty program. An amnesty program did not even become a serious item for discussion in the British political arena.

British Unions: Brief Background

British unions have generally had a reformist and pragmatic orientation in the twentieth century, favoring gradual social change within capitalism. They have displayed somewhat greater interest in social change and more spurts of militancy (for example, 1968-1974) than their American counterparts. However, they have not followed the revolutionary approach that was reflected by a significant portion of the French union movement at various points in time. As will be seen, British unions approached immigration-related issues in the 1990s in a manner that reflected this identity of pragmatism and some progressiveness.

British unions faced great challenges in the 1980s and after.[16] Union density declined from 55.4 percent in 1979 to 30 percent in the late 1990s. British unions shared the problems posed by economic restructuring common to all advanced economies. De-industrialization eroded the post-war base of union strength. However, in the British case these challenges were compounded by the Thatcher government's well-known war against the unions. The government engaged in the "race to the bottom," passed anti-union legislation, and deregulated the economy so as to attract domestic and foreign investors. As pointed out by Chris Howell, the situation was well summarized by *The Economist,* which noted that "Britain comfortably comes bottom in surveys of EU employers' perceptions of the stringency of employment protection regulations."[17] As a result the economy became much more internationalized and foreign investors, particularly from Japan, brought new modes of industrial relations with them, generating the emergence of new forms of worker representation such as works councils.

The labor movement responded to these challenges by relaunching itself under the banner of the "New Unionism" in the early 1990s, replicating the restructuring of the Labour Party. "New Labour" had cut many of its previous close ties with unions, and the "New Unions" engaged in less political activity than their predecessors.

The "New Unionism" involved a major recruitment effort that shared some features with the renewed focus on organizing in the AFL-CIO, and top leaders at the AFL-CIO were invited as speakers at TUC Congresses. British unions re-focused resources away from their traditional and existing members (often white men), and instead placed more emphasis on potential members (women, blacks, and part-time workers). The TUC opened an Organising Academy that was designed to replicate the AFL-CIO's Organizing Institute, and the unions became service providers (for example, legal help and financial/tax advice), rather than just collective bargainers, in their efforts to counter the declining union density.

Unions' Immigration Policy Preferences

Unions, Immigration, and the European Union

Deepening economic integration at the regional European Union (EU) level has at times filtered into the immigration policy discussions of British unions. Economic regionalization (rather than economic internationalization at a global level) presented a challenge for British unions to which they adapted in a pragmatic manner.

The Single European Act (SEA) of 1986, which called for the free mobility of people along with that of capital, goods, and services, was considered by union officials. They did not try to resist this development by advocating national protectionism. In reverse, British unions at times advocated measures that would remove the many practical barriers to migration in the EU. For example, a resolution approved at the TUC's Conference in 1998 called on the government to go beyond removing barriers to the free movement of labor by also promoting information, reciprocity of housing, health, education, and social security programs for intra-EU migrant workers.[18] This position was a change from the 1950s, when the TUC General Council displayed economic nationalism in a statement about a labor code to be signed by members of the Organization for European Economic Co-operation.[19]

On the whole, the TUC responded to the challenge of increased migration arising from EU deepening and widening by favoring organization of migrant workers. This was clear in a campaign to recruit Portuguese workers in London in 2001, jointly undertaken by the TUC and the CGTP-IN (a Portuguese trade union confederation).[20] On the British side the initiative for the campaign came from a policy officer working in the European Union and International Relations Department of the TUC. The campaign was seen as a good way to boost union membership, and fit well with the TUC's general recruitment drive. But to understand why the campaign was initiated, and the timing of the campaign, one needs to look beyond the rejuvenation of TUC recruitment efforts (which began in the early 1990s) and to consider the impact of developments in the external EU arena. The campaign was not initiated by the Organizing Department. It was initiated by the European Union and International Relations Department at the TUC, and by someone who was pushed to consider the subject of migrant workers at that particular time because of EU enlargement negotiations with East European countries, and because of the publication in November 2000 of the EU Commission's communication on drawing up an EU migration policy.[21]

The Portuguese workers campaign included advice surgeries in the London areas of Camden, Brixton, and Portobello, where workers could speak to union representatives (through an interpreter if requested) to find out about a range of employment rights; a major Portuguese cultural festival one Sunday, which was well advertised in bilingual leaflets left in prominent places such as at the TUC's main reception desk; the distribution of bilingual pamphlets giving legal advice on obtaining National Insurance numbers and on rights in the workplace; and a telephone helpline service run by the union where workers could leave messages in Portuguese for union representatives.

Developments in the EU external arena also prompted the TUC's European Union and International Relations Department to submit a grant proposal to the EU Commission in April 2001. The proposal, which was successful and approved by the EU, was entitled "Trade Unions and Migrant Workers in Europe: Free Movement of Labour and EU Enlargement." It noted that "responding in a practical way to the predicted increase in the migrant workforce will require improved knowledge of the relevant EU instruments and their national application, and a greater understanding of the needs of migrant workers and the ways in which trade unions can respond to them. The TUC is already engaged in a project with the CGT-IN from Portugal aimed at providing information and advice on employment rights to Portuguese workers in Britain. It is hoped that this will generate some useful experience of some of the issues, which can then be applied on a larger scale." The more specific goals of the funded project included plans for the production of a trade union handbook on rights and benefits for migrant workers in Britain; holding a major conference (in London) on trade unions and migrants in the EU; holding a series of regional seminars; and setting up multilingual web pages on the TUC site for local unions to download on basic employment and union rights.[22]

While British union officials have considered the implication of deepening regional economic integration for immigration policy issues, their statements do not link broader changes in the international political economy at a global level to immigration issues. In this regard, they differ from their counterparts in France and the United States, both of which considered the challenge of economic internationalization at a global level when forming their immigration policy preferences.

Black Workers Conference
Over time, black British workers have gained some input into the TUC's policy. This began in the mid-1970s, when the TUC took a firmer

position on race relations and moved away from its former position that immigrants needed to assimilate. Instead, the TUC began to stress the need to root out racism in labor's own ranks. A source of change at that time included struggles by black workers, who took a number of industrial actions to express grievances that included discrimination by white trade unionists. The effect of their complaints was broadened by media criticism of the union practices.[23] The struggles of black workers were then further advanced as they engaged in more self-mobilization; and particularly as the TUC embarked on a new recruitment drive in the 1990s, which targeted black workers as a potential block of new members who could stem the tide of declining union density.[24]

The TUC Black Workers Conference (established in the mid-1980s) took a strong stand on immigration issues in the 1990s, at a time when the TUC actively sought to recruit black workers. The input of black British workers increased in the 1990s due to these new recruitment efforts, which targeted black workers, along with women and part-time workers. The TUC changed its rules in 1993 so as to ensure representation of black workers on the General Council, the TUC's policy-making body. By 1998, 72 percent of unions said that they were specifically targeting black and Asian workers as part of their recruitment programs.[25] The TUC undertook a variety of initiatives such as a mentoring program for black and ethnic minority officers in 2001; a series of two day courses for black and Asian officers and staff; and the Southern and Eastern Regional TUC organized a conference entitled "Black Workers and New Unionism" in 2000.

The recruitment campaign involved giving some attention to the concerns of black workers. Their concerns included immigration issues, as noted by the opening speaker of the TUC's Black Workers Conference in 1992 when he described: "... the need for unions to take action in a number of key areas, including the election and appointment of more black officers, taking up race cases, taking up the political issues of immigration and asylum, and meeting the needs of black women members."[26] The same speaker went on to note that the TUC was making progress, as shown by its recent decision to commission a research study entitled "The Involvement of Black Workers in Trade Unions." The second day of the conference was devoted entirely to the subject of "Europe 1992: Race Equality, Immigration and Nationality," and the conference concluded with a call for unions to take seriously the issue of immigration rights.

The TUC Black Workers Conference devoted a considerable amount of attention to immigration and asylum issues in its annual meetings.

Motions on immigration and asylum were regularly approved at the Conference since 1993, the year that the Conference was changed into one that considered motions.

Resolutions approved at the TUC Black Workers Conference have firmly opposed a broad range of restrictionist immigration measures, and have occasionally edged in the direction of advocating open borders. For example, one resolution approved in 1996 called on the TUC: "... to lobby MPs to promote the repeal of the 1962 Commonwealth Immigrants Act and all anti immigration laws (such as the Asylum and Immigration Bill) now and during the term of the next Government."[27]

In 1999 the Black Workers Conference resolutions criticized the Labour Government's proposals and noted that it: "... is disappointed that the Government has failed to address serious weaknesses and human rights violations in the system or to take a more radical approach by proposing new legislation based on the right to equal treatment, justice, dignity and family life."[28]

Part of the explanation for the Black Workers Conference position relates to international considerations—a desire for family reunification of transnational relatives, and normative concerns for the human rights of potential immigrants and refugees. For example, a motion entitled "Human Rights" and approved at the 1995 Conference noted that the: "Conference condemns the British Government's systematic and blatant violation of international law on refugees and asylum seekers ... ."[29]

Domestic concerns have also weighed heavily, as many black workers fear that some of the restrictionist measures heighten racism and discrimination at home in the world of work and beyond. This was particularly clear with regard to the introduction of employer sanctions in 1996, when a motion approved at the Black Workers Conference noted that the:

> Conference rejects and deplores the provisions of the Asylum and Immigration Bill which place a duty on the employer to check the immigration status of job applicants ... . Conference believes that this bill will have disastrous consequences for both racial harmony and for the employment opportunities of ethnic minority groups in this country. We believe that this will be prejudicial to all ethnic minorities seeking employment who will be seen by employers as possible illegal immigrants.[30]

Similar criticisms were reiterated the following year. The subject of employer sanctions placed the Black Workers Conference in coalition with business, as suggested by a motion approved at the 1997

Conference noting that the government's plans were dismissed by business organizations, among others, and that "the Federation of Small Business has warned of race discrimination and The Economist maintains the Government deserved contempt."[31]

The TUC Black Workers Conference has looked beyond British borders in its fight against racism and restrictionism, and it has devoted time to considering the implications of the developments in the European Union for black people in general. A substantial number of resolutions condemning racism and restrictionism in the European Union were approved at the annual conferences. Throughout the 1990s members of the Black Workers Conference within the TUC actively sought to incorporate legislation to uphold non-discrimination on grounds of race into European Union law. These concerns were seriously taken up by the TUC, which actively pushed for the adoption of EU legislation to guarantee equal opportunities and equal treatment for EU and third-country nationals in a variety of EU forums throughout the 1990s.

UNISON

The union that most actively opposed restrictionist immigration measures was UNISON, which emerged as the largest union in the UK when it formed out of a merger of three unions in 1993.[32] UNISON includes over 1.3 million members, who work in public services, or for private contractors providing public services and utilities. The majority of its members are women, who work in areas such as local government, the National Health Service, higher education, and the electricity, gas, and water industries.

UNISON's opposition to the restrictionist measures introduced in the 1990s in part reflected an internationalization of union concerns. With regard to interests, some union members or potential members with transnational relations had an interest in maintaining openings for family reunification. This concern was noted in a guide on immigration published by UNISON that, among other things, advocated measures to facilitate family reunification in accordance with international conventions, and noted that: "This is a fundamental issue for many Black trade union members and their families. Much misery and anguish is caused to families kept separated by racially discriminatory immigration controls."[33] Likewise, a motion submitted to the 1990 TUC Convention by NALGO (one of the unions that later merged to become UNISON) noted that: "Successive British Governments have introduced legislation which has been to the detriment of black people, resulting in divided families, dependants being separated, deportations ... "[34]

Internationalization also spilt over into the ideological realm. Union statements and resolutions often pointed to a concern for the rights of those applying for asylum, and for the rights of family reunion, and often urged respect for international human rights conventions. For example, the UNISON guide on immigration advocated drawing up a new act that: "... recognise[s] the rights to human rights, dignity and family life, enshrined in the European Convention on Human Rights and other international conventions to which the United Kingdom is signatory."[35]

The union's opposition to restrictionism also stemmed from domestic considerations—a concern that restrictionist measures increase racism and discrimination against black British people. This concern was particularly strong with regard to the introduction of employer sanctions in 1996. The union actively campaigned to prevent passage of the bill, and wrote to Members of Parliament urging them to vote against the bill in July 1996.[36] UNISON then firmly condemned the new measures when they were enacted, and it approved, subject to amendments, a motion criticizing sanctions that was submitted to the union's 1997 Convention by its National Black Member's Committee. The motion noted that the: "Conference reaffirms its commitment to campaigning against the provisions of the Asylum and Immigration Act ... [which] in conjunction with changes in social security legislation represents a wide attack on all black people in Britain."

However, those sentences urging a campaign for non-compliance with the law were eliminated from the final motion approved. Likewise a more radical sentence urging a campaign for the Labour Party to repeal all legislation since 1968 on immigration and asylum was deleted in the final version and replaced with a commitment to "consult with the National Black Members Committee to develop a framework within UNISON for reviewing immigration legislation since 1968 ...."[37] A similar result emerged at UNISON'S Conference in 1998.

The TUC

The TUC, like the AFL-CIO, showed some protectionism when it came to high-skilled migrant workers, most of whom entered with work permits to the United Kingdom from such countries as the United States and Japan. Some TUC unions representing high-skilled workers, such as entertainers, musicians, athletes, and ethnic chefs, did apparently at times call for protection against those entering with work permits. However, TUC resolutions and statements in the 1990s did not mention the subject, with the exception of one resolution that was quietly approved at the convention in 2000, when the government was simplifying procedures for obtaining work permits. The resolution, submitted by British Actors Equity Association, urged the government to restore the previously long-standing consultative arrangements with relevant trade unions covering the granting of work permits to enable non-EU nationals to work in the United Kingdom. It noted that consultation had enabled them to "maximise employment opportunities for their own members."[38]

With regard to other immigration policy issues, the preferences of those components of organized labor that opposed restrictionism (the Black Workers Conference and UNISON) were in large part incorporated into the TUC's position in the 1990s, at a time when it sought to recruit new union members, particularly non-whites and women. In the year 2000, 34 percent of Afro-Caribbean employees were unionized, which exceeded the average of about 30 percent for all workers in Britain. Pakistani and Bangladeshi rates of unionization rose from 16 percent in 1997 to 20 percent in 1998 to 22 percent in 2000.[39]

While the TUC became more open to the positions of the more progressive forces, some of the latter's more radical proposals were put aside by the TUC's leadership, apparently so as to avoid whitelash among some existing TUC members.[40] For example, a motion submitted by NALGO to the TUC convention in 1990 included some proposals that went too far in the direction of open borders for the TUC's leadership to accept, and the TUC responded with a compromise position.[41]

The TUC maintained a silent position on the subject of amnesty in policy resolutions and statements in the 1990s. It did not officially support amnesty, and the subject was likewise not an issue on the political agenda of British immigration politics. Nonetheless, the rare unofficial statements by TUC officials that did appear on the subject of amnesty were favorable. For example, a TUC General Council representative, speaking at a European Trade Union Confederation meeting, said that the question of an amnesty for unauthorized workers should be considered positively.[42]

The TUC very actively opposed the employer sanctions legislation introduced in the Immigration and Asylum Act of 1996. The confederation's campaign began when the measure was first proposed and under consideration in Parliament in 1995. At that stage TUC representatives lobbied Members of Parliament and spoke at a range of public meetings and rallies in opposition to the bill, and it supported two national demonstrations against the bill.[43] The TUC also approved a conference motion in 1995, submitted by UNISON, opposing the bill's proposals for new internal immigration controls, including checks on immigration status by service providers, on the grounds that they would increase discrimination and turn public sector workers into immigration officers.[44]

The campaign against the Bill of 1995 brought the TUC into an explicit alliance with business organizations. The TUC and a range of business organizations co-signed a joint letter opposing employer sanctions that was published in *The Times,* a major British newspaper. The letter was signed by the TUC, along with the Association of British Chambers of Commerce, the Federation of Small Businesses, the Institute of Directors, the Institute of Management, and the Institute of Personnel and Development. The co-authored letter noted that:

> We are dismayed that the Home Secretary is persisting in his proposal to place criminal penalties on employers who hire illegal immigrants. Immigration policing in the workplace is not the job of employers.
> Checking immigration status is not straightforward ...
> As well as placing an unjustifiable burden on employers, the proposal threatens to damage race relations. There would be every incentive not to hire black staff or people with foreign sounding names; and to concentrate checks on ethnic minority employees.[45]

The TUC then produced a paper the following month, in December 1995, entitled "Forty New Burdens on Business: Employers and the Asylum and Immigration Act." The paper pointed to numerous problems that the Act would pose for business due to the difficulties of ascertaining who has the right to work, and noted that:

> The complexity of the workplace checks, and the threat of penalties, will inevitably deter employers from employing black and ethnic minority citizens born, bred and settled in this country. Even those with foreign sounding names will find that they face discrimination.[46]

The TUC continued its opposition to employer sanctions after the measure was enacted by the Conservative government in the Immigration and Asylum Act of 1996, and it approved a convention resolution in 1996 that firmly denounced the Act and stressed the discriminatory consequences of the law for black British workers and for those with foreign sounding names. When the Labour government entered office and failed to repeal the employer sanctions legislation in the late 1990s, it likewise became the target of TUC criticism.[47]

The TUC likewise criticized a range of other restrictionist measures that were introduced in the 1990s, first by the Conservative governments and then by the Labour government. Conference resolutions point to the same concerns as those mentioned in the case of UNISON and the Black Workers Conference: a concern that these measures increase racism at home, and undermine the human rights of those seeking family reunion and asylum. The human rights of "economic" migrants were also stressed by some of the speakers at the TUC Convention in 2000. They pointed to the example of their parents, who had come to Britain to improve their standard of living. As noted by one speaker:

> I am an economic migrant. My mother did not come here because of the lovely weather, she came here to improve the standard of living .... Even if it is about economics, human beings have the right to seek improvements. There is nothing wrong with being an economic migrant.[48]

At the same convention of 2000 the guidebook to the conference devoted one of its very few articles on general issues to the subject of Migration and Asylum. The article pointed to the benefits that host countries derive from immigrants and noted that: "Unions worldwide are taking up the challenges presented by the latest wave of migration ...."[49]

Public Policy Relevance

Immigration policy debates have always posed dilemmas for unions, and this was one subject (along with war and colonialism) that brought out deep divisions in the Second International in the early twentieth century. At that time the mainstream of labor movements in countries experiencing immigration for the most part adopted a nationalist response. Deepening internationalization in the global (or regional EU) arena in the late twentieth century presented new challenges for unions on immigration policy, and contributed to their change in coalitions.

Unions have traditionally been important actors in the politics of immigration, and there is a need to give serious attention to this subject today.

The successful incorporation and upward mobility of first and second generation Eastern and Southern European immigrants of the early twentieth century was in part attributable to the organizing wave of the mid-1930s in both France and the United States, two countries with advanced economies that experienced substantial immigration in the early twentieth century. The pre-existing reluctance of the mainstream labor movements to organize immigrants was overcome in the mid-1930s. This unionization provided the immigrants and their children with a crucial means to move up into the economic mainstream. The new union members simultaneously revitalized the labor movements in both countries.

Successful organizing of immigrants and their children as we enter the new millennium generates certain pressures for unions to refrain from the restrictionist coalition and to join the liberal coalition in immigration policy debates.

Notes

Chapter 1

1. Earlier versions of this argument were presented in Leah Haus, "Openings in the Wall: Transnational Migrants, Labor Unions, and U.S. Immigration Policy," *International Organization* 49, 2 (Spring 1995): 285–313; and Leah Haus, "Labor Unions and Immigration Policy in France," *International Migration Review* 33, 3 (Fall 1999): 683–716.

2. Lewis L. Lorwin, *Labor and Internationalism* (New York: The Macmillan Company, 1929), pp. 38–39, and 88–89.

3. Scholarship that reflects the conventional wisdom includes, for example, Richard Rosecrance, *The Rise of the Virtual State: Wealth and Power in the Coming Century* (New York: Basic Books, 1999), p. 59; and Aristide R. Zolberg, "The Main Gate and the Back Door: The Politics of American Immigration Policy, 1950–1976" manuscript, Council of Foreign Relations, New York, 1978; Aristide R. Zolberg, "Contemporary Transnational Migrations in Historical Perspective: Patterns and Dilemmas" in Mary M. Kritz, ed., *U.S. Immigration and Refugee Policy* (Lexington, MA: Lexington Books, 1983); and Aristide R. Zolberg, "Reforming the Back Door: The Immigration Reform and Control Act in Historical Perspective" in Virginia Yans-McLaughlin, ed., *Immigration Reconsidered* (New York: Oxford University Press, 1990).

4. AFL, *Report of the Proceedings of the Forty-First Annual Convention, 1921*, pp. 107–108.

5. AFL, *Report of the Proceedings of the Forty-Forth Annual Convention, 1924*, p. 67.

6. Immigration Committee, LA County Federation of Labor, AFL-CIO, "The Impact of the Immigration Reform and Control Act on Organized Labor in Los Angeles" in U.S. Congress, House, *Hearings on Employer Sanctions*, 103rd Congress, 1st sess., 16 June 1993, p. 433.

7. Jean Bellanger, "Implication du Syndicat dans une Prospective de Mouvements Migratoires" in *Colloque International: Du Travail Pour Tous, Partout Dans Le Monde* (Paris: CGT, 1994).

8. For example Saskia Sassen, *Losing Control? Sovereignty in an Age of Globalization* (New York: Columbia University Press, 1996); and Douglas S.

Massey et al, *Worlds in Motion: Understanding International Migration at the End of the Millennium* (Oxford: Clarendon Press, 1998). These approaches are opposed by Gary P. Freeman, "Can Liberal States Control Unwanted Migration?" *The Annals of the American Academy of Political Science* 534 (July 1994): 17–30.

9. On the impact of changing norms on immigration policy see Peter Schuck, "The Transformation of Immigration Law," *Columbia Law Review* 84, 1 (1984): 1–90; and James Hollifield, *Immigrants, Markets and States: The Political Economy of Postwar Europe* (Cambridge, MA: Harvard University Press, 1992). On the role of changing norms at the global level of analysis on immigrant policy see Yasemin Nuhoglu Soysal, *The Limits of Citizenship: Migrants and Postnational Membership in Europe* (Chicago: University of Chicago Press, 1994); and David Jacobson, *Rights Across Borders: Immigration and the Decline of Citizenship* (Baltimore: Johns Hopkins University Press, 1996).

10. Joseph Carens, "Membership and Morality: Admission to Citizenship in Liberal Democratic States" in William R. Brubaker, ed., *Immigration and the Politics of Citizenship in Europe and North America* (Lanham, MD: University Press of America, 1989).

11. For an example of different views on this debate, see the contributions to Suzanne Berger and Ronald Dore, eds., *National Diversity and Global Capitalism* (Ithaca, NY: Cornell University Press, 1996).

12. See Peter M. Lange, George Ross, and Maurizio Vannicelli, *Unions, Change and Crisis: French and Italian Union Strategy and the Political Economy* (London: George Allen and Unwin, 1982); Peter Gourevitch et al, *Unions and Economic Crisis: Britain, West Germany and Sweden* (London: George Allen and Unwin, 1984); and Andrew Martin, George Ross et al, *The Brave New World of European Labor: European Trade Unions at the Millennium* (New York: Berghahn Books, 1999).

13. Lange, Ross, and Vannicelli, *Unions, Change and Crisis*, p. 6.

14. George Ross, "The Perils of Politics: French Unions and the Crisis of the 1970s" in Lange, Ross, and Vannicelli, *Unions, Change and Crisis*, p. 34.

15. Michael Gordon and Lowell Turner argue that, to the extent that declining union density results from the globalization of capital, the AFL-CIO's domestic response (rejuvenation of the organizing agenda) "constitutes an important international effort." Michael E. Gordon and Lowell Turner, "Going Global" in Michael E. Gordon and Lowell Turner, eds., *Transnational Cooperation Among Labor Unions* (Ithaca, NY: ILR Press, 2000), p. 16.

16. Statement of John J. Sweeney, President, SEIU, in U.S. Congress, House, *Hearings on Employer Sanctions*, 103rd Congress, 1st sess., 16 June 1993, pp. 419–422.

17. SEIU, "Policy Resolutions Adopted by the Twentieth Quadrennial Convention of the SEIU, April 1992," n.d., p. 91.

18. CFDT Press Release, "Immigration," 24 December 1996.
19. For a more enlightening explanation of why these jobs exist in the New York garment industry, see Roger Waldinger, *Through the Eye of the Needle: Immigrants and Enterprise in New York's Garment Trades* (New York: New York University Press, 1986).
20. On the impact of the dynamics of the party system, including the dynamic of inter-party competition, on immigration politics see Martin Schain, "Immigration and Changes in the French Party System," *European Journal of Political Research* 16 (1988): 597–621.
21. Robert Soucy, *French Fascism: The First Wave, 1924–1933* (New Haven, CT: Yale University Press, 1986); and Robert Soucy, *French Fascism: The Second Wave, 1933–1939* (New Haven, CT: Yale University Press, 1995).

Chapter 2

1. For example see Peter A. Gourevitch, *Politics in Hard Times: Comparative Responses to International Economic Crises* (Ithaca, NY: Cornell University Press, 1986); Helen V. Milner, *Resisting Protectionism: Global Industries and the Politics of International Trade* (Princeton, NJ: Princeton University Press, 1988); Ronald Rogowski, *Commerce and Coalitions: How Trade Affects Domestic Political Alignments* (Princeton, NJ: Princeton University Press, 1989); and Robert O. Keohane and Helen V. Milner, eds., *Internationalization and Domestic Politics* (New York: Cambridge University Press, 1996).
   For a study of global social movements' (labor, environment, and women) reactions to, and changing relationship with, international economic institutions (IMF, World Bank, and WTO), see Robert O'Brien, Anne Marie Goetz, Jan Aart Scholte, and Marc Williams, *Contesting Global Governance: Multilateral Economic Institutions and Global Social Movements* (New York: Cambridge University Press, 2000).
2. For Milner, the answer lay in part with increasing international economic interdependence, which changed the trade policy preferences of business firms with international links. Milner, *Resisting Protectionism*.
3. Michael J. Piore, *Birds of Passage: Migrant Labor and Industrial Societies* (New York: Cambridge University Press, 1979).
4. Aristide R. Zolberg, "The Main Gate and the Back Door: The Politics of American Immigration Policy, 1950–1976" manuscript, Council of Foreign Relations, New York, 1978; Aristide R. Zolberg, "Contemporary Transnational Migrations in Historical Perspective: Patterns and Dilemmas" in Mary M. Kritz, ed., *U.S. Immigration and Refugee Policy* (Lexington, MA: Lexington Books, 1983); and Aristide R. Zolberg, "Reforming the Back Door: The Immigration Reform and Control Act in Historical Perspective" in Virginia Yans-McLaughlin, ed., *Immigration Reconsidered* (New York: Oxford University Press, 1990).

5. For a particularly thought-provoking book on this subject, see Susan Strange, *The Retreat of the State: The Diffusion of Power in the World Economy* (New York: Cambridge University Press, 1996).

6. Hans-Henrik Holm and Georg Sorensen, eds., *Whose World Order?: Uneven Globalization and the End of the Cold War* (Boulder, CO: Westview Press, 1995); and Barbara Stallings, ed., *Global Change, Regional Response: The New International Context of Development* (New York: Cambridge University Press, 1995).

7. Aristide R. Zolberg, "International Migrations in Political Perspective" in Mary M. Kritz, Charles B. Keely, and Silvano M. Tomasi, eds., *Global Trends in Migration* (New York: Center for Migration Studies, 1981); and Zolberg, "Contemporary Transnational Migrations in Historical Perspective."

8. Many people stay in Puerto Rico despite the absence of legal barriers to entrance to the United States.

9. Zolberg, "Contemporary Transnational Migrations in Historical Perspective."

10. Aristide R. Zolberg, "Bounded States in a Global Market: The Uses of International Labor Migrations" in Pierre Bourdieu and James S. Coleman, eds., *Social Theory for a Changing Society* (Boulder, CO: Westview Press, 1991), p. 320.

11. Zolberg, "Bounded States in a Global Market," p. 320.

12. Gary P. Freeman, "Can Liberal States Control Unwanted Migration?" *The Annals of the American Academy of Political Science* 534 (July 1994): 29.

13. Janice E. Thomson and Stephen D. Krasner, "Global Transactions and the Consolidation of Sovereignty" in Ernst-Otto Czempiel and James N. Rosenau, eds., *Global Changes and Theoretical Challenges* (Lexington, MA: Lexington Books 1989).

14. Gérard Noiriel, *Workers in French Society in the 19th and 20th Centuries* (New York: Berg Publishers, 1990), English Edition, p. 101.

15. Gérard Noiriel, *Longwy: Immigrés et Prolétaires 1880–1980* (Paris: Presses Universitaires de France, 1984), p. 70.

16. Mark Wyman, *Round-Trip to America: The Immigrants Return to Europe: 1880–1930* (Ithaca, NY: Cornell University Press, 1993); Suzanne Model, "Work and Family: Blacks and Immigrants from South and East Europe" in Yans-McLaughlin, ed., *Immigration Reconsidered;* Ewa Morawska, "The Sociology and Historiography of Immigration" in Yans-McLaughlin, ed., *Immigration Reconsidered.*

17. Victor R. Greene, *The Slavic Community on Strike: Immigrant Labor in Pennsylvania Anthracite* (Notre Dame, IN: University of Notre Dame Press, 1968), pp. 27–28.

18. Morawska, "The Sociology and Historiography of Immigration," p. 194.

19. Piore, *Birds of Passage;* and Wyman, *Round-Trip to America.*

20. Data on immigration is from U.S. Bureau of the Census, *Historical Statistics of the United States: Colonial Times to 1970* (Washington, D.C.: Bureau of the Census, 1975), part 1, pp. 105–107.

21. Data on migration flows is from Ralph Schor, *Histoire de l'Immigration en France* (Paris: Armand Colin, 1996), p. 58.
22. Saskia Sassen, *Losing Control? Sovereignty in an Age of Globalization* (New York: Columbia University Press, 1996), p. 72.
23. Wayne Cornelius, James Hollifield, and Philip Martin, eds., *Controlling Immigration: A Global Perspective* (Stanford, CA: Stanford University Press, 1994).
24. Sassen, *Losing Control?*, p. 86.
25. Saskia Sassen, *The Mobility of Labor and Capital: A Study in International Investment and Labor Flow* (Cambridge: Cambridge University Press, 1988).
26. Sassen, *Losing Control?*, p. 75.
27. Douglas S. Massey et al, *Worlds in Motion: Understanding International Migration at the End of the Millennium* (Oxford: Clarendon Press, 1998), p. 287.
28. Gary Cross, *Immigrant Workers In Industrial France* (Philadelphia: Temple University Press, 1983), p. 149.
29. Douglas S. Massey et al, *Worlds in Motion,* p. 289.
30. For arguments that foreign direct investment intensifies migration by diffusing Western consumption expectations and consolidating ideological links between core and periphery, see Alejandro Portes, "International Labor Migration and National Development" in Kritz, ed., *U.S. Immigration and Refugee Policy;* and Sassen, *The Mobility of Labor and Capital.*
31. Sarah J. Mahler, "Vested in Migration: Salvadorans Challenge Restrictionist Policies" in Max J. Castro, ed., *Free Markets, Open Societies, Closed Borders?: Trends in International Migration and Immigration Policy in the Americas* (Miami: North–South Center Press at the University of Miami, 1999), p. 168.
32. Sherri Grasmuck and Patricia R. Pessar, *Between Two Islands: Dominican International Migration* (Berkeley, CA: University of California Press, 1991), p. 91. On the transnationalization of networks that smuggle illegal immigrants from Fuzhou in China to New York's Chinatown, and on the revival of indentured servitude in New York's Chinatown, see Peter Kwong, *Forbidden Workers: Illegal Chinese Immigrants and American Labor* (New York: The New Press, 1997).
33. For this view see Abram Chayes and Anne-Marie Slaughter, "The ICC and the Future of the Global Legal System" in Sarah B. Sewall and Carl Kaysen, eds., *The United States and the International Criminal Court* (New York: Rowman & Littlefield Publishers, 2000).
34. For this view see Stephen D. Krasner, *Sovereignty: Organized Hypocrisy* (Princeton, NJ: Princeton University Press, 1999), chapter 4.
35. Krasner, *Sovereignty: Organized Hypocrisy,* pp. 106–108.
36. Jack Donnelly, *International Human Rights* (Boulder, CO: Westview Press, 1998).

37. Henry A. Kissinger, "The Pitfalls of Universal Jurisdiction," *Foreign Affairs* 80, 4 (July/August 2001): 86.
38. The Tribunal at Nuremberg rejected state sovereignty as a defense for crimes under international law, and noted that "The very essence of the Charter is that individuals have international duties which transcend the national obligations of obedience imposed by the individual State." Cited in Leila Nadya Sadat, "The Evolution of the ICC" in Sewall and Kaysen, eds., *The United States and the International Criminal Court.*
39. Sadat, "The Evolution of the ICC"; and Chayes and Slaughter, "The ICC and the Future of the Global Legal System," p. 241.
40. http://www.un.org/law/icc/statute/status [7/19/01].
41. Andrew Moravcsik, "The Origins of Human Rights Regimes: Democratic Delegation in Postwar Europe," *International Organization* 54, 2 (Spring 2000): 217–252.
42. Moravcsik, "The Origins of Human Rights Regimes," pp. 218–219.
43. David P. Forsythe, *Human Rights in International Relations* (New York: Cambridge University Press, 2000), pp. 113–114.
44. David Jacobson, *Rights Across Borders: Immigration and the Decline of Citizenship* (Baltimore, MD: Johns Hopkins University Press, 1996), pp. 87–88.
45. Jacobson, *Rights Across Borders,* p. 97.
46. Joseph Carens, "Membership and Morality: Admission to Citizenship in Liberal Democratic States" in William R. Brubaker, *Immigration and the Politics of Citizenship in Europe and North America* (Lanham, MD: University Press of America, 1989).
47. Peter Schuck, "The Transformation of Immigration Law," *Columbia Law Review* 84, 1 (1984): 1–90.
48. James Hollifield, *Immigrants, Markets and States: The Political Economy of Postwar Europe* (Cambridge, MA: Harvard University Press, 1992), p. 187.
49. Yasemin Nuhoglu Soysal, *The Limits of Citizenship: Migrants and Postnational Membership in Europe* (Chicago: University of Chicago Press, 1994), p. 42.
50. Soysal, *The Limits of Citizenship,* p. 4.
51. Soysal, *The Limits of Citizenship,* p. 3.
52. Jacobson, *Rights Across Borders,* p. 2.
53. This point draws on Martha Finnemore's critique of the sociological institutionalist literature. Martha Finnemore, "Norms, Culture, and World Politics: Insights From Sociology's Institutionalism," *International Organization* 50, 2 (Spring 1996): 339.
54. Anthony M. Messina, "The Not So Silent Revolution: Postwar Migration to Western Europe," *World Politics* 49, 1 (October 1996): 147.
55. Amy Gurowitz, "Mobilizing International Norms: Domestic Actors, Immigrants, and the Japanese State," *World Politics* 51, 3 (April 1999): 413–445.
56. Ruth L. Horowitz, *Political Ideologies of Organized Labor* (New Brunswick, NJ: Transaction Books, 1978), p. 18.

57. Chris Howell, *Regulating Labor* (Princeton, NJ: Princeton University Press, 1992), p. 45.

58. George Ross, "The Perils of Politics: French Unions and the Crisis of the 1970s" in Peter M. Lange, George Ross, and Maurizio Vannicelli, *Unions, Change and Crisis: French and Italian Union Strategy and the Political Economy* (London: George Allen and Unwin, 1982), p. 71.

59. Ross, "The Perils of Politics," p. 26.

60. Ross, "The Perils of Politics," p. 69.

61. The scholarship on organizing immigrants in the French case is less focused and less extensive than in the U.S. case. Nonetheless it exists, although at times as brief descriptions within studies that address various other issues pertaining to immigrant workers, such as, for example, Mark Miller, *Foreign Workers in Western Europe: An Emerging Political Force* (New York: Praeger Publishers, 1981), pp. 91–97, and 149–155.

62. Thomas Olszanksi, *Un Militant Syndicaliste Franco-Polonais: la vie errante de Thomas Olszanski 1886–1959* (Lille: Presses Universitaires de Lille, 1993); Noiriel, *Longwy.*

63. René Mouriaux and Catherine Wihtol de Wenden, "Syndicalisme Français et Islam" in Remy Leveau and Gilles Kepel, eds., *Les Musulmans Dans La Société Française* (Paris: Presses de la Fondation Nationale Des Sciences Politiques, 1988). Also see Jacques Barou, Moustapha Diop, and Subhi Toma, "Des Musulmans Dans l'Usine" in Renaud Sainsaulieu and Ahsène Zehraoui, eds., *Ouvriers Spécialisés à Billancourt* (Paris: L'Harmattan, 1995); and Martin Schain, "Ordinary Politics: Immigrants, Direct Action, and the Political Process in France," *French Politics and Society* 12, 2/3 (Spring-Summer 1994): 65–83.

64. CGT union official at Billancourt, cited in Barou et al, "Des Musulmans Dans l'Usine," pp. 150–151.

65. Maryse Tripier, *L'Immigration Dans La Classe Ouvrière en France* (Paris: L'Harmattan, 1990), pp. 190 and 205–206.

66. Greene, *The Slavic Community on Strike.*

67. Hector L. Delgado, *New Immigrants, Old Unions: Organizing Undocumented Workers in Los Angeles* (Philadelphia, PA: Temple University Press, 1993); and Ruth Milkman, ed., *Organizing Immigrants: The Challenge for Unions in Contemporary California* (Ithaca, NY: Cornell University Press, 2000).

68. Gwendolyn Mink, *Old Labor and New Immigrants in American Political Development: Union, Party, and State 1875–1920* (Ithaca, NY: Cornell University Press, 1986), p. 42.

69. Mink, *Old Labor and New Immigrants,* p. 51.

70. Kitty Calavita, "California's 'Employer Sanctions' Legislation: Now You See It, Now You Don't," *Politics and Society* 12, 2 (1983): 205–230; Kitty Calavita, *U.S. Immigration Law and the Control of Labor: 1820–1924* (New York: Academic Press, 1984); Kitty Calavita, *Inside the State: The Bracero Program, Immigration, and the I.N.S.* (New York: Routledge, 1992).

71. Gary Cross, *Immigrant Workers in Industrial France* (Philadelphia, PA: Temple University Press, 1983), pp. 143 and 149.
72. Cross, *Immigrant Workers,* p. 221.
73. Léon Gani, *Syndicats et Travailleurs Immigrés* (Paris: Les Editions Sociales, 1972), p. 77.
74. Gani, *Syndicats et Travailleurs Immigrés,* pp. 65 and 74.
75. Marius Apostolo, "Syndicalisme de Classe et Immigrés" in *Questions de l'Immigration et Syndicat* (Paris: CGT, 1981), p. 65.

Chapter 3

1. William Z. Foster, *History of the Three Internationals: World Socialist and Communist Movements from 1848 to the Present* (New York: Greenwood Press, 1968), pp. 207–208.
2. U.S. Bureau of the Census, *Historical Statistics of the United States, Colonial Times to 1970* (Washington, D.C.: Bureau of the Census, 1975), pp. 105–106. In 1880 there were 2,177 immigrants from Poland and 12,267 from other Central European countries. In 1910 there were 258,737 immigrants from Central Europe (there is no separate listing for Poland that year). In 1880 there were 295,171 immigrants from Britain, Ireland, Scandinavia, and Germany. This figure dropped to 178,346 in 1910.
3. Mark Wyman, *Round-Trip to America* (Ithaca, NY: Cornell University Press, 1993), chapter 2.
4. U.S. Bureau of the Census, *Historical Statistics of the United States, Colonial Times to 1970,* p. 110.
5. Wyman, *Round-Trip to America,* chapter 3.
6. Robert A. Divine, *American Immigration Policy, 1924–1952* (New York: De Capo Press, 1972), p. 22.
7. Divine, *American Immigration Policy,* p. 5.
8. John Higham, *Strangers in the Land,* rev. ed. (Westport, CT: Greenwood Press, 1981), p. 319. The system was subsequently replaced by a method of computing the size of the quotas according to the national composition of the total American population in 1920. This change had negligible impact on the size of the quotas for the new source countries of Southern and Eastern Europe; but it enlarged the size of the quota for Britain and reduced the size of the quotas for Germany and Ireland. Divine, *American Immigration Policy,* chapter 2.
9. Divine, *American Immigration Policy,* chapter 4.
10. Mark Reisler, *By the Sweat of their Brow: Mexican Immigrant Labor in the United States, 1900–1940* (Westport, CT: Greenwood Press, 1976), chapter 9.
11. AFL, *Report of the Proceedings of the Twenty-Ninth Annual Convention,* 1909, p. 316.

12. AFL, *Report of the Proceedings of the Twenty-Forth Annual Convention*, 1904, p. 172.

13. Report by President Gompers to the AFL Convention, December 1901, cited in *American Federationist*, June 1902, p. 276.

14. One member of the Commission, William S. Bennet (a Representative from New York) dissented from this recommendation. The Immigration Commission, *Abstracts of Reports of the Immigration Commission* (Washington, D.C.: U.S. Government Printing Office, 1911), Vol. 1, pp. 47–49.

15. Samuel Gompers, "Immigration—Up To Congress," *American Federationist*, January 1911, pp. 17–21.

16. The Immigration Commission, *Abstracts of Reports of the Immigration Commission*, p. 14.

17. Philip S. Foner, *History of the Labor Movement in the United States*, Vol. 3 (New York: International Publishers Co., 1964), pp. 262–263.

18. Gompers failed to gain majority support for a literacy test at the AFL Convention in 1896, but obtained approval at the AFL Convention in 1897 and thereafter.

19. AFL, *Report of the Proceedings of the Twenty-Second Annual Convention*, 1902, p. 21.

20. AFL, *Report of the Proceedings of the Twenty-Fifth Annual Convention*, 1905, p. 76; AFL, *Report of the Proceedings of the Twenty-Eighth Annual Convention*, 1908, p. 166; AFL, *Report of the Proceedings of the Twenty-Ninth Annual Convention*, 1909, p. 321.

21. AFL, *Report of the Proceedings of the Thirty-Third Annual Convention*, 1913, p. 52.

22. AFL, *Report of the Proceedings of the Thirty-Fifth Annual Convention*, 1915, p. 108.

23. AFL, *Report of the Proceedings of the Thirty-Third Annual Convention*, 1913, pp. 304–305.

24. John Higham, *Strangers in the Land*, p. 151; Kitty Calavita, *U.S. Immigration Law and the Control of Labor: 1820–1924* (New York: Academic Press, 1984), p. 108.

25. Higham, *Strangers in the Land*, p. 164.

26. Higham, *Strangers in the Land*, p. 142.

27. Higham, *Strangers in the Land*, p. 101.

28. Higham, *Strangers in the Land*, p. 102.

29. Statement of the AFL and Statement of the Immigration Restriction League in Report of the Immigration Commission, *Statements and Recommendations Submitted by Societies and Organizations Interested in the Subject of Immigration* (Washington, D.C.: U.S. Government Printing Office, 1911).

30. Higham, *Strangers in the Land*, p. 306.

31. AFL, *Report of the Proceedings of the Thirty-Ninth Annual Convention*, 1919, p. 367.

32. AFL, *Report of the Proceedings of the Fortieth Annual Convention*, 1920, p. 385.
33. AFL, *Report of the Proceedings of the Forty-First Annual Convention*, 1921, pp. 107–108.
34. AFL, *Report of the Proceedings of the Forty-First Annual Convention*, 1921, p. 307.
35. AFL, *Report of the Proceedings of the Forty-Third Annual Convention*, 1923, p. 40.
36. AFL, *Report of the Proceedings of the Forty-Forth Annual Convention*, 1924, p. 67.
37. AFL, *Report of the Proceedings of the Forty-Seventh Annual Convention*, 1927, p. 246.
38. AFL, *Report of the Proceedings of the Forty-Fifth Annual Convention*, 1925, p. 51; AFL, *Report of the Proceedings of the Forty-Seventh Annual Convention*, 1927, pp. 321–339; AFL, *Report of the Proceedings of the Forty-Eight Annual Convention*, 1928, pp. 205, and 257–259.
39. For example, a resolution approved at the AFL Convention in 1929 stated that: "Whereas wage earners not alone of the states bordering on Mexico, but some far removed, find the introduction of these workers contributing to increased unemployment and diminished standards of wages and hours of labor...." AFL, *Report of the Proceedings of the Forty-Ninth Annual Convention*, 1929, p. 304.
40. UMW, *United Mine Workers Journal*, April 1930.
41. AFL, *Report of the Proceedings of the Fiftieth Annual Convention*, 1930, p. 326.
42. AFL, *Report of the Proceedings of the Fifty-First Annual Convention*, 1931, p. 407.
    The same year, 1931, the California State Federation of Labor developed an unemployment relief program that included several proposals to deal with unemployment. The first item in the proposal was unemployment insurance. The second item in the proposal was a call for the total suspension of all immigration for at least two years. Particular emphasis was placed on the need to totally exclude all Mexican and Filipino laborers, who were considered to have "flooded California during the last few years and have seriously aggravated the present unemployment problem." *American Federationist*, March 1931, p. 345.
43. *American Federationist*, April 1931, p. 433.
44. AFL, *Report of the Proceedings of the Fifty-Third Annual Convention*, 1933, p. 103.
45. AFL, *Report of the Proceedings of the Fortieth Annual Convention*, 1920, p. 104.
46. AFL, *Report of the Proceedings of the Forty-Third Annual Convention*, 1923, p. 136.
47. AFL, *Report of the Proceedings of the Forty-Ninth Annual Convention*, 1929, p. 81.

48. AFL, *Report of the Proceedings of the Thirty-Ninth Annual Convention*, 1919, pp. 364–368.

49. AFL, *Report of the Proceedings of the Forty-Third Annual Convention*, 1923, p. 354; AFL, *Report of the Proceedings of the Forty-Sixth Annual Convention*, 1926, p. 250.

50. Foner, *History of the Labor Movement* Vol. 3, p. 259.

51. Cited in Foner, *History of the Labor Movement* Vol. 3, p. 276. Gompers gave a similar response to local efforts at organizing agricultural workers on the West Coast. The Los Angeles Labor Council decided to organize migratory agricultural workers in 1903, including Japanese and Mexican workers into the same union with white American workers, declaring "that the most effective method of protecting the American workingman and his standard of living is by universal organization of wage workers regardless of race or nationality." This stance was endorsed by a high-level official of the California Federation of Labor, who urged the AFL Executive Council to give support, noting that "This is one of the most important resolutions ever brought to the attention of the executive council.... It virtually breaks the ice on the question of forming the Orientals into unions and so keeping them from scabbing on white people, in place of not organizing Asiatics at present." Cited in Foner, *History of the Labor Movement* Vol. 3, p. 278. However, the AFL Executive Council refused to support the organizing effort.

52. Dubofsky, "Organized Labor and the Immigrant in New York City, 1900–1918," *Labor History* 2 (1961): 182–201.

53. Foner, *History of the Labor Movement* Vol. 3, p. 266.

54. Alexander Saxton, *The Indispensable Enemy: Labor and the Anti-Chinese Movement in California* (Berkeley: University of California Press, 1971), p. 265.

55. Saxton, *The Indispensable Enemy*, p. 242; and Michael Kazin, *Barons of Labor: The San Francisco Building Trades and Union Power in the Progressive Era* (Urbana, Chicago: University of Illinois Press, 1989).

56. Higham, *Strangers in the Land*, p. 174.

57. Kazin, *Barons of Labor*, pp. 163–170; Saxton, *The Indispensable Enemy*, p. 252; and Higham, *Strangers in the Land*, p. 166.

58. In his career Tveitmoe also served as national vice-president of the Cement Workers' Union, and third vice-president of the AFL Building Trades Department.

59. Saxton, *The Indispensable Enemy*, pp. 245 and 252; Kazin, *Barons of Labor*, p. 301.

60. Building Trades Department, AFL, *Report of the Proceedings of the Second Annual Convention*, 1909.

61. Building Trades Department, AFL, *Report of the Proceedings of the Fourteenth Annual Convention*, 1920.

62. United Brotherhood of Painters, Decorators and Paperhangers of America, *Official Journal*, September 1903, p. 607.

63. UBC, *Proceedings of the Fourteenth General Convention,* 1906.

64. The UBC's 1920 resolution stated that: "The Japanese menace on the Pacific Coast has assumed such dangerous proportions as to threaten the life of our trade, and the continued peace and prosperity of our country...." UBC, *Proceedings of the Twentieth General Convention,* 1920. A similar resolution was again approved at the UBC's Convention in 1924.

65. See for example, UBC, *The Carpenter,* April 1909, July 1909, September 1909.

66. UBC, *The Carpenter,* April 1909.

67. UBC, *The Carpenter,* September 1909.

68. UBC, *The Carpenter,* March 1916.

69. UBC, *The Carpenter,* August 1923.

70. UBC, *The Carpenter,* February 1924.

71. UMW, *United Mine Workers Journal,* August 1923. While the new immigrant workers increased the labor supply, one should not conclude that this led to displacement of workers already there. The new immigrants came at a time when there was an increase in the demand for mine workers due to a major expansion in coal production at the turn of the century. This expansion allowed a good many of the "old immigrant" workers to move out of the mines into more desirable jobs such as superintendents, mine inspectors, and coal operators. Priscilla Long, *Where the Sun Never Shines: A History of America's Bloody Coal Industry* (New York: Paragon House, 1989), pp. 127–129.

72. Higham, *Strangers in the Land,* p. 48.

73. Cited in Foner, *History of the Labor Movement* Vol. 3, p. 267.

74. John H. M. Laslett, "British Immigrant Colliers, and the Origins and Early Development of the UMWA, 1870–1912" in John H. M. Laslett, ed., *The United Mine Workers of America: A Model of Industrial Solidarity?* (University Park, PA: Pennsylvania State University Press, 1996), p. 49.

75. Union failures were attributed to immigrants acting as strikebreakers. At times mine worker leaders demanded that the new immigrants be restricted from the labor supply, and they supported the certification test that was introduced for anthracite miners in 1889 in the hope that it could be used as a means to block employment of the new immigrants. Victor Greene, *The Slavic Community on Strike* (Notre Dame, IN: University of Notre Dame Press, 1968), pp. 113–118 and 127.

76. At the District level the new immigrants were consistently reserved the position of vice-presidency. Greene, *The Slavic Community on Strike,* p. 182. However, it took longer for them to gain proportional representation in top positions at the District level, and no miner of East European background was elected to the International Executive Board until after World War I. Laslett, "British Immigrant Colliers," p. 48.

77. Greene, *The Slavic Community on Strike,* p. 162.

78. McAlister Coleman, *Men and Coal* (New York: Farrar and Rinehart, 1943), p. 55.

79. John H. M. Laslett, "Introduction" in Laslett, ed., *The United Mine Workers of America*, p. 2.
80. UMW, *United Mine Workers Journal*, 21 and 28 November 1901.
81. UMW, *United Mine Workers Journal*, 22 August 1901.
82. UMW, *United Mine Workers Journal*, 21 November 1901.
83. UMW, *United Mine Workers Journal*, 2 January 1902.
84. UMW, *United Mine Workers Journal*, 5 March 1903.
85. UMW, *United Mine Workers Journal*, 3 January 1907.
86. UMW, *United Mine Workers Journal*, 10 January 1907.
87. Long, *Where The Sun Never Shines*, p. 163.
88. UMW, *United Mine Workers Journal*, 22 September 1904, and 29 September 1904.
89. UMW, *United Mine Workers Journal*, 16 November 1905.
90. UMW, *United Mine Workers Journal*, 4 April 1907.
91. For example, UMW, *United Mine Workers Journal*, 4 May 1911, and 18 October 1917. A major exception to this general pattern was an article by John Mitchell pointing to the severe economic competition generated by European immigrants, particularly for those workers in the unskilled labor market. See UMW, *United Mine Workers Journal*, 28 September 1911.
92. UMW, *Proceedings of the Twenty-Ninth Convention*, 1924.
93. John H. M. Laslett, *Labor and the Left: A Study of Socialist and Radical Influences in the American Labor Movement, 1881–1924* (New York: Basic Books, 1970), p 223.
94. UMW, *United Mine Workers Journal*, February 1919.
95. UMW, *United Mine Workers Journal*, April 1919.
96. AFL, *Report of the Proceedings of the Forty-Seventh Annual Convention*, 1927, pp. 332–333; UMW, *United Mine Workers Journal*, May 1927; and UMW, *United Mine Workers Journal*, March 1930.

Chapter 4

1. Shirley Smith, Roger Kramer, and Audrey Singer, *Characteristics and Labor Market Behavior of the Legalized Population Five Years Following Legalization* (Washington, D.C.: U.S. Department of Labor, 1996), p. 10.
2. For example, 24.8 percent of immigrants to the United States in the 1985–87 period reported their occupations as managerial and professional (the same percentage as that for American workers in 1987). 16.2 percent were in technical, sales, and administrative support; 11.5 percent in precision production, craft, and repair; 22.5 percent in operators, fabricators, and laborers; 20.0 percent in service occupations; 4.9 percent in farming, forestry, and fishing. U.S. Department of Labor, *The Effects of Immigration on the U.S. Economy and Labor Market* (Washington, D.C.: U.S. Department of Labor, Bureau of International Labor Affairs, 1989), p. 27.

3. Joel Perlmann and Roger Waldinger, "Second Generation Decline? Children of Immigrants, Past and Present—A Reconsideration," *International Migration Review* 31, 4 (Winter 1997). For a comparison of the experience of immigrants in New York then and now see Nancy Foner, *From Ellis Island to JFK: New York's Two Great Waves of Immigration* (New Haven, CT: Yale University Press, 2000).

4. The U.S. Department of Labor's review of the INS data on applicants for the regular amnesty program (which excludes the special amnesty program for agricultural workers) showed that 30 percent reported working in the service sector, 15 percent had skilled craft occupations, and 34 percent were employed as operators, fabricators, and laborers. U.S. Department of Labor, *Employer Sanctions and U.S. Labor Markets: First Report* (Washington, D.C.: U.S. Department of Labor, 1991), p. 11. A U.S. General Accounting Office (GAO) study of employer compliance with IRCA identified five non-agricultural sectors that routinely employ illegal aliens, labeled as high alien industries: construction, food manufacturing, apparel and textiles, retail eating and drinking establishments, and services concerned with hotels and other lodging. U.S. Department of Labor, *Employer Sanctions and U.S. Labor Markets: Second Report* (Washington, D.C.: U.S. Department of Labor, 1991), p. 26. A study funded by the U.S. Department of Labor to assess the impact of employer sanctions on local labor markets focused on garments and apparel, construction, building maintenance and cleaning, hotels and restaurants, domestic service, meat packing, and poultry processing as sectors where undocumented immigrants make up a relatively large share of the labor. U.S. Department of Labor, *Impact of IRCA on the U.S. Labor Market and Economy* (Washington, D.C.: U.S. Department of Labor, 1991).

5. The exclusion of Chinese was ended during World War II for wartime geo-strategic reasons. China was granted an essentially meaningless quota of 105. Exclusion of immigrants from other Asian countries was ended in 1952, but these countries were likewise assigned extremely small quotas. Robert A. Divine, *American Immigration Policy, 1924–1952* (New York: Da Capo Press, 1972), p. 147.

6. With regard to legal migrants, a new measure incorporated into the 1996 immigration act stated that sponsors of immigrants through family reunion procedures were required to have a household income of more than 125 percent of the poverty level. In addition to the above legislation, policy pertaining to immigrants already residing legally in the United States was changed under the terms of the welfare reform law of 1996, which cut access to welfare benefits for permanent legal residents.

7. *Interpreter Releases,* 16 March 1998, pp. 364–365.

8. *Congressional Quarterly Almanac* 1996, pp. 5–9.

9. Statement of Walter J. Mason, member, National Legislative Committee, AFL, before the joint hearings of the Senate and House Judiciary Subcommittees on proposed amendments to the Immigration and Naturalization Laws, 9 April 1951.

10. Statement of Walter J. Mason, member, National Legislative Committee, AFL, before the Subcommittee on Immigration and Naturalization of the Senate Judiciary Committee on Immigration Legislation, 21 November 1955.

11. *Constitution of the Congress of Industrial Organizations* cited in May Chen and Kent Wong, "The Challenge of Diversity and Inclusion in the AFL-CIO" in Gregory Mantsios, ed., *A New Labor Movement for the New Century* (New York: Garland Publishing Inc. 1998), p. 216.

12. Statement of Victor G. Reuther on behalf of the CIO, before the Senate Judiciary Committee on Immigration and Naturalization, 21 November 1955.

13. Memorandum for the AFL-CIO Executive Committee on Immigration Policy, n.d., in AFL-CIO Department of Legislation, Legislative Reference Files, Box 27, Folder 17, George Meany Center Archives.

14. Cheng and Wong, "The Challenge of Diversity and Inclusion in the AFL-CIO," p. 217.

15. Interviews in Washington, D.C., January 1993 and June 1993.

16. Interviews in Washington, D.C., January 1993, and in New York, November 1993; and prepared statement of Thomas Donahue, Secretary-Treasurer, AFL-CIO in U.S. Congress, House, *Hearings on Immigration Act of 1989*, 101st Congress, 1st sess., 7 March 1990, pp. 435–436.

17. AFL-CIO "Policy Resolutions Adopted October 1993 by the AFL-CIO Convention," p. 14.

18. Interviews in Washington, D.C., January 1993, May 1993, and March 1994.

19. Interview with the deputy general counsel of the American Federation of Government Employees, Washington, D.C., 25 August 1994.

20. The public employees union, in later years, broadened its organizing horizons to the private sector and passed resolutions on expanding its coverage to the private sector and broadened its membership in the private sector (which is likely to include more undocumented immigrants than the public sector). At the same time the union passed a resolution in 1988 on the need to organize immigrants legalized through the amnesty program, and it adopted a clearly non-restrictionist, liberal resolution on immigration in 1994. See American Federation of State, County, and Municipal Employees, *Proceedings of the Twenty-Fourth International Convention, 1980; Proceedings of the Twenty-Fifth International Convention, 1982; Proceedings of the Twenty-Sixth International Convention, 1984; Proceedings of the Twenty-Seventh International Convention 1986; Proceedings of the Twenty-Eight International Convention 1988; Proceedings of the Twenty-Ninth International Convention 1990; Proceedings of the Thirtieth International Convention 1992; Proceedings of the Thirty-First International Convention 1994.*

21. Moreover, prior to employer sanctions, when undocumented workers were fired illegally for engaging in organizing activities, unions were able to file

a complaint with the National Labor Relations Board. A Supreme Court decision in 1984, prior to IRCA, upheld the Board's interpretation that undocumented workers were covered by the National Labor Relations Act, although the ruling on possible remedies was ambiguous. The decision, stating that undocumented aliens "plainly come within the broad statutory definition of 'employee,'" noted that since the employment relationship between an employer and an undocumented alien was "not illegal under the INA [Immigration and Nationality Act], there is no reason to conclude that application of the NLRA [National Labor Relations Act] to employment practices affecting such aliens would necessarily conflict with the terms of the INA." After the enactment of sanctions, the legal protection available to undocumented workers became more ambiguous because it became illegal for an employer to hire such workers. This increases undocumented workers' risks in joining unions and thus impedes organization. Excerpts of opinion are from *Interpreter Releases*, 20 July 1984, pp. 579–580; syllabus of the opinion prepared by the Supreme Court's Reporter of Decisions is from *Interpreter Releases*, 29 June 1984, pp. 512–514.

22. Interviews in Washington, D.C., December 1993, and in Los Angeles, January 1994.

23. Joe Hansen, International Secretary-Treasurer, UFCW, "UFCW Statement on Immigration—for AFL-CIO Sponsored Forum," 10 June 2000. http:www/ufcw.org/press/viewrelease.cfm [7/18/00].

24. Resolution on Immigration Policy approved at the First Convention of UNITE, 1999.

25. ILGWU, *Proceedings of the Thirty-Ninth Convention of the ILGWU, 1986,* p. 239.

26. On the new ILGWU policy toward undocumented workers that began to emerge in the late 1970s, see North American Congress on Latin America (NACLA), "Undocumented Immigrant Workers in New York City," *Report on the Americas* 13 (November–December 1979), p. 43; and Frank Del Olmo, "Illegal Aliens Target of Union Organizers," *Los Angeles Times,* 30 January 1975.

27. ILGWU, *General Executive Board Report and Record of Proceedings, Thirty-Seventh Convention, 1980,* p. 227.

28. Interview in New York, March 1993.

29. See testimony of Jay Mazur, Vice President, ILGWU, in SCIRP hearings, New York, 21 January 1980; statement of Phil Russo, Director of organization for the Western States Region, ILGWU, in SCIRP hearings, Los Angeles, 5 February 1980; and prepared statement of Frederick Siems, Executive Vice President, ILGWU, in U.S. Congress, House, *Hearings on Immigration Reform,* 97th Congress, 1st sess., 21 October 1981, pp. 362–364.

30. ILGWU, *General Executive Board Report, Fortieth Convention, 1989,* p. 55; ILGWU, *Report of the Proceedings of the Fortieth Convention of the ILGWU, 1989,* p. 48.

31. See Russo, in SCIRP hearings; Mazur, in SCIRP hearings; Siems in U.S. Congress, *Hearings on Immigration Reform;* and interviews in New York, March 1993, and in Los Angeles, January 1994.

32. ILGWU, *Proceedings of the Thirty-Ninth Convention of the ILGWU, 1986,* p. 193.

33. Prepared statement of Muzaffar Chishti, Director, Immigration Project, ILGWU, in U.S. Congress, House, *Hearings on IRCA Anti-Discrimination Amendments Act of 1990,* 101st Congress, 2nd sess., 27 June 1990, p. 438.

34. ILGWU, "Policy Statement Adopted by the Forty-First Convention," June 1992, p. 29.

35. Prepared statement of Charles A. Bowsher, Comptroller General of the United States, in U.S. Congress, Senate, *Hearings on the Implementation of the Immigration Reform and Control Act of 1986,* 101st Congress, 2nd sess., 30 March 1990, pp. 52–64; and Chishti in U.S. Congress, *Hearings on IRCA Anti-Discrimination Amendments Act of 1990,* pp. 434–443.

36. Statement of Russo, in SCIRP hearings; "Court Backs ILG Versus 'Illegal Alien' Shop Raids," *Justice,* January 1993, p. 7; and "Supreme Court Sustains INS on Factory Sweeps," *Interpreter Releases,* 20 April 1984, pp. 296–300.

37. Interview in New York, February 2000.

38. Statement of Joan Suarez, national representative and assistant manager of the San Antonio district, ACTWU, in SCIRP hearings, San Antonio, 17 December 1979, p. 2.

39. Transcript of SCIRP hearings, San Antonio, 17 December 1979, p. 139.

40. Henry Weinstein, "Unions Will Open Six Centers to Assist Aliens with Amnesty," *Los Angeles Times,* 2 May 1987; and ACTWU, *Labor Unity,* April 1989, p. 12.

41. See Suarez, in SCIRP hearings; ACTWU, *Report on the Convention Proceedings: Third Constitutional Convention, 1984,* p. 187; and interview in New York, July 1993.

42. ACTWU, *Report of the Convention Proceedings: Sixth Constitutional Convention, 1993,* pp. 76–77.

43. Michael J. Piore, "Unions: A Reorientation to Survive" in Clark Kerr and Paul D. Staudohar, eds., *Labor Economics and Industrial Relations* (Cambridge, MA: Harvard University Press, 1994).

44. SEIU, "Who We Are: The SEIU Census Report," n.d.

45. SEIU, "SEIU Membership At A Glance" http://www.seiu.org/about/leadway [7/5/00]

46. David Lopez and Cynthia Feliciano, "Who Does What? California's Emerging Plural Labor Force" in Ruth Milkman, ed., *Organizing Immigrants: The Challenge for Unions in Contemporary California* (Ithaca, NY: Cornell University Press, 2000), p. 39.

47. Piore, "Unions: A Reorientation to Survive."

48. See Piore, "Unions: A Reorientation to Survive."

49. http://www.seiu.org [8/21/01]

50. John Sweeney, "Organizing the New Workforce," *Service Employee* April/May 1986, p. 2.

51. Interview in Los Angeles, January 1994.

52. *Labor Education News,* Spring 1999.

53. For example, the resolution on immigration policy that was approved in 1984 noted that "We support the concept of employer sanctions only if they effectively deter unscrupulous employers from hiring undocumented workers." SEIU, *Proceedings of the Eighteenth Convention of the SEIU, 1984,* pp. 251–252.

54. SEIU, "Policy Resolutions Adopted by the Twentieth Quadrennial Convention of the SEIU, April 1992," n.d., pp. 90–93.

55. SEIU, *Proceedings of the Nineteenth Convention of the SEIU, 1988.*

56. SEIU, "Report of the Immigration Committee to the International Executive Board," 2 March 1992, p. 1.

57. SEIU, "Policy Resolutions Adopted by the Twentieth Quadrennial Convention of the SEIU, April 1992," pp. 90–93.

58. Statement of John J. Sweeney, President, SEIU, in U.S. Congress, House, *Hearings on Employer Sanctions,* 103rd Congress, 1st sess., 16 June 1993, pp. 419–422.

59. Interviews in Washington, D.C., May 1993, and in Los Angeles, January 1994; and SEIU, "Report of the Immigration Committee to the International Executive Board," March 2, 1992.

60. SEIU, "Policy Resolutions Adopted by the Twentieth Quadrennial Convention of the SEIU, April 1992," p. 92.

61. Sweeney in U.S. Congress, *Hearings on Employer Sanctions.*

62. SEIU, "Policy Resolutions Adopted by the Twentieth Quadrennial Convention of the SEIU, April 1992," p. 91.

63. Membership had fallen from about 5,000 in 1978 to about 1,800 in 1985 and there was growing competition from non-union contractors for a variety of reasons. In conjunction with this declining membership, non-union contractors hired immigrant workers. Immigrants (primarily from Mexico, El Salvador, and Guatemala) increased their share of the labor force among janitors in LA from 29 percent in 1980 to 61 percent in 1990, bringing the level to a similar level as that of New York City, where immigrants comprised 60 percent of the building service labor force (and where, unlike Los Angeles, union density remained strong throughout the 1980s and after; and wages remained considerably higher than in LA). See R. Waldinger, C. Erikson, R. Milkman, D. Mitchell, A. Valenzuela, K. Wong, and M. Zeitlin, "Helots No More: a case study of the Justice for Janitors Campaign in Los Angeles" in Kate Bronfenbrenner et al, eds., *Organizing to Win* (Ithaca, NY: Cornell University Press, 1998).

64. Interviews in Los Angeles, January 1994; "New Dimensions in Unionism," *Union* May/June 1988, p. 10; and U.S. Department of Labor, *Impact of IRCA on the U.S. Labor Market and Economy,* p. 114.

65. SEIU, "Report of the Immigration Committee to the International Executive Board," 2 March 1992, p. 4.

66. Interview in Los Angeles, January 1994; and Immigration Committee, LA County Federation of Labor, AFL-CIO, "The Impact of the Immigration Reform and Control Act on Organized Labor in Los Angeles" in U.S. Congress, House, *Hearings on Employer Sanctions,* 103rd Congress, 1st sess., 16 June 1994, p. 439.

67. Interviews in Washington, D.C., December 1999, and in New York, February 2000.

68. Interviews in Washington, D.C., December 1999.

69. Steven Greenhouse, "In U.S. Unions, Mexico Finds Unlikely Ally on Immigration," *New York Times,* 19 July 2001.

70. Interviews in Los Angeles, January 1994, and in Washington, D.C., December 1999; and resolution on "U.S. Immigration Policy and Programs" adopted by the 1996 SEIU Convention.

71. Lopez and Feliciano, "Who Does What?" p. 37.

72. Frank Bardacke, "Decline and Fall of the U.F.W.: Cesar's Ghost," *Nation* 26 July/2 August 1993, p. 132.

73. See J. Craig Jenkins, *The Politics of Insurgency: The Farm Worker Movement in the 1960s* (New York: Columbia University Press, 1985), p. 200; and Kitty Calavita, "California's 'Employer Sanctions' Legislation: Now You See It, Now You Don't," *Politics and Society* 12, 2 (1983): 205–230.

74. Prepared statement of the UFW on the subject of amnesty, in U.S. Congress, House, *Hearings on Immigration Reform,* 97th Congress, 1st sess., 14 October 1981, pp. 70–71.

75. See "Preliminary Injunction Denied the UFW," *Interpreter Releases,* 26 September 1988, p. 986; and "1.1 Million Apply for SAW Amnesty" *Interpreter Releases,* 5 December 1988, p. 1,256.

76. Steven Greenhouse, "In U.S. Unions, Mexico Finds Unlikely Ally on Immigration."

77. "Illegal Alien Curbs: House Action Stalled," *Congressional Quarterly Weekly Report,* 20 March 1976, p. 641.

78. The UFW representative at congressional hearings noted that it "concur[s] with the AFL-CIO's position that imposing sanctions on employers who hire illegal aliens would be a good vehicle for controlling the hiring of illegal aliens if the proposed legislation could be effectively enforced." Testimony of Stephanie Bower, coordinator, Legislative Department, UFW, in U.S. Congress, Senate, *Hearings on the Knowing Employment of Illegal Immigrants,* 97th Congress, 1st sess., 30 September 1981, p. 78.

79. Commission on Agricultural Workers, *Report of the Commission on Agricultural Workers* (Washington, D.C.: U.S. Government Printing Office, 1993), pp. 147–153.

80. Interviews in Washington, D.C., July 1992 and June 1993, in New York, March 1993, and in Los Angeles, January 1994. See also Building and Construction Trades Department, AFL-CIO, *Report of the Proceedings of the*

Sixty-Second Convention, 1983, pp. 378–382; Building and Construction Trades Department, AFL-CIO, *Report of the Proceedings of the Sixty-Third Convention, 1985*, pp. 381–390; and statement of Gilbert Kissling, Vice-President, Texas AFL-CIO, in SCIRP hearings, San Antonio, Texas, 17 December 1979.

81. IUBAC, *Proceedings of the Convention of the International Union of Bricklayers and Allied Craftsmen, September 1985*, pp. 178–180, 267–271.

82. UBC, *Proceedings of the Thirty-Fifth General Convention of the United Brotherhood of Carpenters and Joiners of America, October 1986*, pp. 285–86.

83. Building and Construction Trades Department, AFL-CIO, *Report of Proceedings of the Sixty-Second Convention, 1983*.

84. Building and Construction Trades Department, AFL-CIO, *Report of Proceedings of the Sixty-Third Convention, 1985*.

85. Interviews in Washington, D.C., June 1993, and in Los Angeles, January 1994.

86. Ruth Milkman and Kent Wong, "Organizing the Wicked City: The 1992 Southern California Drywall Strike" in Milkman, ed., *Organizing Immigrants*, p. 174.

87. David Lopez and Cynthia Feliciano, "Who Does What?" p. 37.

88. Milkman and Wong "Organizing the Wicked City," pp. 177–178.

89. Milkman and Wong "Organizing the Wicked City" pp. 173–174. The union membership rate was actually over 100 percent of the workforce in the 1950s and 1960s as some union members were self-employed, or employed in other sectors, or unemployed.

90. UBC, *The Carpenter*, June 1987, p. 11.

91. UBC, *The Carpenter*, June 1987, p. 11.

92. UBC, *The Carpenter*, July/August 1992 and November/December 1992; and Milkman and Wong, "Organizing the Wicked City." Since 1992 union density among residential drywallers has again declined.

93. UBC, *The Carpenter*, March/April 1993.

94. Letter from the Executive Secretary of the Los Angeles County Building and Construction Trades Council to the Members of the Los Angeles City Council, 21 October 1992.

95. Letter from the Executive Secretary of the Los Angeles County Building and Construction Trades Council to the Honorable Grace Napolitano, California State Assembly, 10 June 1993.

96. Letter to the Executive Secretary of the Los Angeles County Building and Construction Trades Council from Alan C. Nelson, 21 January 1993.

97. Interview in Los Angeles, March 2000.

98. Interview in Los Angeles, March 2000, and *Labor Education News* Fall 1999.

99. Interviews in Los Angeles, March 2000.

100. Andrew J. Biemiller, Director, Department of Legislation, AFL-CIO, in U.S. Congress, House, *Hearings on Illegal Aliens*, 94th Congress, 1st sess., 5 March 1975, p. 200.

101. Executive Board Minutes of the Building and Construction Trades Council of Greater New York, 11 March 1975, p. 3.

102. Nevertheless, the Building and Construction Trades Council apparently continued to firmly believe in maintaining employer sanctions at the end of the century, shortly before the shift in the AFL-CIO's position. At this level there was no perceived benefit to organizing illegal immigrants. The explanation given was that the union would be wasting its time as it would not refer the illegal immigrants to an employer for hiring, as the employer could not legally hire the worker due to sanctions. Interview, New York City, September 1999.

103. *Labor Notes* November 1999, pp. 1 and 14.

104. AFL-CIO, "Work in Progress," 24 July 2000.

105. Steven Greenhouse, "In U.S. Unions, Mexico Finds Unlikely Ally on Immigration."

106. AFL-CIO, *Policy Resolutions adopted November 1971 by the Ninth Constitutional Convention,* p. 31.

107. AFL-CIO, *Policy Resolutions adopted October 1975 by the Eleventh Constitutional Convention,* p. 27.

108. The quotation is from Biemiller, in U.S. Congress, *Hearings on Illegal Aliens,* p. 197.

109. Prepared statement of Lane Kirkland, President, AFL-CIO, in U.S. Congress, Senate, *Hearings on Immigration Reform and Control Act of 1982,* 97th Congress, 2nd sess., 20 April 1982, p. 415.

110. Statement by the AFL-CIO Executive Council on immigration, 24 February 1983, in U.S. Congress, Senate, *Hearings on Immigration Reform and Control Act,* 98th Congress, 1st sess., 7 March 1983, pp. 521–522.

111. Testimony of Thomas R. Donahue, Secretary-Treasurer, AFL-CIO, in U.S. Congress, House, *Hearings on Immigration Control and Legalization Amendments,* 99th Congress, 1st sess., 9 September 1985, p. 57.

112. AFL-CIO, *Proceedings of the Seventeenth Convention, 1987,* p. 460. Interviews in Washington, D.C. January 1993, and Los Angeles, January 1994.

113. See Jeff Stansbury, "L.A. Labor and the New Immigrants," *Labor Research Review* 8 (Spring 1989): 19–29; "Interview with CIWA and LIAP representatives" in June McMahon, Amy Finkel-Shimshon, and Miki Fujimoto, "Organizing Latino Workers in Southern California," manuscript, Los Angeles, Center for Labor Research and Education, University of California, Los Angeles, 28 June 1991, pp. 17–19; "New Immigration Rules Explored," *AFL-CIO News,* 24 January 1987, p. 2; "Immigrant Aid Spurs Organizing Gains," *AFL-CIO News,* 14 November 1987, p. 1; "Immigrants Turning to Labor for Aid," *AFL-CIO News,* 19 March 1988, p. 1; "Immigrants Hurdle Language Barrier in LA Labor's Study Courses," *AFL-CIO News,* 18 February 1989, pp. 1 and 13; and "Hispanics Respond to Intensified CIWA Effort," *AFL-CIO News,* 28 May 1990, p. 11.

114. AFL-CIO Executive Council Statement, 31 July 2001. http://www.aflcio.org/publ/estatements/jul2001/immigration [8/24/01].
115. Letter from Andrew J. Biemiller, Director, Department of Legislation, AFL-CIO to Peter W. Rodino, Chairman, House Committee on the Judiciary, 23 March 1973 in George Meany Labor Archives, AFL-CIO, Department of Legislation, Legislative Reference Files, Box 27, Folder 34.
116. The Industrial Union Department of the AFL-CIO passed a resolution in 1992 that called for the repeal of sanctions and noted that "Unfortunately, union organizers are running up against an immovable obstacle that is crippling the organizing which otherwise holds so much promise. That obstacle is the employer sanctions provisions of the 1986 Immigration Reform and Control Act." Industrial Union Department, AFL-CIO, *Adopted Resolutions: Nineteenth Constitutional Convention, 1992*, p. 110.
117. Interview in Washington, D.C., January 1993. The AFL-CIO did send a representative to congressional hearings on Legal Immigration Reform Proposals in 1995. The AFL-CIO representative's statement noted that "We support employer sanctions as the most effective way to deter employers from hiring illegal aliens." Prepared statement of Markley Roberts, Assistant Director, Economic Research, AFL-CIO in U.S. Congress, House, *Legal Immigration Reform Proposals*, 104th Congress, 1st sess., 17 May 1995, p. 115.
118. AFL-CIO, *Policy Resolutions Adopted October 1993 by the AFL-CIO Convention*, p. 14.
119. AFL-CIO Executive Council Statement, 10 August 1994, Washington, D.C.
120. *Labor Education News* Spring 1998. Delegates to the AFL-CIO Convention in Los Angeles in 1999 discussed a resolution entitled "Defending the Rights of Immigrant Workers and the Right to Organize." This resolution, which called for the repeal of employer sanctions and the enactment of a new amnesty program, was referred to the Executive Council, and a committee was established to discuss the AFL-CIO's policy on sanctions.
121. Immigration Committee, LA County Federation of Labor, AFL-CIO, "The Impact of the Immigration Reform and Control Act on Organized Labor in Los Angeles," p. 433.
122. AFL-CIO Executive Council Statement, 16 February 2000, New Orleans.
123. Federation For American Immigration Reform News Release, "FAIR Reacts" February 2000. http://www.fairus.org [5/13/2001]
124. John W. Wilhelm, President of HERE, cited in Nurith C. Aizenman, "INS Raids Follow Union Organizing," *Washington Post*, 6 December 1999.
125. Nurith C. Aizenman, "INS Raids Follow Union Organizing."
126. Interviews in Washington, D.C., December 1999, and in New York, February 2000, and Transcript of Discussion on Resolution 17, "Defending the Rights of Immigrant Workers and the Right to Organize," AFL-CIO Convention, October 1999, Los Angeles.

127. Transcript of Discussion on Resolution 17, "Defending the Rights of Immigrant Workers and the Right to Organize," AFL-CIO Convention, October 1999, Los Angeles.
128. Steven Greenhouse, "In U.S. Unions, Mexico Finds Unlikely Ally on Immigration."
129. Steven Greenhouse, "In U.S. Unions, Mexico Finds Unlikely Ally on Immigration."
130. Transcript of Discussion on Resolution 17, "Defending the Rights of Immigrant Workers and the Right to Organize," AFL-CIO Convention, October 1999, Los Angeles.
131. AFL-CIO, "Building Understanding, Creating Change, Defending the Rights of Immigrant Workers: Why People Move Between Countries," http://www.aflcio.org [8/24/01].
132. Resolution on Civil and Human Rights, approved at the AFL-CIO Convention, October 1999, Los Angeles.
133. AFL-CIO Executive Council Statement, 10 August 1994, Washington, D.C.
134. Organized unions such as the ILGWU (UNITE) and the SEIU likewise opposed this collaboration. Thus, for example, the ILGWU in the 1990s avoided filing complaints with the Federal Department of Labor against employers who were breaking laws on issues such as wage and hours. Instead, the union focused on filing complaints at the state level as the Memorandum of Understanding only applied at the federal level. The SEIU similarly opposed this collaborative effort between the INS and Department of Labor to enforce employer sanctions. As noted by John Sweeney, when President of the SEIU in testimony presented at Congressional Hearings in 1993: The "SEIU believes that the Department of Labor's Wage and Hour Division should not be involved in the enforcement of employer sanctions. Nothing in the 1986 IRCA requires DOL to enforce employer sanctions. Sanctions enforcement contradicts Wage and Hour's mission to protect low-wage workers against exploitation because workers fear reporting unscrupulous employers. Unions which play a key role in wage and hour enforcement are deterred from reporting illegal practices for fear of the harmful impact on their members.... Undocumented workers now view the wage and hour division as an extension of the INS and are afraid to file complaints or cooperate with investigators." Statement of Sweeney, U.S. Congress, *Hearings on Employer Sanctions*.
135. As written in the revised Memorandum: "Investigators of ESA's Wage and Hour Division (WH) and Office of Federal Contract Compliance Programs (OFCCP) shall conduct thorough inspections of employers' compliance with their employment eligibility verification obligations (Forms I-9) in conjunction with ESA's labor standards enforcement, *except* in any investigation based on a complaint alleging labor standards violations. (The limitation to conduct employment eligibility verifications

inspections only in "directed"—that is, non-complaint cases—is intended and will be implemented so as to avoid discouraging complaints from unauthorized workers who may be victims of labor standards violations by their employer)." Memorandum of Understanding Between the Immigration and Naturalization Service, Department of Justice and the Employment Standards Administration, Department of Labor, 23 November 1998, p. 10.

136. Interview in New York, February 2000.
137. Resolution on Civil and Human Rights, Approved at the AFL-CIO Convention, October 1999, Los Angeles.
138. AFL-CIO Executive Council Statement, 31 July 2001. http://www.aflcio.org/publ/estatements/jul2001/immigration [8/24/01].
139. Resolution on Civil and Human Rights, Approved at the AFL-CIO Convention, October 1999, Los Angeles.

Chapter 5

1. Georges Mauco, *Les Étrangers en France* (Paris: Armand Colin, 1932), p. 134.
2. Mauco, *Les Étrangers en France,* p. 38; and Ralph Schor, *Histoire de l'Immigration en France* (Paris: Armand Colin), pp. 14 and 58.
3. Gérard Noiriel, *Workers in French Society in the 19th and 20th Centuries* (New York: Berg Publishers, 1990), English Edition, p. 120.
4. Noiriel, *Workers in French Society,* p. 121.
5. Jean-Charles Bonnet, *Les Pouvoirs Publics Français et L'Immigration Dans l'Entre-Deux-Guerres* (Lyon: Centre D'Histoire Economique et Sociale de la Region Lyonnaise, 1976), p. 20.
6. Mauco, *Les Étrangers en France,* pp. 192–194.
7. Mauco, *Les Étrangers en France,* pp. 57 and 494.
8. Noiriel, *Workers in French Society,* p. 101.
9. Noiriel, *Workers in French Society,* pp. 121–122.
10. This duality in the labor market and the divergent interests and demands of French and immigrant workers was reflected by the different union confederations that represented the two groups of workers in Longwy. French workers were represented by the reformist CGT, which often refrained from strikes in the 1920s and pressed for issues such as more say in management. Immigrant workers were represented by the revolutionary CGTU, which focused on issues such as salary increases and often supported strikes. Gérard Noiriel, *Longwy: Immigrés et Prolétaires, 1880–1980,* (Paris: Presses Universitaires de France, 1984), pp. 245–263.
11. Once the immigration process was set in motion by these recruitment agents, the migration process at times became self-sustaining through chain migration, as people moved to reunite with family and friends. Thus in a specific region of France one would at times find immigrants who

originated from the same village or town in the country of origin. Italian migrants to the Longwy region in the North-East of France often continued to come from the same villages over the course of a number of years. Noiriel, *Longwy*, pp. 70 and 221. There were also people who moved to France for political reasons (for example, anti-fascists from Italy, and "white" Russians from the Soviet Union).

12. Bonnet, *Les Pouvoirs Publics Français*, pp. 121–124; Noiriel, *Longwy*, p. 171.

13. Bonnet, *Les Pouvoirs Publics Français*, p. 47.

14. Mauco, *Les Etrangers En France*, pp. 118–125; and Janine Ponty, *Polonais Méconnus: Histoire Des Travailleurs Immigrés En France Dans L'Entre-Deux-Guerres* (Paris: Publications de la Sorbonne, 1988), p. 77.

15. Mauco, *Les Etrangers En France*, p. 118.

16. Gary Cross, *Immigrant Workers in Industrial France: The Making of a New Laboring Class* (Philadelphia, PA: Temple University Press, 1983), p. 149.

17. Bonnet, *Les Pouvoirs Publics Français*, pp. 262–268 and 304.

18. Catherine Wihtol de Wenden, *Les Immigrés et la Politique: Cent Cinquante Ans D'Evolution* (Paris: Presses de la Fondation Nationale des Science Politiques, 1988), p. 55.

19. Noiriel, *Longwy*, pp. 267–268.

20. Mauco, *Les Etrangers en France*, p. 129.

21. Wihtol de Wenden, *Les Immigrés et la Politique*, p. 30.

22. Bonnet, *Les Pouvoirs Publics Français*, p. 134.

23. Tomas Hammer, "Introduction" in Tomas Hammer, ed., *European Immigration Policy* (New York: Cambridge University Press, 1985), p. 7.

24. Bonnet, *Les Pouvoirs Publics Français*, pp. 148–149 and 273–280.

25. Annie Kriegel, *Les Communistes Français* (Paris: Editions du Seuil, 1968).

26. Robert Wohl, *French Communism in the Making, 1914–1924* (Stanford, CA: Stanford University Press, 1966). It has been argued by Peter Stearns that the belief in revolutionary syndicalism was limited to the leadership level of the CGT, and did not reflect the views of the workers except perhaps in the Parisian building trades. See Peter Stearns, *Revolutionary Syndicalism and French Labor: A Cause Without Rebels* (New Brunswick, NJ: Rutgers University Press, 1971).

27. Kriegel, *Les Communistes Français*, pp. 101–103.

28. David J. Saposs, *The Labor Movement in Post-War France* (New York: Columbia University Press, 1931), p. 74.

29. CGT, *La Voix du Peuple* 1923, p. 128.

30. Saposs, *The Labor Movement in Post-War France*, p. 89.

31. CGT, *La Voix du Peuple* 1921, p. 173; 1923, p. 127; 1925, pp. 29 and 230; 1926, p. 127.

32. CGT, *La Voix du Peuple* 1925, p. 195.

33. Cross, *Immigrant Workers in Industrial France*, p. 143.

34. CGT, *Le Peuple*, 21 January 1927.

35. Cross, *Immigrant Workers in Industrial France*, pp. 149–152.

36. Note from the Ministry of the Interior, 21 January 1927 in the National Archives F/7/135 23.
37. CGT, *La Voix du Peuple* 1927, p. 275.
38. Ralph Schor, *L'Opinion Française et Les Etrangers En France 1919–1939* (Paris: Publication de la Sorbonne, 1985), p. 563.
39. Cross, *Immigrant Workers in Industrial France,* p. 189.
40. Cross, *Immigrant Workers in Industrial France,* p. 189; Schor, *Histoire de L'Immigration en France,* pp. 128–129.
41. On Coty and Solidarité Française see Robert Soucy, *French Fascism: The Second Wave, 1933–1939* (New Haven, CT: Yale University Press, 1995) chapter 3.
42. *L'Ami du Peuple,* 22 December 1931, cited in Schor *L'Opinion Française et Les Etrangers en France,* p. 592.
43. Schor, *L'Opinion Française et Les Etrangers en France,* pp. 593–594.
44. Léon Gani, *Syndicats et Travailleurs Immigrés* (Paris: Les Editions Sociales, 1972), pp. 17–18.
45. CGT, *La Voix du Peuple* 1926, pp. 538–539.
46. CGT, *La Voix du Peuple* 1925, pp. 4–5.
47. For a study of why people in Bobigny, and the Paris suburbs more generally, voted heavily and consistently for the French Communist Party in the inter-war years see Tyler Stovall, *The Rise of the Paris Red Belt* (Berkeley: University of California Press, 1990).
48. Jean Bellanger, "La Centenaire de la CGT: La Place de l'Immigration" (Paris: CGT, n.d.), pp. 26–29.
49. CGTU, *La Vie Ouvrière,* 27 January 1933.
50. Resolutions on foreign labor at the CGTU Congresses of 1931 and 1933, cited in Gani, *Syndicats et Travailleurs Immigrés,* p. 21.
51. Cited in Gani, *Syndicats et Travailleurs Immigrés,* p. 11.
52. Intervention by J. Racamond, 6th Congress of the CGTU, 1931. Cited in Gani, *Syndicats et Travailleurs Immigrés,* p. 21.
53. CGTU, *La Vie Ouvrière,* 4 March 1927.
54. Gani, *Syndicats et Travailleurs Immigrés,* p. 17.
55. Saposs, *The Labor Movement in Post-War France,* p. 139. By contrast, a significantly greater proportion of CGT members were government workers.
56. CGTU, *La Vie Ouvrière,* 3 December 1926; 4 March 1927; 19 December 1930; 6 November 1931; Cross, *Immigrant Workers in Industrial France,* pp. 181–182.
57. George Ross, *Workers and Communists in France* (Berkeley, CA: University of California Press, 1982), p. 10.
58. Commentary by Mylene Mihout in Thomas Olszanski, *Un Militant Syndicaliste Franco-Polonais: la vie errante de Thomas Olszanski 1886–1959* (Lille: Presses Universitaires de Lille, 1993), p. 350. The CGT also had a Department for Foreign Workers and published some pamphlets and papers in a foreign language such as Polish, but showed much less concern for such issues than the CGTU.

59. Ponty, *Polonais Méconnus,* p. 196.
60. Commentary by Mihout in Olszanski, *Un Militant Syndicaliste,* p. 352.
61. Olszanski's memoirs, translated from Polish into French by Mylene Mihout, are available in Olszanski, *Un Militant Syndicaliste.* Olszanski's activities are also discussed in Ponty, *Polonais Méconnus.*
62. Mihout's commentary in Olszanski, *Un Militant Syndicaliste,* p. 362; and Wihtol de Wenden, *Les Immigrés et la Politique,* p. 51.
63. Olszanski, *Un Militant Syndicaliste,* pp. 215 and 248; and Mihout's commentary in Olszanski, *Un Militant Syndicaliste,* p. 365.
64. Olszanski, *Un Militant Syndicaliste,* p. 266. David Saposs has also noted that immigrant workers carrying a Communist union card were liable for deportation. Saposs, *The Labor Movement in Post-War France,* p. 130.
65. Noiriel, *Longwy,* p. 243.
66. Mihout's commentary in Olszanski, *Un Militant Syndicaliste,* p. 367; Ponty, *Polonais Méconnus,* p. 204.
67. Wihtol de Wenden, *Les Immigrés et la Politique,* p. 64.
68. Noiriel, *Longwy,* pp. 234 and 244.
69. Olszanski, *Un Militant Syndicaliste,* p. 224.
70. Mihout's commentary in Olszanski, *Un Militant Syndicaliste,* p. 19.
71. Andre Vieuguet, *Français et Immigrés: Le Combat du P.C.F.* (Paris: Editions Sociales, 1975), p. 111.
72. Jean Bellanger, "Centenaire de la CGT: La Place de L'Immigration" (Paris: CGT, 1995, n.d.), p. 21.
73. Gani, *Syndicats et Travailleurs Immigrés,* p. 16.
74. Cited in Mihout's commentary in Olszanski, *Un Militant Syndicaliste,* p. 359.
75. Bellanger, "Centenaire de la CGT: La Place de l'Immigration," p. 23.
76. CGTU, *La Vie Ouvrière,* 12 September 1930.
77. CGTU, *La Vie Ouvrière,* for example, 11 January 1924; 29 August 1924; 4 January 1929; 19 December 1930.
78. Cross, *Immigrant Workers in Industrial France,* p. 160.
79. Albert Fau, *Maçons Au Pied Du Mur* (Paris: FNTC-CGT), CGTU, *La Vie Ouvrière,* 7 September 1923; and 7 December 1923; Stearns, *Revolutionary Syndicalism and French Labor,* pp. 12 and 16; Olszanski, *Un Militant Syndicaliste,* pp. 186–187.
80. *L'Ouvrier du Bâtiment,* May–June 1924, July–September 1924, August 1925, June 1926.
81. CGT, *Le Peuple,* 14 May 1924.
82. CGT, *La Voix du Peuple,* September–October 1925, p. 369.
83. *L'Ouvrier du Bâtiment,* September–October 1925, February 1926.
84. *L'Ouvrier du Bâtiment,* June 1926.
85. *L'Ouvrier du Bâtiment,* January–February 1927.
86. *Le Bâtiment Syndicaliste,* February 1931.
87. *Le Bâtiment Syndicaliste,* April 1931.
88. *Le Bâtiment Syndicaliste,* December 1933.

89. *Le Bâtiment Syndicaliste*, May–June 1933; December 1933.
90. CGTU, *La Vie Ouvrière*, 29 August 1924.
91. CGTU, *La Vie Ouvrière*, 3 October 1924; 14 November 1924.
92. Saposs, *The Labor Movement in Post-War France*, p. 123.
93. CGTU, *La Vie Ouvrière*, 11 December 1931; 17 June 1932.
94. Letter from Prefect of Rhône to the Ministry of the Interior, 30 March 1923, in National Archives F/7/13651; *L'Humanité*, 1 April 1923 in National Archives F/7/13651.
95. *L'Effort*, March 15 1927.
96. For example *L'Effort*, 15 July 1927; 15 August 1927; 15 December 1927; 1 January 1928; 15 January 1928.
97. *L'Effort*, 1 October 1929.
98. Fau, *Maçons Au Pied Du Mur*, pp. 108–109; and interviews with retired construction union officials in Lyon, June 1998.
99. Schor, *L'Opinion Française et Les Etrangers En France 1919–1939*, p. 559.
100. Schor, *Histoire de l'Immigration en France*, p. 121.
101. Schor, *Histoire de l'Immigration en France*, p. 121.
102. Schor, *Histoire de l'Immigration en France*, p. 123.
103. Wihtol de Wenden, *Les Immigrés et la Politique*, p. 53.
104. Bonnet, *Les Pouvoirs Publics Français*, pp. 74–75; 224–25; and 235.

Chapter 6

1. Institut National de la Statistique et des Etudes Economiques (INSEE), *Les Immigrés En France: Portrait Social* (Paris: INSEE, 1997), p. 17.
2. Italians, and then Spaniards, were the largest immigrant groups in France in the 1950s and 1960s. By the 1970s they were outnumbered by Algerians (800,000) and Portuguese (700,000). Other major immigrant groups in the 1970s were the Italians (580,000), Moroccans (220,000), and Tunisians (120,000). Catherine Wihtol de Wenden, *Les Immigrés et la Politique* (Paris: Presses de la Fondation Nationale des Sciences Politique, 1988), p. 157.
3. SOPEMI, *Trends in International Migration* (Paris: OECD, 1999), p. 138.
4. Wihtol de Wenden, *Les Immigrés et la Politique*, p. 301.
5. INSEE, *Les Immigrés En France: Portrait Social*, p. 17.
6. Mark J. Miller and Philip L. Martin, *Administering Foreign-Worker Programs* (Lexington, MA: D.C. Heath and Co., 1982), pp. 53–61; Ralph Schor, *Histoire de l'Immigration en France* (Paris: Armand Colin, 1996), p. 197. The precise details on these modes of recruitment were laid out in bilateral treaties between France and the source country. Algerians were exempted from going through these procedures until 1964 because there was free movement between Algeria and France.
7. Ralph Schor, *Histoire de l'Immigration en France*, p. 201.
8. Wihtol de Wenden, *Les Immigrés et la Politique*, p. 158.

9. The Secretary of State did consult with several leaders of businesses that were large employers of foreign labor. They approved the decision to suspend labor migration in 1974. Patrick Weil, *La France et Ses Etrangers* (Paris: Editions Calmann-Levy, 1991), p. 126.

10. Weil, *La France et Ses Etrangers*, p. 138.

11. Wihtol de Wenden, *Les Immigrés et La Politique;* and Weil, *La France et Ses Etrangers.*

12. Cited in Wihtol de Wenden, *Les Immigrés et La Politique,* p. 206.

13. FNCB-CFDT, "Rapport D'Activité," Nineteenth Federal Congress, 1978, p. 15.

14. The administration's attempt to gain passage of a law that would make it easy to refuse to renew permits did not gain approval at that time. Weil, *La France et Ses Etrangers.*

15. This law also included a section that was intended to protect the irregular immigrant workers. This part of the law stated that irregular immigrant workers had rights equal to regular workers on such issues as health and safety legislation, length of work, salaries, and the right to one month salary if the employer ended the employment relationship. However, this law appears to have been rarely used by unions to protect irregular workers. An article on the subject in 1996 noted that "the unions use this power very rarely, if ever." Fabienne Doroy, "Les Droits du Salarié Employé Illégalement" in GISTI *Plein Droit* 31 (April 1996), p. 34. Also see Danièle Loschak, "Les Nouveaux Textes Sur Les Travailleurs Immigrés," *Alpha Info,* November 1981.

16. The criteria for regularization in the 1997–98 program made regularization particularly difficult for unmarried immigrants, and for others who had problems obtaining documents that proved that they had lived in France in an undocumented status.

17. *Le Monde,* 3 July 1998, 4 July 1998, 5–6 July 1998, 22–23 August 1999.

18. Weil, *La France et Ses Etrangers,* pp. 144–148.

19. Cited Weil, *La France et Ses Etrangers,* p. 146.

20. The third labor confederation in the post-war years has been Force Ouvrière (FO), which covers the public sector and thus does not cover sectors where immigrants are concentrated. FO split from the CGT in 1948. It was anti-Communist and had an identity similar to American "business unionism." For a discussion of relations between FO and the National Front in France see Nicolas Sauger, "Force Ouvrière et le Front National," Working Paper no. 87, FNSP-CEVIPOF, Paris, 1997.

21. Léon Gani, *Syndicats et Travailleurs Immigrés* (Paris: Editions Sociales, 1972), p. 48. Gani suggests that the real reason for union opposition to immigration in the 1950s was a fear that it would weaken unions, p. 57.

22. Gani, *Syndicats et Travailleurs Immigrés,* p. 74.

23. M. Dufriche statement at the 34th Congress of the CGT, 1963, cited in Gani, *Syndicats et Travailleurs Immigrés,* p. 74.

24. Gani, *Syndicats et Travailleurs Immigrés,* p. 65.

25. For example, the report of the CGT's first National Conference on Immigrant Workers in 1963 noted that "With the massive and accelerated introduction of immigrant labor, the monopolies and the gaullist government expect to weaken the French labor movement. They want to form a reserve army of labor ... ." Report of the CGT's First National Conference of Immigrant Labor, March 1963, available in CGT, *Le Peuple* March 1963.

26. Marius Apostolo, "Syndicalisme de Classe et Immigrés" in *Questions de l'Immigration et Syndicat* (Paris: CGT, 1981), p. 65.

27. Report of the CGT's Fifth National Conference on Immigration, Paris, November 1980.

28. With regard to immigrants already in France (immigrant policy), the CGT reiterated French unions' longstanding call, going back to the early twentieth century, that immigrant workers be granted equal pay and equal rights as those accorded to French workers on all issues such as the right to be union officials and the right to social security benefits. For example, see the reports of the CGT's First National Conference on Immigrant Labor, March 1963 (available in CGT, *Le Peuple* March 1963); and the Second National Conference on Immigrant Labor, March 1969 (available in CGT, *Le Peuple* April 1969). Equality of treatment would simultaneously improve the situation of immigrant workers and block employers from being able to exploit immigrant workers to undercut wage rates and rights of French workers. Some rights were then extended to immigrants in the 1970s. For example, immigrant workers gained the legal right to become union officials. New laws in 1972 and 1975 permitted immigrants to be elected to works councils and to become union officials providing that they could express themselves in the French language, and providing that immigrants did not represent more than one third of officials in a union. Finally, union statements in the years of prosperity and productivity at that time often stated opposition to racism, and at times noted that immigrants worked in the least desirable jobs that French workers did not want and were thus not a cause of unemployment.

29. George Ross, *Workers and Communists in France* (Berkeley: University of California Press, 1982), p. 27.

30. CGT Statement, "La Déclaration Des 'Droits De L'Homme' a 50 ans" in CGT, *Le Peuple,* 23 December 1998, p. 77; for a collection of articles on the Universal Declaration of Human Rights see CGT, *Tribune de l'Immigration,* January 1999.

31. CFDT, *Le Monde Bouge: Les Hommes Aussi,* February 1996, pp. 6 and 10.

32. CFDT, *CFDT En Direct,* September 1997.

33. Gérard Chemouil, "Les Flux Migratoires" in CGT *Tribune de l'Immigration,* November 1997, p. 5.

34. For example, see "Pression Migratoire" in CGT, *Tribune de l'Immigration,* July 1998, p. 4.

35. Jean Bellanger, "Implication du Syndicat dans une Prospective de Mouvements Migratoires" in *Colloque International: Du Travail Pour Tous, Partout Dans Le Monde* (Paris: CGT, 1994).

36. Gérard Chemouil, "Syndicalisme et Immigration" in CGT, *Tribune de l'Immigration,* May 1996.

37. Interview with Didier Niel, Secretary of the CGT in *Tes Papiers! Questions d'Immigration* (Montreuil: CGT, 1997), pp. 49 and 53.

38. Jacques Trégaro, "Les Mouvements Migratoires Dans Le Monde" in CGT, *Tribune de l'Immigration,* November 1997, pp. 7–9.

39. Jean-Christophe Le Duigou, "Europe" in CGT, *Tribune de L'Immigration,* November 1997, p. 15.

40. CFDT, *Syndicalisme,* 10 April 1980, p. 5.

41. CFDT Press Release, "Immigration," 24 December 1996.

42. CGT, *Le Peuple,* 9 November 1995, pp. 61–62.

43. CGT, *Le Peuple,* 16 May 1996, p. 3.

44. CGT Statement, "Les Immigrés de Nouveau Mis en Cause" in CGT, *Le Peuple,* 9 November 1995, pp. 61–62.

45. José Pinto, "Regroupement Familial, Des Règles Assouplies" in CGT, *Tribune De L'Immigration,* August 1999, p. 25.

46. Note to the Prime Minister concerning immigrant workers in CGT, *Le Peuple,* 3 December 1987, pp. 12–13.

47. Gérard Chemouil, "Immigration et la CGT" in CGT, *Tribune de l'Immigration,* September–October 1998, p. 5.

48. CGT, *Courrier Confédéral,* 31 July 1991, p. 16.

49. CFDT, *Syndicalisme,* 14 April 1994, p. 7.

50. CGT, *Le Peuple,* 15 January 1997, pp. 57–58; 26 February 1997, pp. 54 and 57–58; 12 March 1997, p. 57.

51. CFDT, Executive Commission Statement, 7 November 1991.

52. L'UD CFDT de Paris, *Des Salariés Parisiens Sans Papiers* (Paris: Paris Commune Dossier, 1994), p. 108.

53. In an unusual display of differences with the Communist Party, the CGT promptly denounced the Vitry affair in 1980, when local communist authorities expelled several hundred Malian workers from their lodgings.

54. See, for example, CGT, *Le Peuple,* 1–15 May 1981, p. 25; 15 January 1997, pp. 57–58.

55. CGT Statement, "Immigration: La Répression Doit Cesser" in CGT, *Le Peuple,* 29 April 1998, p. 39.

56. Joint Statement of CGT and CFDT in CGT, *Le Peuple,* 16–31 January 1973, p. 31.

57. Report of the CFDT's National Meeting on Immigration, Paris, 14–15 April 1973.

58. CFDT, *Syndicalisme,* 24 March 1983, p. 4.

59. CFDT, *Syndicalisme,* 11 August 1983.

60. See, for example, CFDT, *Syndicalisme,* 21 August 1997, p. 3; CGT, *Tribune de L'Immigration,* November 1996, p. 5.

61. CGT, *Le Peuple,* 5 February 1997, p. 56; and CFDT, *Syndicalisme,* 13 March 1997, p. 4.

62. L'UD CFDT de Paris, *Des Salariés Parisiens Sans Papiers,* p. 104; and interviews in Montreuil, May 1995, and in Paris June 1995.
63. CFDT, *Syndicalisme,* 21 February 1980, p. 5; 6 March 1980, p. 6; 10 April 1980, pp. 4–5; 17 April 1980, pp. 17–18; 24 April 1980, pp. 16–17; 22 May 1980, p. 5; 5 June 1980, p. 2.
64. CGT, *Le Peuple,* 11–20 September 1981, pp. 7–8; CFDT, *Syndicalisme,* 9 July 1981, p. 12; and interviews in Montreuil, May 1995, and in Paris June 1995.
65. CFDT, *Syndicalisme,* 5 November 1981, p. 9; CGT, *Le Peuple,* 11–12 September 1981, p. 8; Weil, *La France et Ses Etrangers,* p. 237; and interviews in Montreuil, May 1995, and in Paris, June 1995.
66. CGT Statement, "Sans-Papiers: L'Enjeu Des Droits De L'Homme" in CGT, *Le Peuple,* 5 September 1996, p. 47.
67. CFDT Press Release, "Etrangers Sans Papiers," 12 July 1996.
68. Joint Statement of CGT, CFDT, FEN, and FSU, "Sans-Papiers" in CFDT, *Syndicalisme,* 22 August 1996, p. 2.
69. Common platform adopted in December 1996, in Dossier de Presse, Collectif de Soutien aux Sans-Papiers de Seine-et-Marne.
70. Report of the Tenth Congress of the UD-CFDT de Paris in *Paris Commune,* May 1998, p. 17; and interview in Paris, May 1998. In the 1980s undocumented immigrants constituted an increasing portion of private household domestic workers in Paris (as in the building service sector in Los Angeles in the 1980s). This generated a coincidence of interests between the undocumented workers who wanted their rights recognized and the union representing declared workers who wanted to defend the collective contract by legalizing and unionizing the undocumented workers. The union thus chose to help the undocumented private household workers regularize their status—a task that was apparently made easier by the employers, many of whom were apparently prominent people living in the sixteenth arrondissement who, seeking to avoid publicity of their names, became unusually eager to help the Parisian Department of the CFDT. Union militants helped the undocumented immigrants prepare their files and several hundred obtained legal status at the earlier stages. The union's efforts to regularize the status of undocumented private household domestic workers obtained less results in the late 1990s. Interviews in Paris, June 1995, June 1996, and May 1998.
71. CGT Statement, 20 June 1997; CGT, *La Vie Ouvrière,* 20–27 June 1997, p. 17.
72. CFDT, *Syndicalisme,* 2 July 1998, p. 2; and CFDT, *CFDT En Direct* No. 28, July 1998.
73. "Le Projet Chevènement N'est Pas Acceptable" in CGT, *Le Peuple,* 22 October 1997, p. 56.
74. Fédération de la Construction, CGT, *Lettre Fédérale,* July 1998, p. 17.
75. FNCB-CFDT, *La Vie Fédérale,* May 1999, p. 5.

76. J. Ramos, "Immigration," in Fédération de la Construction, CGT, *L'Aplomb*, June 1997.
77. CGT, *Informations Fédérales*, October 1996, p. 10.
78. CGT, *Informations Fédérales*, October 1996, pp. 8–9.
79. Interview in Montreuil, June 1998.
80. Interview in Lyon, June 1998.
81. Interview in Montreuil, June 1996.
82. Interviews in Paris, June 1997, and June 1998.
83. FNCB-CFDT, *Syndicalisme*, 17 April 1997.
84. CFDT, *Syndicalisme*, 9 April 1998, p. 13; FNCB-CFDT, *La Vie Fédérale* Supplement No. 1 December 1997, p. 7; FNCB-CFDT, *Syndicalisme*, 9 April 1998.
85. The book is Philippe Bataille, *Le Racisme au Travail* (Paris: La Decouverte, 1997).
86. CGT, *Le Peuple*, 4 June 1997, pp. 27–29; CGT, *Tribune de L'Immigration*, December 1997; interviews in Paris and Montreuil, 1997.
87. CFDT, *Syndicalisme*, 17 October 1996, p. 4; 20 March 1997, p. 13; CGT, *Le Peuple*, 5 February 1997, p. 57; CFDT, *CFDT En Direct* April 1997; CGT, *La Vie Ouvrière*, 20–27 June 1997, p. 7.
88. CFDT, *Syndicalisme*, 16 April 1998, p. 4; CGT, *Le Peuple*, 29 April 1998, p. 40.

Chapter 7

1. Guy Groux and René Mouriaux, "The Dilemma of Unions without Members" in Anthony Daley, ed., *The Mitterand Era* (New York: New York University Press, 1996), p. 175.
2. Kate Bronfenbrenner et al, "Introduction" in Kate Bronfenbrenner et al, eds., *Organizing to Win* (Ithaca, NY: ILR Press, 1998), p. 3.
3. For an assessment of the impact of union policy on the legislative outcome see Leah Haus, "Openings in the Wall: Transnational Migrants, Labor Unions and U.S. Immigration Policy" *International Organization* 49, 2 (Spring 1995): 285–313.
4. George Ross and Peter Gourevitch, "Conclusion" in Peter Gourevitch et al, *Unions and Economic Crisis: Britain, West Germany and Sweden* (London: George Allen and Unwin, 1984), p. 363.
5. Groux and Mouriaux, "The Dilemma of Unions Without Members," p. 172.
6. On the liberal and individualistic philosophy underlying international human rights conventions, see Jack Donnelly, *Universal Human Rights in Theory and Practice* (Ithaca, NY: Cornell University Press, 1989).
7. George Ross and Andrew Martin, "Through A Glass Darkly" in Andrew Martin and George Ross, eds., *The Brave New World of European Labor: European Trade Unions at the Millennium* (New York: Berghahn Books, 1999), p. 381.

8. Wuokko Knocke, "Sweden: Insiders Outside The Trade Union Mainstream" in Rinus Penninx and Judith Roosblad, eds., *Trade Unions, Immigration, and Immigrants in Europe, 1960–1993* (New York: Berghahn Books, 2000), pp. 166–167.

9. Rinus Penninx and Judith Roosblad, "Conclusion" in Penninx and Roosblad, eds., *Trade Unions, Immigration, and Immigrants in Europe, 1960–1993*, p. 204.

10. August Gachter, "Austria: Protecting Indigenous Workers From Immigrants" in Penninx and Roosblad, eds., *Trade Unions, Immigration, and Immigrants in Europe, 1960–1993*.

11. For earlier versions of some of the arguments presented here see Leah Haus, "Openings in the Wall," Leah Haus, "Opposing Restrictionism: Labor Unions and Immigration Policy in France," paper presented at the International Studies Association Annual Meeting, March 1998; and Leah Haus, "Labor Unions and Immigration Policy in France," *International Migration Review* 33, 3 (Fall 1999): 683–716.

12. Gamze Avci and Christopher McDonald, "Chipping Away at the Fortress: Unions, Immigration and the Transnational Labour Market," *International Migration* 38, 2 (2000): 191–213.

13. Julie Watts *Strange Bedfellows: How Labor Union Leaders and Employers Find Common Ground on Immigration in Spain, Italy and France*, Ph.D. Dissertation, New York University, 1999.

14. SOPEMI, *Trends in International Migration Annual Report 2000* (Paris: OECD, 2001), p. 306.

15. For a summary of the history of British immigration policy, see Zig Layton-Henry, "Britain: The Would-Be Zero-Immigration Country" in Wayne Cornelius et al, eds., *Controlling Immigration: A Global Perspective* (Stanford, CA: Stanford University Press, 1994).

16. This brief background section on British unions draws heavily on Chris Howell, "Unforgiven: British Trade Unionism in Crisis" in Martin and Ross, eds., *The Brave New World of European Labor*.

17. *The Economist*, 24 July 1993, cited in Howell, "Unforgiven," p. 32.

18. TUC, *Congress Report 1998*.

19. R. Miles and A. Phizacklea, "The TUC, Black Workers and New Commonwealth Immigration, 1954–1973," S.S.R.C. Research Unit on Ethnic Relations, University of Bristol, Working Paper on Ethnic Relations no. 6, 1977.

20. Similar reasoning came from NALGO, one of the unions that later merged to become UNISON, in its report on the European Community and 1992. The report anticipated that the SEA would not generate a dramatic increase in migration due to the existence of barriers to mobility such as language and lack of access to housing. But it did anticipate that progress toward mutual recognition of qualifications might over time mean that job vacancies in the United Kingdom would increasingly be filled by southern Europeans such as Portuguese. NALGO's response was that "it will be vital

to recruit into the union all new staff coming from abroad and to make certain that the collective strength of the membership is maintained at both local and national level." NALGO "The European Community and 1992: The Report of the National Executive Council's Single European Act Working Party" 1990, p. 82.

21. Interview, London, June 2001.
22. TUC grant application to the EU Commission, 26 April 2001.
23. Ron Ramdin, *The Making of the Black Working Class in Britain* (Aldershot: Gower Publishing Co. 1987).
24. On the role of black self-organization see Satnam Virdee and Keith Grint, "Black Self-Organization in Trade Unions," *Sociological Review* 42, 2 (1994): 202–226.
25. TUC Press Release, "Unions Target Black and Asian Workers," 14 November 1998.
26. TUC Black Workers' Conference "Report of the 1992 Conference," p. 2.
27. TUC Black Workers' Conference, "Report of the 1996 Conference," p. 15.
28. TUC Black Workers' Conference, "Report of the 1999 Conference," pp. 24–25; TUC Black Workers' Conference "Report on the 1998 Conference."
29. TUC Black Workers' Conference, "The Race Relations Committee Report of the 1995 TUC Black Workers' Conference," pp. 29–30.
30. TUC Black Workers' Conference, "The Race Relations Committee Report of the 1996 TUC Black Workers' Conference," p. 14.
31. TUC Black Workers' Conference, "The Race Relations Committee Report of the 1997 TUC Black Workers' Conference," p. 8.
32. The three unions were COHSE (Confederation of Health Service Employees), NALGO (National and Local Government Officers), and NUPE (National Union of Public Employees).
33. UNISON, "A Campaigning Guide to Asylum and Immigration," n.d., p. 11.
34. TUC, *Report of 122nd Annual Trades Union Congress, 1990*, p. 472.
35. UNISON, "A Campaigning Guide to Asylum And Immigration," n.d., pp. 11–12.
36. UNISON, *UNISON FOCUS*, 28 June 1996.
37. UNISON, "National Delegate Conference 1997: Decisions, Motions and Amendments," n.d., pp. 18–20.
38. Interview, London, June 2001; and TUC, "Congress Decisions: 2000," http://www.tuc.org.uk/congress/tuc [6/5/01].
39. TUC Press Release, 27 June 2000.
40. Interview, London, June 2001.
41. TUC *Report of 122nd Annual Trades Union Congress, 1990*, pp. 471–474; and 585–589.
42. TUC, "General Council Report, 1993," pp. 71–72.
43. TUC, "General Council Report, 1996," pp. 42–43.
44. TUC, "Congress Report 1995," p. 40.

45. *The Times,* 30 October 1995, cited in TUC, "Forty New Burdens on Business: Employers and the Asylum and Immigration Act," 1995.

46. The paper showed that proof of possession of a National Insurance (NI) number was inadequate for the task at hand, and noted that government statements conceded that there are people with NI numbers who lack the legal right to work, and that there are people who have the legal right to work but lack NI numbers, and that fraudsters can easily acquire false NI numbers. The paper pointed out that there were 20 million more National Insurance numbers in circulation than there were U.K. residents over sixteen and that the two government databases of National Insurance numbers differ by 3 million in counting the number of NI numbers in circulation.

47. TUC, "Congress Decisions: 1998," http://www.tuc.org.uk/congress/tuc [6/5/01].

48. Glenroy Watson in TUC, "Congress 2000: Verbatim Report" http://www.tuc.org.uk/congress/tuc [6/5/01].

49. "Migration and Asylum" in TUC, *Congress Guide 2000,* p. 29.

Index

National Council of Labor (France)
  CGT, 112, 121–2
  CGTU, 116
National Front (France), 12, 13
  CFDT, opposition to, 152–3
  CGT, opposition to, 152–3
  see also radical right
National Immigration Forum (United
  States), 63, 72, 73
National Origins Act (United States),
  21, 43, 66
  AFL, 48
Noiriel, Gérard, 119
non-immigrant workers, temporary
  AFL-CIO, 102–3
  business, 101–2
  occupations in the United States, 66

"odd-couple" coalition
  expectations for, 17
  in France, 113, 124–5
  in the United States, 46–7, 54, 55,
    59, 89, 93
Office Nationale d'Immigration. *See*
  ONI
Olszanski, Thomas, 118–19, 120
ONI (Office Nationale d'Immigration),
  129, 130
organizing immigrants, 2, 5–7, 30–5
  ACTWU, 80, 81
  AFL, avoidance, 52–3
  AFL-CIO, 96, 98
  CFDT, 146
  CGT, 146
  CGTU, 116–20
  HERE, 99
  ILGWU, 78, 79, 80
  SEIU, 82–7
  TUC, 167–8
  UBC, 92
  UMW, 57–8

Pasqua, Charles, 132
Pasqua Laws (France), 131
Plyer v. Doe, 28

radical right (France), 13, 113
  see also National Front
raids. *See* inspections

regularization, 130, 131
  CFDT, 145–9
  CGT, 145–9
  see also amnesty
restrictionism
  conventional wisdom, 3, 16–17
  economic issues, 43–50, 55, 60–1,
    89–90, 92–95, 97, 102,
    111–14, 120–4, 133–4, 144,
    172–3
  racial issues, 44–7, 53–6, 58–9
Rodriguez, Arturo, 89
Ross, George, 8, 117

San Francisco Building Trades Council.
  See SFBTC
"sans-papiers" movement
  CFDT, 147–8
  CGT, 147–8
Sassen, Saskia, 21–2
Saxton, Alexander, 53
Schor, Ralph, 125
Schuck, Peter, 28
SCIRP (Select Commission on
  Immigration and Refugee Policy),
  74
SEA (Single European Act), 167
Second International, 3, 39
SEIU (Service Employees International
  Union)
  amnesty, 87
  economic internationalization, 85
  employer sanctions, 83, 84–5
  human rights, 84
  language issues, 83
  membership growth, 82
  organizing immigrants, 82–7
Select Commission on Immigration and
  Refugee Policy. *See* SCIRP
Service Employees International Union.
  See SEIU
SFBTC (San Francisco Building Trades
  Council), 53–4
  AEL, 54
  Chinese Exclusion Act, 54
SGI (Société Générale d'Immigration),
  106, 107
Single European Act. *See* SEA
Social Security Administration. *See* SSA